I0211227

# Available by Joe Mahoney

**Fiction:**

A Time and a Place

Other Times and Places

**Nonfiction:**

Adventures in the Radio Trade

**Editor:**

The Deer Yard and Other Stories (by Tom Mahoney)

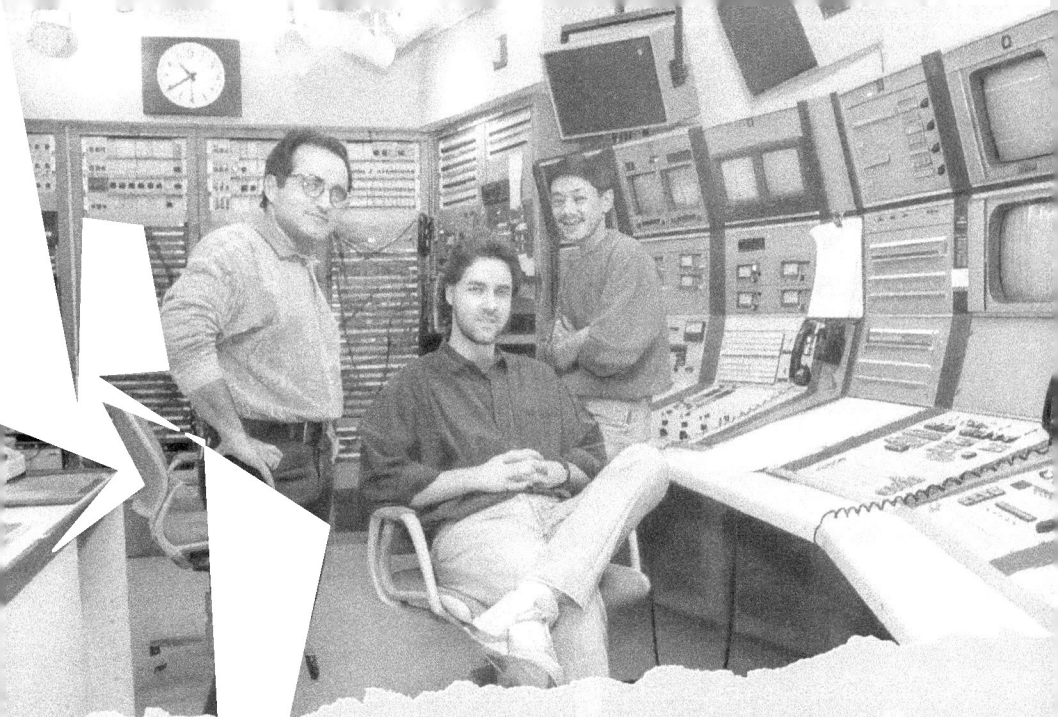

# ADVENTURES IN THE

ON AIR

Radio
Trade

A MEMOIR

## JOE MAHONEY

DONOVAN STREET PRESS

# Copyright © Joe Mahoney

All rights reserved. Without limiting the rights under copyright reserved above, no part of this publication may be reproduced, stored in or introduced into a retrieval system, or transmitted in any form or by any means (electronic, mechanical, photocopying, recording or otherwise), without the prior written permission of both the copyright owner and the publisher of the book.

Library and Archives Canada Cataloguing in Publication
Title: Adventures in the Radio Trade/ Joe Mahoney —First edition.
Names: Mahoney, Joe, 1965 - author
Issued in print and electronic formats.

**ADVENTURES IN THE RADIO TRADE: FIRST EDITION**

Donovan Street Press Edition / 2023
Adventures in the Radio Trade
Published in Canada

ISBN (Paperback) 978-1-0690965-9-3

The author and publisher would be glad to amend in future editions any errors or omissions brought to their attention.

Edited by Arleane Ralph.

Cover Photo by John Lewis

Cover Copyright © 2023 by Avery Olive

Interior design and layout by Avery Olive of Bibliofic Designs

Published by Donovan Street Press Inc.

www.donovanstreetpress.com

For my parents,
Tom and Rosaleen Mahoney

# Table of Contents

# I

## Something Technical

June 1988. My roommate Paul White came home with a car. I'd been bumming around for a couple of months, enjoying a summer off after working as a lab assistant at Ryerson Polytechnical Institute in Toronto. Paul had been bumming around too, but then he got a job at GM, and one day he came home with a car. It seemed so grown up. The guy could afford a car. A brand-new car. I still remember what kind of car it was. A red Chevy Beretta. I decided I wanted a car, too. That meant enough loafing around. It was time to find a job.

I applied for a position at Sony where I'd make twenty-five thousand dollars a year. This seemed like a huge amount. My job at Ryerson had paid thirteen thousand for eight months of work. I was still living off that because my lifestyle cost virtually nothing. I lived in an apartment with three other guys and milk crates for furniture. I had nothing. Up until then I'd wanted nothing. Until Paul came home with a car.

I also applied at a post-production facility. I forget the name. They interviewed me (Sony didn't). They were willing to pay me eighteen thousand dollars a year.

"If you were offered both jobs, this one and the one at Sony, which one would you take?" the interviewer asked me.

I didn't even blink an eye. "The one at Sony."

"Why?"

"Because it's seven thousand dollars more a year!"

I didn't get either job. The post-production facility phoned me up to give me the news.

"Do you know why we didn't give you the job?" the fellow who called asked me.

"No, why?"

"It's because you said you'd take the Sony job over ours for the money."

"You're penalizing me for being honest," I said.

He didn't care. He was trying to tell me that they wanted to hire someone with a passion for what they were doing, but I didn't clue in. It wasn't where my head was at just then. I wanted a job, and the more money the better. I'd figure out the passion bit later.

I crossed the street from where I lived—Jarvis Street—to the CBC Radio Building and gave the receptionist June Shafi my resume.

"What kind of job do you want?" June asked.

"Something technical," I told her.

I have no idea why I said that. It just came out. I could have said, "Something that will earn me a lot of money," or "Something that will make me famous," but I didn't. Probably any other answer wouldn't have gotten me a job. I said, "Something technical," and June picked up the phone right away and called someone.

It was Don Burgess. He was the manager in charge of radio technicians at the time. No idea what his exact title was. I don't think he did the job very long. But he did it long enough to hire me. We chatted a bit about my background: plenty of experience in private radio, a degree in radio and television arts from Ryerson, and so on. After our chat, just to cover all bases, I also dropped a copy of my resume off to the CBC HR department.

Don Burgess set up an interview. A week later he sat at one end of a boardroom table with a woman from Human Resources while I sat at the other. It was a friendly interrogation as they did their best to figure out who I was.

I told Don and his colleague that I could read music, that I'd been an announcer/operator for private radio stations in Prince Edward Island off and on since the age of sixteen, and that I'd listened to CBC Radio since I'd been a kid. I could name shows and hosts dating back a decade and a half. My favourite shows had been *Variety Tonight* with Vicki Gabereau, *The Entertainers*, and the *Royal Canadian Air Farce*.

At the end of the interview, the woman from HR asked me, "Do you have any questions?"

"Just one," I said. "What have you been interviewing me for?"

They laughed. Nobody answered the question. I guess they thought I'd been joking. But I hadn't been. Nobody had taken the time to explain the position to me. All I knew was that it was something technical to do with CBC Radio. (I've conducted many interviews since then and I always take time off the top to make sure the applicant completely understands what they're applying for.)

A week later Don Burgess called to tell me I'd been hired.

A few days after that I received a letter from CBC Human Resources in response to the resume I'd dropped off. The letter said that they couldn't hire me because there were no jobs available. The HR department didn't want me. Fortunately, the technical folks did.

I'd been working for CBC Radio an entire week before I really started to get a sense of what the job was. It was a job that hadn't existed in any of the private radio stations I'd worked for. In private radio you did it all. At the CBC you just did a piece of it all. You specialized. And I was going to specialize in the technical stuff. Not fixing equipment, operating it. Consoles, microphones, tape recorders, all technical equipment having to do with the recording and broadcast of sound.

*Something technical.* Those two words have defined my life for over three decades now. I never did get around to buying a car. Married into one, later—but that's another story, for a different book.

# II
## CJRW

In July 1988, CBC Radio acquired a twenty-three-year-old with a lot of growing up yet to do. I wasn't completely green, though. I'd been in broadcasting since the age of fourteen, the age at which I'd begun volunteering at the local cable television affiliate, Cable 5, in Summerside, Prince Edward Island.

I loved working at Cable 5. I learned to operate the cameras and the big clunky Video Tape Recorders (VTRs) and I was especially fond of "switching" the shows on the cool-looking video switcher. My friends and I produced our own shows and worked on other peoples' shows, often about music. I also worked at Three Oaks Senior High School's brand-new and exceptionally well-run radio station under the leadership of teacher Ralph Carruthers, who launched at least two careers in broadcasting that I know of, and probably more.

That was all volunteer, though. I was a teenager. I needed a part-time job that actually paid money. In 1981 I got a job at McDonald's. I hated it there. The managers, only a little older than I was, yelled and screamed at the rest of us, especially me. I cursed them angrily under my breath. Luckily, after one month they fired me.

"It's not for everyone," the franchise manager told me, not unkindly.

She meant that it wasn't for immature fifteen-year-olds who couldn't be bothered to memorize what went on a Big Mac.

Getting fired from McDonald's was one of the happiest days of my life.

Had I not been fired from McDonald's I might never have got my first real job in radio. One cold November afternoon I cruised down Water Street in an Oldsmobile with my friend Justin Hickey at the wheel and two other pals, the four of us probably listening to classic Genesis. We passed CJRW, Summerside's local radio station, a 250-watt day-timer located at 1240 AM on the dial. It had been broadcasting since 1948, seventeen years before I was born. I'd grown up listening to CJRW.

"Stop the car!" I shouted to Justin.

He stopped. I jumped out, crossed the street, and entered CJRW's front door. I climbed up a flight of stairs to CJRW's reception area, walls festooned with plaques attesting to the station's long history of community activity. Elton John was playing on a set of speakers: "Goodbye Yellow Brick Road," not a new release at the time, but the first time I'd ever heard the song. I've loved it ever since.

A woman in her forties greeted me at the reception desk, super friendly. Summerside is a small town—probably she knew my mother.

"I'd like to apply for a job," I told her.

She furnished me with an application. I filled it out as best I could. A man took me to a studio booth and gave me several sheets of thin yellow paper with dot-matrix type. News, weather and sports. I recorded an audition tape on the spot. A month later, at home, the phone rang.

"Joe, this is Llowell Huestis, calling from CJRW radio."

I recognized Llowell's voice immediately. He was the first famous person I'd ever spoken to. Famous on PEI, anyway. He'd worked for CJRW since its opening in 1948, and for its predecessor CHGS for two years before that. "I'd like to offer you a job as a disc jockey. When can you start?"

I could barely believe my good fortune. Llowell and CJRW hired me to work two shifts each week. I hosted a six-hour long country music show on Friday nights and a rock show on Saturday nights. I hated country music. I grew to like it in time. Well, some of it. I worked at CJRW all through high school. I would have done it for free. I almost did do it for free: I earned $3.35 per hour, minimum wage at the time.

I darned near didn't show up for my first shift (I was still the same kid who couldn't memorize hamburger ingredients). I got confused about which week I was supposed to start. One of my fellow disc jockeys was Peter Arsenault (he went by Peter Scott on air). Peter happened to drive down High Street—my street—in his gold Pontiac Firebird Trans Am shortly before the start of my shift. Spotting me, he pulled up beside me and rolled down the window.

"You do realize you start tonight, don't you?"

"I do?"

"Get in the damned car!"

He drove me to the station and put me on the air before a big silver console with rotary pots and two huge turntables. I learned how to cue up 7" 45 single records so they'd start an instant after introducing them (about one quarter turn back from where the needle hit the first sound). We played IDs and promos on cartridges (called "carts"). There was a quarter-inch tape machine that looked rather daunting. For my first few shifts I got the guy who worked before me to cue it up. His name was Jim Murray and like me he'd go on to work for the CBC (they'd call him James Murray there).

I got nervous before every shift, but I was never nervous on air. I loved every second of it. I got to choose my own music. I played other peoples' requests. Once, I sneezed on air. I learned not to do that. Another time, introducing a record, I choked on a potato chip. I learned not to do that. I had two laughing fits on air—I never learned not to do that (I was a giddy teen-ager). With a mere 250 watts, CJRW didn't have a strong signal, but it seemed to reach a lot of people. I grew close to my audience. I got calls from all over western PEI as well as Cap Pele, in New Brunswick, across the Northumberland Strait. They'd call to make requests. They'd call to say hi. They'd call week after week. They'd tell me I knew them but wouldn't tell me who they were. Once, phoning a friend during a show, I accidentally called the wrong number. A girl answered the phone. "Hey, you're the guy on the radio!" she exclaimed.

We had a good chat.

I learned to take a compliment by working at CJRW. One day shortly after starting there, I went shopping at Summerside's flagship department store, Holman's (the "largest store in the world for a small-town").

"I recognize your voice," a cashier told me. "Are you on the radio?"

I allowed that I was.

"You have a nice voice," she said.

I had no idea how to respond. I was embarrassed. My first instinct was to deny it.

My mother advised me later, "Just say thank you."

And that's how you respond to a compliment.

The name of the Friday night country show was *The Ranch Party*. I always opened it with Bobbie Nelson's "Down Yonder" from Willie Nelson's album *Red Headed Stranger*. The station didn't own that record; my father did. I always brought in a lot of my own stuff. I mixed the country up with folk music. The Clancy Brothers & Tommy Makem were favourites. I used to play this one song by them. One night after I played it a *Ranch Party* regular called up, an older Acadian woman.

"That song you just played?" she said. "You must never play it again."

"Why not?"

"It's too sad."

She wasn't wrong:

> Isn't it grand, boys, to be bloody well dead?
> Let's not have a sniffle, let's have a bloody good cry
> And always remember the longer you live
> The sooner you'll bloody well die.

I had always gotten a kick out of it. Young and fully alive, it didn't apply to me. I could see how it might be considered a little morbid, though. I respected my listeners. I never played it again.

Another night, during the Saturday night rock show, a girl called up. Not someone I knew.

"I love you!" she said, before hanging up.

I laughed. It was just some kid in town having fun, probably hanging out with a bunch of other kids. For a few short years I supplied the soundtrack of their lives, and we all had fun together. A lot more fun than grilling hamburgers.

# III
## A Brief History of Radio

Radio is a tiny, white, battery-operated device I snuck into my bed at night at the age of eleven to hear static and people and music from distant lands. It's a clock radio I got for Christmas when I was twelve. It's the shortwave radio my grandfather listened to after a hard day's work on the farm, and it's the one that kept my father company in northern New Brunswick during the long cold winters of the forties. It's the radio my parents kept on our kitchen counter when I was growing up, that played our local radio station before school, that played top forty music and told us the news and the weather and the ferry schedule and that regretted to make the following announcement: "in lieu of flowers a donation to a society of your choice would be appreciated."

Radio is all the stations that ever broadcast my voice, or anyone's voice, via radio waves that are now up to two hundred light years away from the Earth the last we checked, where (I like to think) some alien race has surely heard it and is busy crafting a polite response.

Radio is communication by a type of electromagnetic radiation, but don't worry because it's non-ionizing radiation, meaning that it doesn't turn atoms into ions, and it isn't sufficiently powerful to cause the molecules in human cells to break apart and burn people and cause cancer. Rather, radio employs benign electromagnetic radiation, the friendly kind, the non-ionizing kind, the kind that powers the radios, televisions, mobile phones, and microwaves that furnish our homes and our lives. Radio wields sound like a sorcerer, displacing invisible particles of air that tickle the diaphragms of microphones, converting energy into electrical currents that, amplified, become radio waves that antennas fling to receivers that transmute them back into electricity that vibrates speakers to create sound waves to journey once more through the air to our ears.

We know all this because Scottish physicist James Clerk Maxwell began figuring it out back in the 1870s, proving that electric and magnetic fields, properly choreographed, make excellent dance partners, performing sophisticated pas de deux in electromagnetic ballets.

We know it because German physicist Heinrich Hertz, who lived a tragically short life, a mere thirty-six years, made good use of his abbreviated time on this earth, applying Maxwell's theories in 1886 to successfully transmit and receive radio waves for the first time in human history, though to what end he could not say: "Nichts denke ich," he replied, when asked what good it all was. (That is, "Nothing, I guess.")

In 1893, Nikola Tesla demonstrated a wireless radio to the fine people of St. Louis, Missouri. Three years later Guglielmo Marconi patented wireless telegraphy technology. Four years after that, in 1900, Canadian Reginald Fessenden spoke on the radio for the first time, over a distance of fifty miles (eighty kilometres), asking: "Is it snowing where you are, Mr. Thiessen?" The following year, not to be outdone, Marconi sent radio waves all the way across the Atlantic Ocean, from Cornwall in the United Kingdom to Signal Hill, overlooking St. John's, Newfoundland, in the form of Morse Code. (That's not why it's called Signal Hill, though. It's been called that since 1762, when Lt. Colonel William Amherst changed its name to "Signal Hill" from "The Lookout" after the role the hill played in signaling the forces under his command during the defeat of the French during the final battle of the Seven Years' War.)

Six years after Marconi's transatlantic Morse Code feat, Reginald Fessenden topped it by making the first ever two-way radio broadcast using the human voice across the Atlantic Ocean, from Boston to Scotland. Still, it was a while before radio really caught on. Darby Coates worked for the Canadian Marconi Company in 1920. He gave public demonstrations of radio and telephone radio equipment that had been built for troops in France for the First World War.

"People were skeptical," he recalled later. "They could accept the idea of sound waves but couldn't see how they could come through the walls of buildings."

Coates went on to become the manager and announcer for the first publicly owned radio station in Canada, CKY, set up by the Government of Manitoba in 1923 and run by the Manitoba Telephone System. The Canadian Broadcasting Corporation was still a few years away.

Graham Spry was a journalist and Rhodes Scholar from St. Thomas, Ontario. He was also the national secretary of something called the Association of Canadian Clubs, which had been formed in 1897 by a journalist from Hamilton to "foster interest in matters affecting the welfare of Canada." In 1927, at twenty-seven years of age, Spry, in his capacity as Association secretary, made a bold proposal. He suggested a Diamond Jubilee broadcast originating from Parliament Hill in Ottawa to celebrate Canada's sixtieth anniversary. It would be broadcast from coast to coast using telegraph and telephone lines to link many of the fifty-seven private radio stations operating in Canada at that time.

Prime Minister William Lyon MacKenzie King participated in the broadcast, which was a huge success. Impressed, King wrote, "On the morning and evening of July 1st all Canada became for the time being a single assemblage, swayed by a common emotion, within the sound of a single voice... Hitherto for most Canadians, Ottawa had seemed far off but henceforth all Canadians will stand within the sound of the carillon and within the hearing of the speakers of Parliament Hill."

The bit about the carillon was made possible by the intrepid engineers who comprised the recording team, including Jack Carlyle. In 1986, the CBC Radio show *Ideas* interviewed Jack for an episode celebrating the network's own fiftieth anniversary:

"I remember going up in that tower and the clock struck, just when I got near the bells," he recalled. "And of course, it was carbon mikes in those days, and you couldn't put it on the ground and pick up the sound. So Charlie Findlay, the chief engineer, he climbed out among the gargoyles, you know, the gargoyles on the clock and the Peace Tower. He climbed up and sat out there for an hour with the microphone in his hand. He was never allowed to do it again, of course."

By 1929 religions had discovered that independent radio stations were handy for publicly bashing one another over the airwaves. Jehovah's Witnesses were particularly fond of hammering Roman Catholics via their independent stations. The federal minister responsible for broadcasting revoked the Jehovah's Witnesses broadcasting license, making religious censorship a hot-button political issue.

With this in mind, along with warm memories of the Diamond Jubilee national broadcast, Prime Minister King asked John Aird to set up a Royal Commission on Radio Broadcasting. You might think, of course! That makes complete sense. It's Canada. That's what we do. We set up Royal Commissions to figure out this sort of thing. But the Aird Commission was the first-ever public consultation of its kind in this country; only after the Aird Commission did we as a nation routinely approach cultural governance this way.

A banker by trade, Aird set up his commission with Augustin Frigon, an electrical engineer, and Charles Bowman, editor of the *Ottawa Citizen*. They were asked whether a public broadcasting entity should be a private enterprise with a government subsidy, a federally owned and operated system, or one that was provincially owned and operated. The Aird Commission delivered a nine-page report to King. In it, the commissioners shared King's concerns about religious radio. They were also worried about US radio stations gobbling up radio frequencies before Canadians could get their hands on them. And like King, they were especially interested in the ability of a national radio broadcasting network to foster Canadian unity. They recommended a federally owned and operated national public broadcasting system. This was at a time when fewer than forty percent of Canadians outside of Toronto and Montreal could hear any Canadian radio station at all.

Six weeks after the Aird Commission delivered its report, the stock market crashed, plunging the world into the Great Depression. The creation of a national radio network became less of a priority for Prime Minister King. On July 28, 1930, he was voted out of office. Richard Bedford Bennett, known as R. B. Bennett, replaced him. Bennett led a majority Conservative government, one not interested in the Aird Commission's recommendations, at least not right away.

In 1930, Graham Spry (originator of the Diamond Jubilee broadcast) and fellow broadcasting pioneer Alan Plaunt created the Canadian Radio League. Its goal? Pressure Bennett's government into implementing the Aird Commission's recommendations. Spry asserted that "Radio broadcasting is no more a business than the public school system, the religious organization or the varied literary, musical and scientific endeavours of the Canadian people. It is a public service."

In May 1932, Bennett's government formed the Canadian Radio Broadcasting Commission ("the CRBC"), at least partially in response to the Canadian Radio League's efforts.

By May 1933 the CRBC was broadcasting nationally an hour a day. The number of hours the CRBC broadcast grew over time. The network grew as well. Eventually the CRBC came to consist of eight network-owned and operated stations and fourteen privately owned stations operating as network affiliates.

Unlike its modern-day incarnation, though, the CRBC did not operate at arm's length from the government. Before the October 14, 1935 federal election, the CRBC broadcast a series of fifteen-minute soap operas called *Mr. Sage* criticizing the opposition Liberals and their party leader, William Lyon MacKenzie King. If the soap operas were intended to help the Conservatives win the upcoming election, they failed. On October 14, 1935, the Liberals trounced the Conservatives. Just over a year later, on November 2, 1936, King's government reorganized the Canadian Radio Broadcasting Commission as a Crown Corporation, perhaps in part to address concerns over its perceived lack of impartiality. The CRBC became the CBC, or the Canadian Broadcasting Corporation, which promptly got on with the business of making "the home not merely a billboard, but a theatre, a concert hall, a club, a public meeting, a school, a university," in the words of Graham Spry.

Fifty-two years later, the CBC hired me.

# IV
## Net Testing

The first work I would ever do for CBC Radio was not typical of what I'd come to do. Technically it wasn't even in the job description. It was a maintenance job, not a radio technician's job, which is the work that I was supposed to be doing. That the first work I would ever do for the CBC was maintenance work is an intriguing bit of foreshadowing, as I would find myself involved in maintenance work again nineteen years later as the manager of Audio Systems, one of the broadcast maintenance departments.

The work they had me start with was called Net Testing. I was taught how to do it by a fellow by the name of Ron Grant. Ron Grant was a Radio Master Control technician. Probably he'd been many things before that, but he'd wound up working in Radio Master Control on Jarvis Street, and that is where he'd finish his career. He was probably less than four years away from retirement when I met him.

The first thing Ron said to me was, "I'm supposed to teach you how to do this in a week. I don't think it's possible to teach you in a week. The last guy I tried to teach how to do this ran screaming out of here in two days with his tail between his legs. But I'll give it a go."

It was a brilliant speech. I don't think it was premeditated. Ron was the kind of guy who said what was on his mind, usually loudly. Once upon a time he'd been a wrestler. The other guys in Radio Master Control called him "Boomer."

Ron's speech had a terrific impact on me. Up until that time I was the kind of guy who got by. I was smart enough that I could coast through school, and coast through university, without ever really applying myself. I did fine—sometimes really fine if something captivated my imagination, occasionally not so well if I underestimated some challenge. Ron's speech put the fear of God in me. This was a real job, not something I wanted to screw up. There would be no coasting here. And it was obvious from the get-go that what Ron was teaching me was complex. I hung on his every word. Took lots of notes. Asked plenty of questions. By the end of the week I knew how to do what I needed to do. The week after that I was on my own.

My job was to test all the audio lines from coast to coast on a strict schedule. The tools of my trade were audio tapes full of a series of tones from frequencies so low a human could barely hear them to frequencies so high most mature adults couldn't hear them. I don't remember the exact range, but it was something like 25 hertz up to 25 kilohertz. (Many adults can't hear past 12 or 15 kilohertz. When I started at CBC Radio, I was twenty-three years old and I could hear up to at least 20 kilohertz).

The idea was to patch the audio down these lines one after another and work with other audio engineers across the country to measure the frequency response. I would record the results using a pen and paper. If the results were in any way awry, I would contact an engineer with Bell Canada who would investigate the problem on his or her end, as the lines were all Bell lines. They had names like 1P West (also known as 1PW, a mono line to points west from Toronto), 1P East (1PE, a mono line to points east from Toronto), 1E5 (an emergency circuit), 1H59, and other lines starting with the number 6, which denoted stereo for some reason, and so on. This was a great education. For the rest of my career I always knew all the lines, what they meant, and where they went. At least I did until CBC Radio decided not to renew the contract with Bell and replaced the lines with something called the NGCN (Next Generation Converged Network) which is basically all data, spitting files across the country instead of actual audio.

I was surprised to learn that I needed math for this work. Integers, no less. I had always considered myself a creative type and had never imagined ever having to do a job involving actual math. I once told my Grade Twelve math teacher, Mr. Winston Yeo, that math would not be a part of my future.

"You never know," Mr. Yeo told me.

He was right. I didn't know.

I conducted these tests all summer long, the summer of 1988, after which someone else took over, probably Ron Grant again. Much later these network tests were automated, and nobody did them, although real live human beings still had to look at the results.

In the fall my contract lapsed for three weeks. I went home to Prince Edward Island for a vacation. While I was there the CBC contacted me. They asked me if I could come back to work until Christmas, this time as a Radio Technician Group 4. I was only too happy to do so, though I had no intention of working for CBC Radio forever, or even for much longer. It was just work for the time being. One day not long after being hired back I found myself working in Tape Reclaim (more on this hellhole later) with another radio technician—a pleasant fellow a few years older than me—by the name of Mike Ewing. As we laboriously stripped quarter-inch tape off reels to recycle the tape and reclaim the reels, Mike asked me about my future plans.

"Two years max," I told him. "Won't be staying here any longer than that."

"Oh? What will you do?"

"Write. Or direct films. Both, maybe."

Unlike Mr. Yeo, Mike didn't challenge my assertion. "Great," he told me. "Good for you."

But some thirty years later Mike and I were still saying "hi" to one another in the halls of the CBC Toronto Broadcast Centre.

# V

# The Radio Building

When I started at CBC Radio in Toronto in July 1988, I worked out of the Radio Building at 354 Jarvis Street. The Radio Building was a sprawling ancient structure originally constructed in 1898. Before housing CBC Radio it had been the Havergal College for girls. Brick on the outside, it was surrounded by gates and guards and kiosks—some people referred to the whole set-up as "Stalag CBC."[1]

Inside, the Radio Building was people and wood and consoles and tape machines, and it smelled like my grandparents' old wooden farmhouse in rural New Brunswick. It was huge and had a lot in it, including an abandoned pool in the sub-basement that nobody swam in much except for a few rats.

Studio C was a tiny studio that was mostly used for voice tracking and two-ways. "A" might have been for Aardvark, as Lister Sinclair used to say, but his show *Ideas* used Studio D. *Basic Black*, *The Arts Tonight*, and *Stereo Morning* came out of Studio E. *As It Happens* used Studio F from 11am to 7pm. Studio H was on the verge of being renovated into a high-end production studio featuring an AMS Neve Audio File and Logic 1 console, a state of the art mixing facility so advanced its inventor was said to have gone insane shortly after inventing it. *Arts National* was packaged in Studio J. Studio K was a multi-purpose packaging studio—*Listen to the Music*, *Sunny Side Up*, and *My Kinda Jazz* with Jeff Healey were packaged in there, among others. *Prime Time* with Ralph Benmergui (later with Geoff Pevere) came out of Studio L. CJBC (French services serving

---

1 Security maybe wasn't as solid as it seemed. There's a famous story, possibly apocryphal, involving thieves who successfully stole a grand piano from one of the radio studios by disguising themselves as movers. They told the security guards that the piano needed to be tuned, then wheeled the instrument out of the building and hauled it off in a white, unmarked truck. It's said that the security guards held the doors open for them. The thing is you can't move a piano to tune it; moving it will make it go out of tune.

the Franco-Ontario community) broadcast live out of Studio M. Studio R was used for *Morningside* and *Sunday Morning*. Of course, many other shows also came out of these studios over the years.

The Technician's Lounge was located on the main floor directly across from Studio M. Many were the friendships I forged in that lounge while waiting for my next booking, and many were the television shows about bugs and animals I was forced to watch because of the old-timers controlling the TV remote—at least, those old-timers not absorbed in their never-ending card games.

I hardly set foot in Studio G, which seemed the domain of engineers infinitely more capable and ambitious than I was. Radio drama would come later in my career, in a different studio in a brand-new building.

One floor down was the cafeteria. I ate a lot of Banquet Burgers in there, prepared by a friendly woman named Laurel who later became a popular security guard at the Toronto Broadcast Centre.

Down the hall from the cafeteria was Radio Master Control. Also down that hall were the Radio Operations Office, Studio B, Studio W, Tape Reclaim, the Delay Room, the Recording Room, and Audio Systems. Tech Stores, the Mail Room, and the sound effects department were in the basement on the other side of the cafeteria. The machine shop was also down there somewhere, though I don't quite remember exactly where.

The inhabitants of the Radio Operations Office were genial frontline supervisors who performed a host of technical supervisory functions and kept the radio technicians in line. If a technician was near the end of their shift and was bored and wanted to go home, they would ask the Operations Officer on duty if they could leave early. Some officers you could count on to say yes, and others you could count on to say no. If you needed to call in sick, you called an Operations Officer. Operations Officers were usually well-respected, some even well-loved. It was almost a prerequisite of the job.

Tape Reclaim (where, you might recall, I told Mike Ewing I had no intention of working at CBC Radio any longer than I absolutely had to) was my least favourite place to work. There, radio technicians would cut used quarter-inch tape from audio reels to recycle the tape and free up the reels. They would hang the reel on a primitive slab of a machine and then haul down on a great lever to pierce the tape with a sharp steel point. Particularly feeble radio technicians usually had to yank on the lever once or twice to completely pierce the tape, which fell into a great bin of used tape. The process required a certain amount of strength and energy, energy I frequently lacked in the mornings after skipping breakfast. I didn't recycle much tape. Making matters worse, some frequenters of this cramped space tended to work up a sweat and accompanying body odour, making working in Tape Reclaim a unique kind of purgatory.

Studio B was a small control room with a McCurdy console and a tiny announce booth. It was used for simple production tasks, such as interviews and basic packaging. One day I found myself recording Patrick Watson in there. The broadcaster, not the singer. The man who created the Canadian Heritage Minutes. And who happened to be Chairman of the CBC at the time.

Before I go on, you're going to need to know about 1K reference tone.

There are different types of tone. The tone I'm talking about here is 1 kilohertz tone (often referred to simply as 1K tone). The idea is to play the 1K tone through the various pieces of broadcast equipment in the studio to "line them all up" (adjust playback and record levels). It's also used to establish continuity, to ensure that the audio signal is travelling successfully from the studio to wherever you want to send it. For example, if you were doing an interview between one person in Halifax and another in Toronto, you would want confirmation that the audio signal from your console was reaching Halifax, and vice versa. So 1K tone is quite useful. It can also be quite annoying. Especially if you're wearing a pair of headphones and some fool technician happens to blast tone through the board into your headphones, deafening you.

Which is the only thing I remember about the Patrick Watson interview: me accidentally blasting 1K tone into his headphones, and Watson whipping off his headphones as fast as he could. I've accidentally done that to two or three people in my career, but it was probably not a good idea to do it to the Chairman of the place where I worked.

Another memory of Studio B was working in Master Control and looking down the hall to see Canadian actor, writer, and director Sarah Polley hanging around the studio waiting to be interviewed. Seventeen years later I would escort her to Studio 203 in the Broadcast Centre for an interview on the show *Q*.

Right across the hall from Radio Master Control was Studio W, which maybe stood for weird, because it had a weird, one-of-a-kind console in it. I did a two-way with academic, broadcaster and well-known environmental activist David Suzuki in there once.

Down the hall from Studio W, one wall west of Radio Master, sat the Recording Room. Two guys alternated working in there. Techs like me would replace them on meal breaks and annual leave. We used the Recording Room to record everything we broadcast. We also used it to record "feeds" (audio content) from across Canada, and sometimes other countries, to be used on our various shows. The job consisted of setting up tapes to do these recordings and boxing them up when they were done. In those days, recordings were done on quarter-inch tape and DAT (digital audio tapes), defunct mediums today. The CBC recently transferred many of those recordings—the ones deemed valuable for posterity—to the digital realm. What little time I spent in the Recording Room proved most useful for getting a lot of reading done. I read much of Stephen King's *The Stand* in there.

The Delay Room was little more than a closet, its size inversely proportional to its significance. There was an A and a B tape delay system, or a main and a backup. Each consisted of a couple of heavy-duty tape machines that recorded certain programs, such as Morningside, upon their initial broadcast out of Toronto. Usually we broadcast such programs to the east first before the rest of the country got to hear them. The idea was to stagger the broadcast of these programs in such a way that every Canadian would hear their favourite show at exactly the same time, subjectively at least, because in reality someone in Vancouver would be hearing Morningside and certain other shows (except for the news) hours later than it was originally broadcast. Because in those days this content was recorded on the medium of tape, this process affected the sound quality slightly. Probably most people couldn't really tell, but the sound quality of the programs broadcast in Vancouver, one tape generation after the original broadcast, wouldn't be quite as good as the quality in Newfoundland, where audiences heard everything live, straight from the studio.

On the other hand, Eastern Canadians heard all our mistakes. If Peter Gzowski experienced a slip of the tongue during *Morningside*, everybody in the Maritimes heard it. If the mistake was serious enough, we would try to fix it for the rest of the country. If we got to it in time, we might be able to fix it in time for Ontario. We tried hard to do this because most, if not all, of the English Senior Executive Team lived in Ontario. Producers wanted our programming to be the best it could possibly be for all Canadians, but they especially wanted it to be the best for the Senior Executive Team. Depending on the nature and the timing of the fault, sometimes the best we could do was fix it for Vancouver. If Peter Gzowski accidentally spilled his coffee and swore on air during the first half hour of *Morningside* (just an example—he never actually did this, at least as far as I know) it might have been possible to restrict the damage to the Maritimes by broadcasting the show over again live in the studio while the first part of the show played to more westerly time zones via the delay system. We called this sort of thing a "remake," and we did it a lot. *As It Happens* producers were particularly fond of "remaking" their show if they got something wrong.

I don't have much to say about the rest of the denizens of the basement, such as those in the mailroom, the audio maintenance technicians, and the sound effects engineers. I never worked in the mail room. I would go on to become the Manager of Audio Systems, but that was years in the future. I would also eventually spend a lot of time creating and performing sound effects, but those days were also a long way off.

# VI
## Studio Q

All new radio technicians at the CBC spend a lot of time booked with more experienced techs to watch them work, and hopefully learn from them. This is officially called "observing."

"I call it ob-swerving," fellow technician Barry Spray told me one day up in Studio Q. "Cuz I spend so much of my time swerving out of the way."

Barry demonstrated the concept of "ob-swerving" by rolling his chair out of veteran technician Fred Park's way as Fred retrieved a tape from a producer for that evening's newscast.

Whether you learn anything observing depends largely on whom you're observing. We learned a thing or two from Fred. He warned Barry and I about a curious phenomenon that we were bound to experience sooner or later: in the middle of a show we'd push a button or flick a switch and at that exact instant silence would descend–dead air, the arch-nemesis of all makers of radio– and it would seem to us as though we'd caused the dead air by pushing that button. But in fact it would have nothing to do with us, and a second or two later the show would resume as though nothing had happened, because, in fact, nothing had happened, the silence was just a coincidence, somebody had paused in the middle of a thought, "un ange était passé" (an angel was passing). Fred was right–in the years to come I would experience this all the time.

We learned from many other technicians as well. Joe Lawlor demonstrated how to cue up a tape for news in ten seconds. Greg DeClute taught me how to destroy old tape with pencils (in lieu of disposing of it in Tape Reclaim). I learned from Jan Wright that you could knit sweaters, scarves and mittens and do crosswords while doing *As It Happens* live, and from Peter Beamish, that it was possible to mix complicated items for *Sunday Morning* using ump-teen different sources (music, sound effects, interviews, clips, etc.) with a mere two arms. (This was back in the days of analog, before computers. I never even came close to Peter's abilities.) In short, I learned how to do everything I needed to do to be a proper radio technician from my eighty or so colleagues.

I suppose there were techs who weren't all that keen to help you, who kept their years of experience close to their chests. At least I've heard that there were, but thinking about it now, I can't think of a single one. I found everybody to be generous and helpful.

Studio Q, where Fred Park pretty much worked full time, was located on the second floor of the Jarvis Street building. It was a news studio. We did *World Report, The World This Weekend, The World at Six*, and short four-and-a-half minute-long newscasts called *Hourlies* out of there. Like every other facility in the Canadian Broadcasting Corporation's Radio Building on Jarvis Street, Q was dusty and dingy. It had an analog console, probably a McCurdy, in the control room. Directly behind Fred and his audio console were a couple of industrial strength quarter-inch Studer A810 tape machines. To cue up tape on these beasts, Fred would have to turn completely around. Several news items during the newscast would rely on audio from these tapes, so Fred frequently had his back to the console.

A news editor functioning as show director would sit on Fred's right. A glass window separated the control room from an announce booth big enough to accommodate two news announcers. *Hourlies* and *World Report* only had one announcer but a show like *The World at Six* had two. A small recording room to the right of the control room contained four Studer A810 quarter-inch tape machines. A second technician always worked in there; it was their job to take in audio feeds from all over the world.

About ten minutes before every newscast, Fred would "line up" with somebody two floors below in Radio Master Control using a dedicated phone line. After checking tone to ensure continuity, the Master Control technician would relay the time, counting up a few seconds, to ensure that the clock in Studio Q was correct. Shows switched according to a strict automated schedule in Master

Control, meaning that if Fred started the news early, the beginning of the show would be clipped.

One day I found myself observing a technician other than Fred in Studio Q. Busy explaining to me how things worked, the tech forgot to line up a newscast. The phone from Radio Master Control rang: the Master Control tech was wondering why the news hadn't started. The news tech cursed and leapt into action, hitting the news theme, but it was too late. We already had had about a minute of dead air. Afterward Radio Master phoned back and asked for the tech's initials, which would be included on the inevitable fault report. I wasn't implicated that day, but my own initials MO (JM was already taken) would wind up on a few fault reports over the years.

There was usually a fair amount of excitement in Studio Q before a major newscast such as *The World at Six*. Providing the most up-to-date news reports meant that reporters often filed their stories at the last possible instant. For example, as soon as Fred finished recording a reporter's "voicer," an editor would appear and snatch the tape from Fred's hands to prepare it for broadcast. This meant editing out mistakes and inserting a piece of leader tape—tape upon which it was not possible to record sound—before the actual audio to be played back. This would make it easier for Fred to find the item on the tape and cue it up. Sometimes, if it was seconds before the tape was to air, the recording room technician would simply hand the tape to Fred, who would cue it up as fast as possible before whirling around to stab at the "play" button when the news announcer finished reading the intro.

We moved fast but cared about quality. Everything needed to sound as good as it possibly could. One day, in pursuit of this perfection, someone decided that a certain news announcer sounded "off mic." He needed to be closer to the microphone. The announcer accepted this criticism. He did his best to improve his technique like the professional he was. But after several newscasts of being told this he grew frustrated. "What do you want me to do? Eat the fucking thing?"

Studio Q wasn't my first exposure to radio news. At my first station, CJRW in Summerside, Prince Edward Island, I was required to read the news every hour on the hour. Before each newscast I would put on a long song and go down the hall to rip the news, sports, and weather off the wire machine. Over the previous hour the news wire machine would have spit out a ribbon of cheap yellow paper, sometimes thirty-seven or so metres in length. It was my job to scan that scroll of paper for the information I was looking for. Fortunately, the news always came in distinctive blocks of print that made it easy to find. I ripped off the sections I required and returned to the studio to read it live on the air.

I never read the copy ahead of time. I was a pretty good sight reader, and because I was busy hosting a show all alone I didn't have the time. Usually this wasn't a problem, but I did get into trouble twice. Once, glancing up from reading the news, I saw my friend Andrew Fortier (visiting me at the station) making a face at me. I immediately burst into a big belly laugh right in the middle of the newscast. Another time I was reading an item about a contest to come up with a name for a new sports dome in Vancouver. After listing several serious suggestions, I came to the suggestion "The Unknown Dome." Coming from out of nowhere, it struck me as funny, and I dissolved into gales of laughter live on air and giggled my way through the rest of the news.

A few years later I hosted an overnight show at CFCY/Q-93 in Charlottetown.[2] At CFCY/Q-93, instead of reading the news myself, I used a news service called CKO. I opened a line and someone in Toronto read the news for me, after which I resumed my hosting duties live.

After completing my degree at Ryerson Polytechnical Institute in Toronto, I applied for a job at CKO. Someone from CKO phoned me up to offer me an interview. I was in the bathroom at the time.

"He's taking a shit," one of my roommates (not Paul White) told the caller.

Despite my roommate's idiotic remark, they offered me a job, but it was only part-time, so I declined. A good thing, too—CKO went out of business shortly afterward, in 1989.

---

2 CBC news correspondent James Murray also worked at both CJRW and CFCY/Q-93. There was a sign on one of the doors at CFCY/Q-93 when I worked there: "Please do not prop this door open with useless objects such as Jim Murray's head."

Back to Studio Q.

After my stints in private radio I was rather taken aback by all the effort that went into making news at CBC Radio. I didn't understand why it was necessary to have two people at the console (one operating, the other directing) while a whole other person—sometimes two—read the news. They made it all seem like such a big deal. There was a real sense of gravitas. The work wasn't all that difficult for the tech—the serious atmosphere made it feel harder than it was—but we did create quality newscasts.

Still, mistakes happened. One memorable night Helen Hutchinson filled in for one of our regular hosts. Her presence completely flustered regular co-host Russ Germaine.

"The World at Six," Russ intoned to the nation in his authoritative voice. "Good evening, from the national newsroom of CBC Radio, this is Helen Hutchinson."

He gasped audibly.

"I'm Helen Hutchinson," Helen gently corrected him. "And you're Russ Germaine."

In between newscasts, when not mixing items and taking in feeds, techs created makeshift tape reclaims around the console. Employing pencils as axles, we'd spin the reels with our fingers and easily spool the tape off. Or we'd take a few minutes to see who could cue up tapes the fastest.

It's no coincidence that the show *q* (formerly *Q*), hosted by Tom Powers (formerly hosted by Shadrach (Shad) Kabangois, and before that, Jian Ghomeshi), is called *q*. When we were trying to come up with names for that show, one of the suggestions on the whiteboard was Studio Q. From this the final name of the show is obviously derived and was, at least in part, an homage to a certain hallowed news studio back in the Radio Building on Jarvis Street.

# VII

## "Joe, We Have a Problem"

Just before Christmas 1988, scheduling assigned me to work the evening shift in Radio Master Control. I worked there solid for about six months, prefaced by a week or two of training.

Radio Master Control sounds kind of impressive. It looked impressive, even back then, when it was run in part by computers using cassette tapes, technology dating back to the seventies, if not earlier. Radio Master Control in Toronto was, indeed, impressive. It was the central hub. All CBC Radio shows coming out of Toronto passed through Radio Master. Many shows originating in the regions (by which I mean throughout Canada other than Toronto and Montreal) passed through Radio Master in Toronto, at least if they were national shows. When you worked in Radio Master you had a fair amount of responsibility. Much of what went on was automated, but the automation only worked if the radio master control tech set it up properly, and maintained it properly, and dealt with it properly when things went horribly wrong. Which they always did, usually at least once a day.

People who have never worked in Radio Master sometimes find it difficult to understand. When you walk by the place, which used to be located in the basement of the Jarvis Street facility, and later the third floor of the Toronto Broadcast Centre (and yet later the sixth floor), you often saw technicians doing what appeared to be, well, nothing. In fact, they were only at rest if all their preparations were complete, if nobody in any studios or other master controls across the country were calling them, if everything was going to air properly. In a sense, master control techs are like fire-fighters, waiting for something to go wrong. And every properly trained master control technician is poised to leap into action at the first sign of trouble.

Back when I started in the eighties, if a show wasn't being broadcast live, odds were it was being played back off quarter-inch tape. It was the job of the radio master control technician to put up the tape, check it for any issues, make sure the levels were good, and confirm that the first sounds on the tape were what they were supposed to be—in other words, that it was the right program.

Putting up the final tape ever for the show *Eclectic Circus*, hosted by Alan McFee (a show I had enjoyed while growing up in vacuum land, as McFee would have put it), I thought, wow, I'm the last link in the chain of the last-ever episode of this show.

During the first week of my six-month gig in Radio Master Control I worked the evening shift on New Year's Eve. Early in the shift I put up the tapes for a show called *Two New Hours*, which featured modern Canadian composers and was produced for many years by David Jaeger (until its cancellation in the spring of 2007). The show consisted of three one-hour long reels of tape. I put each of them up carefully, checked their levels, listened to the first words, and was not at all concerned about any of them.

Here's how it worked. When the technician was recording the show in the studio he or she added what was called a "swap tone" to the end of the first and second hours. The swap tone was something like 25 Hz at -6 dB. Listeners at home were not supposed to be able to hear the swap tone—it was at the bottom edge of human hearing. It was there for the Radio Master Control systems to detect and trigger a "swap" from one tape to the next (it was loud enough for me to hear it when I put the tapes up, but the swaps happened pretty quickly, so even if listeners could hear something, they wouldn't hear it for long).

I was working with Peter Chin that night. In his early thirties, slim and unpretentious, Peter always dressed casually, usually in blue jeans, and sported a thin, dapper moustache. Everybody liked

Peter. He had grown up in downtown Toronto and was infinitely cooler than I could ever hope to be.

About three hours into my shift I was on a break in the technician's lounge when Peter called me. "Joe, you'd better get down here. There's a big problem with *Two New Hours*."

"What's going on?" I asked.

"It finished forty-five minutes early."

Yikes!

I ran from the lounge on the first floor of the Radio Building to Radio Master in the basement where Peter was trying to figure out what had happened. It didn't take long to sort out. When radio master control techs put up tapes they were supposed to read a form that accompanied each tape with information about the program in question. I had done this but had neglected an important part of the form: a comments section in which the producer David Jaeger had written: "There are low organ notes in this show. Please take this into consideration when playing back the show."

I was supposed to have programmed the Radio Master Control computer to severely limit the amount of time it could detect the swap tone, so that it wouldn't confuse extremely low organ notes with the swap tone. Not having noticed the comment, I had not done this, so the computer detected the organ notes and swapped one of the tapes forty-five minutes early. This meant that the show finished forty-five minutes early, and there was nothing for us to do but play fill music for forty-five minutes on Radio Two. Because of the way programming is played back in Canada—that is, time delayed so that all programming airs at the same time on the clock if not the same actual time—we were able to fix the show for Vancouver, but not before that.

The shit hit the fan.

The phone started ringing off the hook, with people wanting to know what happened. I felt absolutely terrible for being responsible for forty-five minutes of incorrect programming from (almost) coast to coast.

The following week people in the Music Department wanted blood. My boss at the time, Kel Lack, told me that they wanted whoever was responsible fired. But Kel felt that if I wrote a letter of apology it might smooth things over, so I did.

Many years later, shortly after I became a manager myself, I was shown a filing cabinet containing personnel files for all radio technicians dating back many years. Naturally there was a file on me and it included that letter.

Here is what I wrote:

January 4, 1989

I'm writing you regarding the incident concerning Two New Hours. I was the technician responsible for the disruption in the broadcast of that show.

For a number of reasons I am sorry for what occurred. I realize my mistake, which took place as a result of negligence, affected a lot of people. I'm aware of the amount of work and effort required to construct a show such as Two New Hours, and I can imagine the dismay all involved must have felt. I feel particularly bad for the Vancouver composer who almost missed hearing his work broadcast.

I have been reprimanded and questioned thoroughly as to why the incident occurred. Steps have been taken both departmentally and personally to ensure that it is not repeated. I make no excuses for my mistake. I do ask that you accept my apology.

Thank you for taking the time to read this.

Sincerely,

Joe Mahoney

Attached to the letter was a note that I had never seen, hand-written by Kel Lack and addressed to Karen Keiser, Head of Serious Music Programming at that time (a position that no longer exists). Kel had written:

Karen Kieser: (See attached)

Joe Mahoney is a new and very promising tech who needless to say was devastated by what happened with Two New Hours.

The tone of his note speaks for itself and I know he learned a good lesson. I propose to leave the matter there.

Once again our apologies

Kel

*Joe Mahoney is a new and very promising tech who needless to say was devastated by what happened with Two New Hours.*

*The tone of his note speaks for itself and I know he learned a good lesson. I propose to leave the matter there.*

*Once again our apologies.*

*Kel*

A good guy, Kel. I never heard of any response from the Serious Music Department.

A couple of other comments about that infamous night. Once we knew what had happened and that it had been my fault, Peter Chin said to me, "You need to bear down, Joe. You need to bear down." He said it to me several times. The line became a joke between the two of us. Over the next several years we laughed about it many times, and I've even had occasion to repeat it back to him. "You need to bear down, Peter!"

The Operations Officer on duty that night, Malcolm MacKinney, took pity on me. It was New Year's Eve, after all. The friendliest of a friendly bunch, Malcolm had a unique gravelly voice and a good sense of humour. He gave me half a bottle of wine and took me across the street to the Hampton Court Hotel, where we rang in the New Year together. A parade of elderly women lined up to give me a peck on the cheek when the clock struck twelve.

Good times.

I've made plenty of other mistakes in my career, but no other doozies quite like that. A good thing, or it probably would have been a short career.

# VIII
## Riding the Faders

After my stint in Radio Master Control, management made me a Group 4 Radio Technician and started booking me regularly in the studios. The radio studios were challenging because there were a lot of them, each one unique. They had different consoles, different patch racks, different tape machines, different outboard gear. In them you would encounter different producers, different talent, and different requirements depending on the booking. You could be working on a McCurdy console, or a Studer, or a Ward-Beck, or an Audioarts, or some weird one-off I'd never heard of before (or since).

It was about two years before I could handle myself in any situation in the studio without having to run to the tech lounge to find someone to help me figure out why the speakers weren't working or why the microphone sounded funny. That's just the run-of-the-mill studios—there was a whole other class of high-end studios used for recording music and radio plays that I didn't set foot in for years, also with a completely different set of consoles, equipment, personalities, and expectations.

What I loved about working in the studios was that every day was different. If you didn't like a gig, no problem: an hour, or a day, or a week later you would be on to something different. Many bookings in a studio lasted only an hour or two. Sometimes you'd be booked to a news or sports studio for a few days. Often a day consisted of multiple bookings for multiple shows. Only after you'd proven yourself would you get something resembling a regular gig with the same show and/or producers.

In the beginning, I worked on everything they threw at me. I recorded and mixed promos. I subbed for other folks who had regular gigs. I worked on shows for both Radio One and Radio Two. On shows I can no longer remember. Music shows, magazine shows, science shows, arts shows, French shows, sports shows. I worked on many remotes. I worked mostly out of the Jarvis Street facilities, but I also did time on Parliament Street, where they produced *Metro Morning* and *Later the Same Day*.

It was work but it was also fun and interesting, though not all my gigs were successful. For instance, I do not remember my time on *Basic Black* fondly. It was my first regular stretch. I was filling in for their regular tech, Kathy von Bezold, for two weeks while she was on vacation. The show was produced in Studio E. I got along well with the host Arthur Black and two of the show's producers, Colleen Woods and John Stinchcombe, but the Studio Director made me nervous. He didn't talk much. I never knew what he was thinking. I was clumsy and slow in his presence. One day the console didn't work properly so I called maintenance. All the maintenance tech had to do was breathe on the console to make it work again. I looked like an idiot. At the end of my two-week stretch the Studio Director took me aside and critiqued my performance.

"You were slow finding patch points," he told me. "You were slow setting up the day we recorded Danny Marks." And so on.

Although not a disaster, my work had left a bit to be desired. Young and not great at taking criticism, I was quite put off by his comments. But I got over it and learned from my mistakes.

Another show that gave me a bit of trouble was *Sunday Morning*. It was a current affairs show that could be quite nerve-wracking to work on. Journalists arrived in the studio with complicated mixes. These days you would do such a mix on a computer. Back then you did it all manually. You pre-recorded sound effects and ambiance and voice clips onto carts. What are carts? Well, they resemble eight track cassettes, which are—well, never mind: look them up in a history book alongside pterodactyls and other extinct species. Other sound elements you recorded onto quarter-inch tape (also extinct). You had to be organized. You had to strategize how to make all these elements accessible for when you needed them. The journalist sat in the announce booth and read his or her script, and you played back all these sonic elements at the appropriate times according to cues on the script. The entire process could be quite a juggling act.

*Sunday Morning*'s regular tech, Peter Beamish, was a genius at this sort of thing. He had tons of experience, so naturally all the journalists wanted to work with him. Guys like me looked like a klutz next to Peter. I remember making a mistake during a mix with one journalist—probably playing a sound effect late or getting a cue wrong.

"Why me, God?" she exclaimed, sighing heavily and laying her head in her arms.

She made me feel like crap.

Still, there were many friendly producers on the show, and the host Mary Lou Finlay was pleasant, and Peter Beamish was never anything less than friendly, humorous, and helpful.

A great hurdle all new technicians had to face was the intimidating presence of experienced producers. You walked into a studio as a new technician and the first question you got from the producer was, "Who are you?" There are many wonderfully flippant responses to this inane question, but you choked them back. Intelligent, mature producers simply dealt with the situation and helped you make the booking a success, whether it was a simple recording or a two-way or what have you.

It was frequently an intimidating experience. There were over twenty studios in the old Jarvis Street radio facilities, and as I've mentioned earlier, almost every studio was set up differently. Every patch rack was different, usually with a spaghetti-like tangle of patch cords, and the rack itself cryptically labeled.

One day I did a booking in Studio F. Studio F was reserved for the show *As It Happens* between 11am and 7pm. This was outside those hours, so this particular booking was for the show *Sunday Morning*. I was working with a prickly producer whom I shall call Maurice. I needed to make a patch, but I didn't know where the patch point was, so I started at the top left-hand corner of the patch rack and worked my way down to the bottom right-hand side.

I said to Maurice, "You'll have to excuse me. It may take me a couple of minutes to find the right patch point."

He said, "Have you considered the possibility that you're stupid?"

Flabbergasted, I resolved to take the high road and said nothing. I found the patch point and continued with the booking. At one point I offered Maurice some gum to illustrate that I had no hard feelings about his harsh remark, and at the end of the booking, I said, "Better make a point of remembering where that patch point is lest it ever be implied again that I'm stupid."

"How you guys remember all these different studios is beyond me," Maurice mumbled.

I accepted this oblique apology, though I never forgot how Maurice's words made me feel.

Working as a Group 4 Radio Technician was trial by fire. You paid your dues until you got up to speed. Until you earned peoples' trust, which took some doing. On yet another night I arrived for a random booking in Studio F to find a producer I'd never seen before.

"Who are you?" he asked.

"I'm your tech," I told him.

He turned on his heels and skulked off to scheduling to complain about having to work with someone new. I had the confidence of the folks in scheduling and they wouldn't have any of it. The producer returned to the studio and we completed the booking without incident. I worked with this producer several times later and it was always friendly enough, but we never became friends.

Fortunately, the positive experiences far outweighed the negative. Such as one memorable booking in the spring of 1992.

The scheduling department had asked me to work overtime in Studio K. It turned out to be a two-hour booking packaging a disc show called *My Kinda Jazz*, hosted by Canadian blues musician Jeff Healey. Healey played antiquated jazz on the show, dating back well into the thirties.

I arrived at the studio before Healey, who settled into the studio's booth shortly afterward. The producer, David Cavlovic, informed him of my presence in the control room. Healey greeted me over the talkback. I thought this was a friendly thing for him to do, as the talent sometimes ignored us technical types until it became absolutely necessary to acknowledge our presence. I said hi back.

Healey remarked that he couldn't hear me very well over the talkback. This didn't really matter as I knew I probably wouldn't be talking to him during the show, but I decided to look at it anyway. I went to the booth and pointed out a certain knob that I suspected might have control over the talkback volume. Healey had his hand partially over the knob in question, preventing me from turning it up myself. As Healey was blind, I was pretty sure that he didn't know which knob I was talking about, so I did a sort of stupid thing, I said, "It's the one just to the right of your hand," and then I reached out and touched the knob, also brushing his hand slightly to let him know the position of the control I was talking about.

He said, "No, that doesn't have anything to do with it, that's the monitor control," giving me the impression that I'd annoyed him.

Without having solved the problem, I adjusted his mic and returned to the control room. (I found out later that you couldn't adjust the level of the talkback in that studio. It was pre-set.)

If Healey really was annoyed with me it didn't last long. There was a bit of friendly banter before we started the show. The packaging went well. It was a straightforward sort of affair—chatter, song, chatter, song, with all the songs pre-recorded by Healey, one right after the other on a DAT (digital audio tape), which made my job easy.

It just so happened that it was March 25, 1992, Healey's twenty-sixth birthday.

Healey was quite knowledgeable about his subject matter. I couldn't tell how much he was reeling off the top of his head or how much he derived from his notes (all in braille). All the tunes were from old 78s, that were his own; apparently he had a collection of about 6000 or so.

We played a song from Duke Ellington and his Orchestra, one of four versions the Duke recorded of this particular song, called "The Mooche." There was a muted trumpet solo in the song, and

Jeff remarked in his intro that the trumpet player used a plunger for a mute.

"Is he joking?" I asked David.

"No," David told me. "It's true."

Via the talkback system, David asked Jeff, "Was it a used plunger?"

Jeff laughed. "If it was, it was probably a shitty plunger."

Jeff sat with his eyes closed the entire booking, rocking a bit to the music. When he left he didn't say goodbye, and David left as well to hail a cab for him.

After a couple of years of gigs like that one, I finally landed a regular studio gig, on a show about books. This worked out well as I'm a big fan of books. The show in question was *Writers & Company*.

The regular technician for *Writers & Company* had been a fellow by the name of Derek Stubbs. When Derek left the CBC, producer Sandra Rabinovitch asked me if I would be interested in replacing him. Flattered and keen to have a show I could call my own, I accepted at once and remained the show's regular tech until shortly before taking a ten-month leave of absence in October 1993 to study abroad.

In June 1993, Knopf Canada published *Writers & Company: In Conversation with CBC Radio's Eleanor Wachtel*. By then I wasn't *Writers & Company*'s regular tech anymore. Just the same, Eleanor kindly included me in her acknowledgements, writing, "We work with many technicians in actually recording and broadcasting interviews—too many to name here—but I am happy to mention our once regular studio engineer, Joe Mahoney."

It wasn't necessary. But I appreciated the gesture.

Nor was it the last kind gesture on Eleanor's part.

When Eleanor found out that I was taking time off to study French in Aix-en-Provence, she told me that I really ought to read the memoir, *Two Towns in Provence: Map of Another Town and A Considerable Town, A Celebration of Aix-en-Provence & Marseille*, by M. F. K. Fisher. I thanked her for the suggestion but never got around to purchasing the book.

Before leaving for France I stayed with my friend and fellow radio technician Joram Kalfa for a few weeks. One wet, blustery day

I got a phone call from Eleanor asking me for Joram's address. An hour later she showed up on Joram's doorstep with a gift. It was Fisher's book. She had gone out of her way to make sure that I had the book for the trip. And what a great book. Thanks to Eleanor I was able to read about Fisher's experience in Aix-en-Provence while living there myself.

Many years later I had a novel published by the small independent Canadian publisher Five Rivers Press. The Merril Collection of Science Fiction, Speculation & Fantasy in Toronto hosted the launch. Even though I hadn't worked as a radio technician on any of their shows for at least a decade, my old pals from *Writers & Company*, *The Arts Tonight*, and *Canada Reads* (Nancy McIlveen, Mary Stinson, Ann Jansen, and Sandra Rabinovitch) all showed up for the launch.

More often than not the people you work with in the studios of CBC Radio become your friends.

# IX
## Radio Techness

When I started at CBC in 1988 there were over eighty radio technicians working in Toronto. We were not the kind of techs who fixed stuff. That was a different kind of tech. Our job was to record, manipulate and broadcast sound.

We came in all shapes and sizes and at least two different genders but we were strikingly similar. We dressed casual but not too casual. It was radio; nobody cared what we looked like. At least, not much—there was a guy who wore sweatpants and another guy who wore a tie. They didn't last long. A couple of the older techs wore blazers and dress pants. They got away with it because they were old. Like, fifty something. I was twenty-something. I wore jeans and T-shirts and sneakers and shaved every second day.

A tech's time was not his or her own. Techs lived and died by the schedule. The schedule told us where to go when:

> Studio B at 9:00 for Infotape promos.
>
> Studio W at 9:30 for a *Quirks & Quarks* two-way.
>
> Studio D at 10:00 to voice track Lister Sinclair for *Ideas*.
>
> Studio L at 11:00 to package *Writers & Company*.
>
> After that, an hour of standby in the lounge.
>
> And so on.

If you wanted a meeting with me, you needed to talk to my scheduler, not me. This wasn't usually a problem. Techs didn't go to many meetings.

I picked up my schedule in my mailbox just outside the scheduling office. My mailbox was one of eighty or so other metal mailboxes, many with weird paraphernalia taped to them, like headlines from newspapers such as "Beware of Doug," and "Mysterious Face Found on Moon" (that one had my face photocopied beneath it). One day we got our schedules in a new format. Days off were indicated by the letters SDO.

"What does SDO stand for?" I asked Master Control guru Gerry Samson.

"Stupid Day Off," Gerry told me.

We didn't have a boss. We had many bosses. We all reported to someone somewhere on paper, but we rarely saw or heard from them. In the studio, everyone was our boss, or thought they were. Everyone from thirty-year veteran producers to associate producers six weeks on the job. Somebody had to tell you what songs and clips to play, when to fade the music up and down. This was fine at first, but it grew old after a couple of decades.

Most techs played at least one musical instrument. Everything from guitars to pianos to bagpipes to hurdy-gurdys. Maybe because they screened for that in the job interview. "Can you read music?" they asked me. I could—I played piano, baritone, and trombone, skills I used a few times on the job, playing organ for a radio play and piano for many sound checks. (Fellow radio technician Mike Furness did not think highly of my keyboard skills. He used to organize a jam session for CBC staff at the Red Lion across Jarvis Street. When I hit a few wrong notes during the opening chords of a Van Morrison song he was trying to cover, he leaned over and whispered, "Don't play.")

There were techs we all admired. Impossibly experienced and competent techs. Super techs. Today super tech means something different—supervising technician. Back then it meant just what it sounded like: a super tech. Superman, only smarter and maybe not as strong, with laser hearing instead of laser vision. There was even a tech who looked like Superman. There were techs rumored to have maintenance backgrounds, who could fix their own gear. Techs who knew how to operate anything from a Shure FP42 to a Neve VR to a McCurdy Turret System. Who knew when to use an AKG 414 and when to switch to a Neumann U-87. Who had four arms for analog mixes and golden ears for concert recordings and the know-how to put together a live pickup of a six-piece band including a full set of drums in Studio R at the last minute. Techs not afraid to share their hard-won knowledge with lesser, mortal technicians like me.

As a tech, if you wanted to, if you were lucky enough and ambitious enough, you could travel from show to show peddling your technical wares, no two days the same, getting to do everything and know everyone. Some days you were a hero, performing difficult mixes for journalists, trotting out long-distance phone codes from memory for associate producers, fixing technical problems at the last possible instant. But the day after that you might be a complete fool, accidentally playing the wrong piece of tape at the wrong time, maybe over a host's introduction for all the world to hear.

On live radio, I felt like a goalie. Nobody noticed when I made the save, but when the puck got past me, the whole country heard the puck go in the net.

Sometimes I got blamed when it wasn't my fault. Many was the time I heard a host tell the world, "Having some technical problems," when in fact the problem had nothing to do with me or my equipment.

During my time as a tech we endured one strike and two lockouts. Because we were in a different bargaining unit than everyone else, we endured two of these labour actions alone. While everyone else was inside, we were outside marching around the building or huddled around oil barrels in sub-zero temperatures. It's water under the bridge, but for anyone who lived through all that, it's a part of our DNA.

It's worth mentioning that radio techs had better Christmas parties than anyone else, at least at Jarvis Street, and that's probably all I ought to say about that.

The job barely exists now, at least the way I remember it. There are only a handful of radio techs left (though some good ones to be sure). Most of the techs I worked with are gone now. Of the ones still around, many have moved onto different positions.

I like to think that a bond remains between those of us who worked as CBC Radio technicians—an invisible thread of quarter-inch Ampex tape, maybe. We're not quite the same as everyone else. Our hearing is notched at 1K, but we still listen better than most. And if you ever need someone to plug in a few cables and adjust some settings here and there, you could do worse than to ask a radio tech for help.

# X

## *As It Happens*

The first few years I worked for CBC Radio I lived across the street from the Radio Building. It was brilliant. No commute. Five minutes to work. I could, and did, eat lunch at home many days. But there was a downside. If someone called in sick I was often the first one they called to replace them. Or maybe it was a good thing, creating opportunities that might not have arisen otherwise.

One morning the phone rang about eight o'clock, waking me up. I answered groggily. It was Heather Rowe from the scheduling department. "Jan Wright has called in sick. Can you do her shift?" Jan Wright was the radio technician for *As It Happens*.

The *As It Happens* shift was from 11am until 7pm. Most of the day was spent recording interviews, followed by an hour and a half long live show. I'd never done *As It Happens* before, though I'd observed the show. I'd never done any live show with CBC Radio before, other than the news, which was pretty straightforward.

The thought of doing *As It Happens* scared the dickens out of me. I was still a relatively new, inexperienced tech. *As It Happens* had been on the air since the time of Moses (having debuted November 18, 1968). It's considered a flagship show (many shows are considered flagship shows, especially by those who work on them, but *As It Happens* really is). It's broadcast nationally. If I made a mistake the entire country would hear it. Screwing it up would sink my entire budding CBC career, I figured.

"Sure," I told Heather.

I slept a bit more, by which I mean I tossed and turned for a bit. I got up and showered. I may have shaved. At five minutes to ten, I marched across the street to Studio F, the *As It Happens* studio.

*As It Happens* is a current affairs show. Chase producers reach out to guests, usually by telephone, pre-interview the guests, and arrange for them to be interviewed by the *As It Happens* host while the guests are actually living the news, or as soon as possible afterward. Most of the interviews are pre-taped the day of the show. Those that aren't are broadcast live during the show, frequently in the first slot (at least when I worked on the show).

In my day the hosts were Michael Enright and Alan Maitland. Alan introduced the guests while Michael did all the interviewing. Michael was in and out of the studio all day. Alan pre-taped the odd little bit but was mostly just in the studio during the live portion of the show. Alan was over seventy when I worked with him, and I was in my mid-twenties. I remember thinking that he would have been in his mid-twenties during the Second World War. For many years you could still hear Alan Maitland on *As It Happens* every Christmas Eve when they replayed his superb reading of "The Shepherd" by Frederick Forsythe.

I don't remember a single interview we recorded the first day I worked on the show. For one thing, I was a nervous wreck. For another, technicians frequently finish shows they're working on with no clue what they just broadcast. This isn't because they aren't paying attention. Quite the contrary: it's because techs are listening extremely closely, just not to the same things as everyone else in the studio. Producers are listening to the content. They want to know if all the information is getting out, and whether the narrative makes sense. Techs are listening to the sound. What's the phone line like? Is it intelligible? Can you make out the guests' words? Is there too much background noise? Are the levels okay? Why is the host sitting so far back from the microphone? Why are they putting their hand in front of their mouth? What's that sound? Is someone hitting the table with their knee?

Once we finished recording the interviews on quarter-inch tape, the producers took them back to their desks to edit them for length and clarity. They also "top and tailed" them—inserting leader tape before and after the interview to make it easier for the technician to cue them up for the live show. We also recorded other little bits between Michael and Alan—special segments, end credits, and so on.

At five-twenty (ten minutes before the show start time), I phoned Radio Master Control and lined up with tone and a time check. By this point on my first day with the show I was a bundle of nervous energy, convinced that the next hour and a half would be my undoing. Nevertheless, I was prepared. I had the first interview tapes cued up on the four Studers lining the back wall of the control room. I had three carts in the cart machine: the opening theme, Moe Koffman's "Curried Soul," edited for *As It Happens* by producer Volkmar Richter (he also did the closing theme), and a couple of stings (brief pieces of music) that we would use as interstitials between Alan Maitland's live extros and his intro to the next piece of tape. Studio director Alan Guettel was seated on my left (when he wasn't hovering behind me), and both Michael and Alan were ensconced in the announcer's booth before us.

Ten seconds before air the studio's confidence clock counted down the time: ten, nine, eight...

When the countdown hit zero a red light would come on and our studio would be live to the East Coast (the delay system would broadcast to the rest of the nation.) At the top of the clock I hit the opening theme. At the appropriate point in the music, Alan Guettel indicated with a hand gesture that I should lower the theme. Our hosts introduced the show over the music. When they were finished, I brought the theme back up for a few seconds before fading it gradually out as Alan Maitland introduced the first item, which was live on the phone.

While Michael interviewed the first guest, Guettel decided to change the sting music we had picked out to follow the interview. I piped the sound to a tiny "cue" speaker on the console that only those of us in the control room could hear. We auditioned several carts before he finally picked one appropriate to the tone of the interview (this would happen frequently throughout the show) and I loaded it into the top slot of the cart machine.

I was establishing several protocols that would serve me well operating live shows for the next nineteen years. For example, I always pushed the fader associated with the next source I was about to play (e.g., cart, tape machine, etc.) up ever so slightly on the console, and only brought it up to full level just before hitting the play button. That way I always knew what I was supposed to play next. It was easy to get distracted in the heat of battle. Also, with the fader mostly down I wouldn't ever accidentally broadcast something at the wrong time (which could easily happen if I auditioned something such as a sting without realizing that I'd left the fader up).

I soon learned that operating *As It Happens* wasn't anywhere near as difficult as I'd feared. In fact, the show worked like clockwork: intro, interview, extro, sting. Intro, interview, extro, sting (there were always a few extra elements thrown in as well, such as caller talkback, a bit called "For the Record," etc.). Each interview, whether live or on tape, was like an island, an oasis of calm. I could sit back for five or eight minutes and calmly survey the script for what needed to be set up next. Alan Guettel was crystal clear in his directions, telling me what to play when. There were moments he got distracted; in those times I needed to pry the information I required out of him, but as it was important to keep me informed about what was going on, usually this wasn't a problem.

There was a fun little piece of business at the end of the show that I liked. During the extro to the last interview, I faded up the closing theme, which was another Moe Koffman song called "Koff Drops (Allegro Sonata II)." After a few seconds, I faded it down, allowing Michael and Alan to close the show. Immediately following their last word, I hit another cart, playing another section of "Koff Drops" at full volume. This other section began with a great drum riff ("BUMPA BUMPA bumpa BUMPA BUMPA bumpa") that completely took over, allowing me to quickly and discretely fade out the first part of the theme. It was a simple but satisfying piece of business. I would go on to operate *As It Happens* many times, and every time I did I savored that moment.

One time, though, when I hit the cart to bring in the drums, the result didn't sound right. It was not entirely inappropriate—it was just wrong, somehow. Everyone in the control room went silent as we tried to figure out what was the matter. Then I realized: instead of playing the closing theme, "Koff Drops," I'd play the opening theme, "Curried Soul." I'd cheated myself (and everyone else) out of that moment with the drums. I was embarrassed at my mistake. But it didn't sound all that bad, so we left it, and I'm probably the only one on the planet that even remembers the day *As It Happens* finished with the opening theme instead of the closing theme.

These days *As It Happens* uses an updated version of the theme. I have to be honest: I miss the original themes.

# XI

## *Morningside*

John Johnston was *Morningside*'s regular technician. It had been Jim Summerfield before John. After John, it was Trish Thornton. Many others had done the show, too. All of them worked on the show a lot more than I did. I just filled in from time to time and worked on a summer version of the show with a couple of replacement hosts: Denise Donlon and Ian Brown. I did the actual show with regular host Peter Gzowski just three times. The show looms large in my memory, though.

The summer replacement version of *Morningside* was called *Summerside*. Having grown up in the town of Summerside, Prince Edward Island, I got a kick out of the name. By the time I came to work on the show *Summerside*, I had a fair bit of experience operating shows like *As It Happens*, but *Morningside aka Summerside* was rather more challenging. *As It Happens* was microphones, phones, and tape. *Morningside/Summerside* was microphones, phones, tape, wireless microphones, two-ways, three-ways, live bands, and any number of other weird setups depending on the guests.

John Johnston trained me the week before I took over *Morningside/Summerside*. Thanks to John, by the time I worked on the show alone, I knew every strip on Studio R's McCurdy console inside and out. I knew every aux and group, every patch point, all the (limited) outboard gear, and every inch of every wallbox in the booth. John instructed me on control room protocol, too. He advised me to keep the chatter to a minimum during the show and to insist on clarity of direction. He suggested that I keep the monitors in the control room at a consistent level, but I was never able to do that—I considered it a courtesy to turn down the volume if the studio director needed to be on the phone.

I didn't get the full week of training from John that I was supposed to, though. My shadowing was interrupted when we showed up Wednesday morning to find the console fried. We called Audio Systems (radio maintenance) and technologist Don Paterson arrived to help. Don quickly determined that the console's power supply was toast. This wasn't good, as we needed to be on the air in an hour, and an hour wasn't enough time to fix the problem.

We had no choice—we would have to do the show out of another studio. The logical choice was Studio F next door, which had a similar McCurdy console. Because I'd done *As It Happens* out of there recently and was more familiar with the console and the studio, it made sense for me to do the show. In the fine CBC tradition of trial by fire, I did. I have absolutely zero memory of what happened that day, suggesting that I may have done the show in a kind of fugue state, but both the show and I appear to have survived intact.

Thanks to Don Paterson of Audio Systems, Studio R was back in service the following day. By Monday, John Johnston and Peter Gzowski were off playing golf while I flew solo with guest host, Ian Brown. He would do the first two weeks of *Summerside,* and Denise Donlon would do the second. Memorable guests included Michael Enright (host of *As It Happens* at the time) and Canadian actor Kenneth Welsh (fresh off the television show *Twin Peaks*, with more recent credits in *The Day After Tomorrow* and *The Aviator*, among others).

Michael Enright had been invited on the show to demonstrate Tai Chi. Yes, that's right, Tai Chi on the radio, but if anyone could make that work it was Michael. I had to figure out how to mic him while he was standing up and demonstrating the moves. Tech Stores had recently acquired some wireless microphones so I used a wireless Lavalier, which did the job.

The Kenneth Welsh interview didn't work out quite so well. The actor was quite pleasant, but a third of the way through the interview his AKG 224 microphone cut out. I punched the mic button on the console off and on and played with the gain but it didn't help. I could still hear Welsh through Ian Brown's mic, which meant that the problem was likely limited to the strip on the console, a cable, or the mic itself.

I tore out of the control room and into the booth. Brown and Welsh kept on talking even though Welsh sounded like he was in another room. There were four AKG 224s on the table: Brown's, the one that wasn't working, and two others not in use, which were presumably fine. Ian treated the nation to a play-by-play as I swapped out the bad mic for one of the spares. I plugged it in, skedaddled back to the control room, and brought the fader up. It worked.

On another occasion I had a bit of a problem with a two-way.

Two-ways consist of a host in a studio in one location and a guest (usually in a studio) in another. The second location could be just across the city or it could be a studio on the other side of the world. You have to master a little something called the "mix/minus" to perform a proper two-way. This is just making sure that you're not sending the person on the other end of the line back to themselves. Say I have a two-way between Toronto and Vancouver. The voice of the guest in Vancouver is sent down a line to my studio in Toronto. At the same time, I must send the voice of my host down the line to the studio in Vancouver. But both the technician in Vancouver and I need to make sure that we don't send our signals back to one another. If I send the guest in Vancouver back to himself, it will come back to him delayed by as much as half a second. He or she will hear this in the headphones and find it very distracting. Although straightforward once you know how, people often get the mix/minus wrong.

On this instance, while broadcasting the show *Summerside* live, we had a guest about to appear on the show from a studio in Moncton. About twenty minutes before the interview was to start, when I thought there was a good chance that the guest had settled into the Moncton studio, I pressed a button on the console and spoke down the line:

"Hello Moncton, this is Toronto."

No response.

We were already live on air with another guest and the clock was ticking. I didn't waste any time. I called Radio Master Control on our dedicated phone line.

Peter Chin answered. "Master."

"Hey Peter, we have a two-way with Moncton and I'm not hearing anything down the line."

"No prob, Joe. I'll give them a call."

A couple of minutes later Peter called me back. "It's a summer replacement tech. Sounds like he doesn't know how to split the board."

What Peter meant is that the tech in Moncton, probably just a couple of weeks into the job, didn't know how to set up his console for the two-way. Peter gave me the phone number to the studio in Moncton. With our show live on air and mere minutes to the interview, I called the Moncton tech.

"Hey there, it's Joe in Toronto. I'm the tech for *Summerside*. You have a guest there waiting to do an interview with us in a few minutes."

"Yes. I can hear you down the line."

"Good. Unfortunately, we can't hear you. Are you sending the guest down the aux?"

Together we figured out how to make his console do what it needed to do. Fortunately, he was a quick learner and got it working seconds before we would have been forced to cancel the interview. It was a tense few moments for both of us, but live radio is always full of challenges like that.

These sorts of issues are not all that unusual. It is said that no plan survives contact with the enemy, and this certainly applies to live radio. Equipment breaks, bands show up late for sound checks, somebody doesn't split the board properly in another part of the country, guests don't show up at all, or when they do show up they behave erratically, and it's up to the team behind the show, particularly those in the control room, to deal with it all. It's not life or death. It's not like somebody will die if you screw up. But it sure feels important when you're sitting in the hot seat. The listener experience is on the line. Ratings are on the line. And if you don't get it right, your job might be on the line—or at least the plum gigs.

I wasn't some kind of super tech, constantly saving the day. John Johnston could easily have done the show from Studio F. Any tech can swap out a microphone. The summer relief tech in Moncton ultimately figured out how to split the console himself. I am well aware of where I sat in the pantheon of the eighty or so techs working in CBC Toronto at the time. I was neither the best nor the worst of the lot. These are just a few real-life examples of the kinds of challenges one faces attempting to cobble together live radio.

Still, despite the occasional bit of stress, I found working on live radio therapeutic. Live radio is frequently all-consuming, deeply immersive, and even cathartic. On a busy show you don't have time to think about anything else. You're completely in the moment. Something knocks you sideways and you need to produce a rabbit out of a hat and you're not sure you can pull it off but somehow you do. It completely clears your mind. Whatever mood you're in when you go to air, the show spits you out in a completely different mood. If you survive—and you usually do—you emerge calm and happy.

I didn't work on *Morningside* (or *Summerside*) again until we moved out of the Jarvis Street Radio Building to the new Toronto Broadcast Centre on Front Street. There I did the show live twice, both times with the man himself, Peter Gzowski. Pop singer Kim Stockwood performed live. Pierre Berton and Dr. Spock both dropped by for a chat.

The first day Gzowski and I never spoke. That just seemed to be the dynamic with him. Halfway through the show on the second day, during a piece of tape, Gzowski finally addressed me from the booth via the talkback.

"Hi," he said.

"Hi," I replied.

"You're doing a great job," he said.

"Thanks," I said.

It's the only thing Peter Gzowski ever said to me.

It's all I needed him to say.

# XII

## Freelancing

Despite the challenges and occasional rewards of working behind the scenes, I missed being on air. Four years in, I was getting tired of being the tech. The bottom of the food chain. First came the talent, then the producers, then the mice, then the cockroaches, and finally the techs.

I had been the talent once. I wanted to be the talent again.

I began by applying for on-air jobs within CBC. I applied to be host of the afternoon show in Charlottetown. It didn't seem much of a stretch. I had already broadcast from three of the five radio stations on Prince Edward Island (CJRW, CFCY, and Q-93). I only had CHTN and CBCT-FM left to go. I didn't even land an interview. Instead I got a rejection letter addressed to someone else (who presumably got my letter).

I applied for another host job, this time in Prince Rupert, British Columbia. They asked me to provide a sample of an on-air interview. As a disc jockey, I'd read the news, weather, sports, and ferry reports, introduced records, and dealt with other, less pleasant tasks ("At this time we regret to make the following announcement"), but I'd never conducted interviews. I needed to get an interview on tape. Friend and fellow tech Trish Thornton offered to help me.

"Who can I interview?" I asked her.

"Someone famous," she suggested.

"Who?"

By then I'd already met several famous people, but I didn't actually know any of them. We batted around a few names, but none seemed right.

"What about Ray Lund's father?" Trish suggested finally.

Ray Lund was a fellow radio tech also in his twenties, a wonderfully laid-back guy who loved to fish. We called him "the fishin' technician."

"The fishin' technician's father is famous?"

"Ray's father is Alan Lund," Trish explained. "You should know this. You're from Prince Edward Island! He choreographed and directed the first-ever *Anne of Green Gables* musical."

I was impressed. I'd seen *Anne of Green Gables* at Confederation Centre in Charlottetown at least twice. It was pretty good. I'd had no idea that the fishin' technician was descended from such renowned stock.

Ray spoke to his father. Alan Lund kindly agreed to let me interview him via phone. I prepared a bunch of questions, and one evening, Trish, Ray and I commandeered Studio C to record the interview. Trish operated the console. Alan Lund waxed loquacious about his illustrious career. He was terrific. Unfortunately, his tales knocked me completely off script. I could not figure out how to segue from his answers to my follow-up questions with anything resembling grace. Interviewing, I discovered, was a lot harder than it looked.

I edited the interview into something palatable and sent it off to the folks in Prince Rupert. I never heard back. At least Charlottetown had sent me a rejection letter, even if it had been addressed to someone else.

Applying for host jobs wasn't getting me anywhere. I needed to try something else.

Maybe, I reflected, I could start by freelancing. By which I mean producing content for CBC Radio on the side as a freelancer.

CBC Radio is always on the lookout for content. That's because radio is insatiable. It requires content twenty-four hours a day, seven days a week, fifty-two weeks a year with no end in sight. In the constant, unrelenting effort to satisfy the appetite for content, freelancers are a critical component. Back in the early nineties, when I was plotting my return to on-air status, one of the best ways into CBC Radio as a freelancer was via a department called Infotape (later called The Content League, and then Syndication). Infotape produced and distributed short audio features to CBC

Radio morning and afternoon shows across Canada to help flesh out their content.

As a Group 4 Radio Technician, I often worked with Infotape producers. We helped freelancers produce commentaries, financial and historical columns, and so on. How difficult could it be to come up with some content of my own that I could sell to Infotape to get my foot in the door?

Film reviews, for instance. I often recorded film reviewer Michael Skeet's reviews for Infotape. I enjoyed his reviews, but as a movie buff myself, I always rather cockily thought that I could do just as well. That is, until one day I recorded his review for the movie *Nine and a Half Weeks*. During his read, Michael pronounced the director's name, which is Adrian Lyne, as Adrian "Lin." Now, I knew my directors.

"It's pronounced 'line,' not 'lin,' I told producer Ian Hamilton.

Ian hit the talkback. "Joe thinks his name is pronounced 'Line.'"

"No, it's pronounced 'Lin,'" Michael assured us.

This was well before the Internet. We had no way of instantly verifying the pronunciation, but it turned out Michael was right.

So, maybe movie reviews weren't the way to go, then.

One day I got booked to record a commentary (opinion piece) from a freelancer. The freelancer arrived at the studio unaccompanied by a producer. This was unusual, but I accepted his script and helped him get comfortable in the booth. I'd learned that many freelancers and guests come from backgrounds far removed from radio; anything you can do to help them get comfortable in a radio environment improves their performance. So, I asked this freelancer if he knew how to turn his mic off and on, whether he knew how to adjust the volume of his headphones, and so on. He indicated that he did without letting on that maybe I was telling him something he already knew.

To my surprise, the freelancer performed a single pass on the script with no pickups. This was almost unheard of. Still, I had two issues with his performance. One was a slight vocal stumble. The other was a questionable word choice. I mentioned both when he emerged from the booth. Usually everyone involved in the process wants to get things right. Pointing out mistakes so that they might be corrected is just part of the job.

Instead of responding to my constructive criticism, the "freelancer" thanked me for recording him and left the studio. Only afterward did I discover that the man I had taken for a freelancer was in fact a well-established broadcaster in Newfoundland on the cusp of becoming a national personality by the name of Rex Murphy.

No doubt he had been bemused by my attempt to "produce" him.

But recording him encouraged me to pursue my own on-air aspirations. I couldn't write like Rex Murphy; nor was I as opinionated, so instead of pitching a commentary, I pitched an idea for an item called a "streeter" to Infotape producer Laurie Townsend. Streeters are short, snappily edited interviews with people out in the real world, "on the street," as it were. I thought it would be fun to do a streeter about Prince Edward Island. Being from PEI, I had discovered that people "from away" had a lot of funny ideas about Canada's smallest province. (Islanders refer to anyone not from PEI as "from away." My parents moved to PEI from New Brunswick in 1966 and are still considered from away.)

Laurie liked the idea. Trish Thornton found me a Shure SM58 microphone and a professional cassette recorder—this was long before digital. The cassette recorder was a professional Sony unit, the TCM-5000 Three Head Portable Cassette Recorder. Sturdy, reliable, easy to use. Comfortable shoulder strap. Pressing play and record on that baby was very satisfying, a solid mechanical two-finger crunch. Mono but that was all I needed for my modest purposes.

So armed, one evening after work I made my way downtown to the corner of Yonge and Dundas where I stood at the northeast corner of the Eaton Centre, Toronto's downtown shopping mall and office complex. The idea was to flag down passersby to get their thoughts on Prince Edward Island. I was horribly self-conscious. I could barely bring myself to approach anybody.

"Excuse me... excuse me..."

People just ignored me, everyone in a rush, zero interest in talking to the strange young man waving a microphone about. But

I couldn't leave without getting a few interviews. Finally, a young woman consented to speak with me. Over the hustle and bustle of Yonge Street, I told her, "I'm with CBC Radio doing a piece on Prince Edward Island. What do you think of when I say Prince Edward Island?"

She thought for a bit. "Potatoes."

Emboldened, I approached others.

"Potatoes."

"Potatoes."

"Potatoes."

"Anne of Green Gables."

"Gorgeous scenery, seafood."

I approached a well-dressed man in his late thirties. "I just want to throw something at you, get your immediate reaction. Prince Edward Island, what do you think of?"

"Uh, I'm not familiar with him."

"You've never heard of Prince Edward Island?"

"Prince Allen? No, I haven't, no."

"Prince Edward."

"Prince Edward? Yeah, I've heard of Prince Edward, right."

"Prince Edward Island? It's a province of Canada."

"Oh, oh, I'm sorry, Prince Edward... Island. No, I can't say that I have."

Turned out he was from the States.

I stood at Yonge and Dundas long enough to get plenty of tape. I talked to people about PEI potatoes ("they're creamier or something"). Nobody knew who the premier of PEI was, though one man came close, guessing "Ghizzie." (The correct response was Joe Ghiz.) I asked people about the population of PEI. Guesses ranged from ten million to three or four thousand. The actual population at this time (late summer 1991) was about 130,000.

Back in the studio, I edited all the responses together. Trish helped me write a script around it. As usual, she operated the board as I recorded the piece. We mixed in a bit of Stompin' Tom's "Bud the Spud" for good measure, and I presented the finished product to Laurie. She liked it. She took it to her colleagues in Infotape. I waited for it to be fed to the regions for broadcast, and for my on-air career to take off.

I waited, and waited, and waited.

One day during all this waiting the fire alarm in the Jarvis Street Radio Building went off. I stood in the parking lot with Ray the fishin' technician waiting to be allowed back in the building. A radio show host I'll call Jimmy waited with us. Both Ray and I had operated Jimmy's show for him. Ray and Jimmy got to chatting.

"So, what do you do here?" Jimmy asked after a few minutes.

Ray's eyes narrowed. "I'm a radio tech."

"Oh," Jimmy said. "What shows do you work on?"

Ray stared at him. "Yours."

I wandered off and bumped into Laurie from Infotape. "There's an election coming up," I told her. "Ghiz might not be Premier much longer. If he's not Premier, my piece will be out of date."

Laurie finally convinced her colleagues to syndicate the item, and it played on a few markets around the country. As luck would have it, I was visiting Prince Edward Island when they finally played it in February 1992. Hearing it broadcast out of Charlottetown I was pleased as punch. I felt pretty good about myself. The day after the piece was broadcast, I drove Lynda (my future wife) to the ferry terminal in Bordon to take the boat over to Moncton to visit her sister. I thought I'd impress her by showing her a shortcut to the ferry terminal, one I often took in the summer. It was a dirt road. This was the dead of winter. In PEI they don't plough all the dirt roads in the winter. I didn't know that. I got Lynda's brand-new Pontiac Sunbird stuck in the snow. Stuck real good. We had to get a farmer with a tractor to tow us out.

Afterward, Lynda's father, Dave Beach, asked me, "You couldn't see that it wasn't ploughed?"

Turns out that despite having been raised in PEI I was just as ignorant about certain aspects of the province as the people I'd been poking fun at in my streeter.

Still, my first attempt at freelancing had been a success. Over the years I produced several more pieces: streeters, documentaries, and so on. One of my favourite streeters was about the impending retirement of cartoonist Gary Larson, the man behind the comic strip *The Far Side*. People enjoyed sharing thoughts about their favourite *Far Side* comics with me. I interspersed their reminiscences with funny sound effects, and the item played in various markets across Canada, including *Metro Morning* in Toronto.

The day it played on *Metro Morning* I was working for the French radio services (CJBC) on the fifth floor. During one of our live shows the studio phone rang. It was someone from *Metro Morning*, who told me that Gary Larson had heard my piece about him on their show. He was upset about the item. So upset, in fact, that he was considering legal action. I would be hearing from his representative soon.

I hung up thinking, that can't be right. There wasn't a damned thing the least bit objectionable about the piece. I had quoted some of the gags from the comics, but that was it. Was Gary Larson crazy? I was seriously bummed.

By the end of the following day I hadn't heard from anyone. I called an acquaintance on *Metro Morning*. Turned out it had all been a practical joke. Ha ha.

All my freelancing eventually generated listener emails. Two, to be precise. After *The Arts Tonight* broadcast a radio documentary I produced about science fiction, an associate producer for the show promised to forward them to me. Naturally I was keen to see the emails. Several days went by. No emails.

"What, does she have to build a computer from the ground up before she can forward them to me?" I complained to another producer via email, and then hit send.

Moments later the associate producer from *The Arts Tonight* plunked a piece of paper down in front of me. Not the listener emails. My email.

"Maybe you meant to send this to someone else," she suggested.

I had accidentally emailed my griping about her, to her. If she held it against me, she didn't show it. It was better than I deserved. I have respected her ever since. She finally forwarded me the listener emails.

I never did get that on-air job I'd been looking for, though.

# XIII

## Studios from Scratch

M ost of the time, CBC Radio shows (such as *Morningside, As It Happens,* and so on) are broadcast out of special, purpose-built radio studios, all carefully designed, built, and equipped by experienced broadcast engineers. In studios like that all you have to do to get your show on the air is go in, sit down, and turn on a piece of equipment or two.

Other times, studios are built from scratch.

Sometimes this is as simple as a microphone attached to a recording device by an XLR cable, along with a pair of headphones.

Sometimes it's rather more complicated than that.

When we go off site and cobble one of these transient radio studios together, whether it's simple or complicated, we call it a "remote."

Some remotes are more remote than others. If a remote is just a few blocks away and the tech happens to forget a piece of gear, maybe a microphone stand or a clip, he or she can just dart back to the plant and get it. If a remote is hours away, maybe halfway across the country, or in a completely different country, the tech had better have all the right gear.

Some remotes last only an hour or two; others never seem to end. Sometimes a show will broadcast live right from their remote location. Other times they'll record what they want and edit the content later and broadcast it sometime after that.

My first remote was a music pickup in the Church of the Holy Trinity in downtown Toronto, not too far away from the Radio Building on Jarvis Street. Recording engineer Dave Burnham was recording a choir there to be broadcast later on a show called *Listen to the Music.* The Cowboy Junkies had recorded their superlative album *The Trinity Session* in that same church a few months earlier. My job was to help Dave, which mainly meant lugging all his equipment. Remotes almost always involve a lot of lugging.

It was a simple enough remote, on the surface: recording one small choir. Dave's setup consisted of a handful of microphones connected to a small console. Still, there were several questions that needed to be answered. Just how exactly to make this choir sound as good as possible? What kind of microphones to use? How many? Where to place them? What kind of outboard gear to use, if any? An experienced high-end recording engineer like Dave had plenty of tricks up his sleeves and employed his own unique strategies. Recording music out in the field was an art, and although I accompanied engineers like Dave out on a few remotes and did some remote music recording of my own, I never acquired anything resembling the expertise of someone like Dave.

After a couple of years of lugging gear for other techs and learning what I could, I started getting my own remotes. Despite my time observing, I was initially a bit handicapped. Unlike many other techs, I never did a stretch in Radio Technical Stores. Radio Tech Stores was where techs got equipment for their remotes. Working in Stores you assembled equipment for more senior techs and accompanied them on their remotes. If you paid attention, you learned what gear was best and how to make it work.

Motivated by a profound fear of failure, I overcame my handicap by spending time in Stores on my own, hooking up gear and figuring out how to make it do what I needed it to do. Over time my preparation paid off, though the knowledge of gear I acquired didn't entirely compensate for certain other massive deficiencies, such as an inability to find my way around Toronto.

One of my first solo pickups was for a show on politics called *The House*, broadcast out of Ottawa. My job was to record the second-last mayor of Scarborough, Joyce Trimmer, on a Nagra tape recorder in her office for one half of a double-ender. A double-ender consists of an interviewer back in the studio talking to a guest on the phone while somebody like me records the guest out in the field. Afterward, back in the studio, a tech eliminates the poor phone-quality recording of the guest, replacing that recording with the high-fidelity recording done in the field.

I needed to be at Trimmer's office by two in the afternoon. We had the studio in Ottawa booked until two-thirty only. Unfortunately, I didn't own a car and wasn't used to driving in Toronto. I didn't know my way around the streets of Scarborough at all. Driving a Stores van, I got hopelessly lost. I couldn't find Trimmer's mayoral office (this was long before the days of GPS). Somebody had told me it was in the Scarborough Town Centre shopping mall, but I couldn't even find that. Finally, I arrived at Mayor Trimmer's office in an adjacent building. Panting and sweating and lugging my equipment, I got there twenty minutes late. Back in the studio the producer and host must have been freaking out. Trimmer herself was the epitome of graciousness. She offered me a glass of water, which I gratefully accepted, and we managed to get the recording done in the time remaining.

My remote skills (such as they were) really came together while working for the folks at CJBC. CJBC is a part of CBC Radio-Canada. An affiliate of the *ici Radio-Canada Premiere* network, they broadcast to Franco-Ontarians at AM 860 out of studios on the fifth floor of the Toronto Broadcast Centre. I was loaned to them for four and a half years after I took the better part of a year off to live in France. More about France later, but in my time with CJBC I did a lot of remotes.

The first big remote I did for CJBC was for something called a *Salon du livres*, held in one of the big halls in the Toronto Convention Centre. Basically it was a book fair. We did one of those a year. Because the *Salon du livres* was a relatively big remote and because I really didn't know what the heck I was doing, I asked for help. I was assigned fellow technician Carlos Van Leeuwen, who happened to be working in Stores at the time.

The remote consisted of a host and three guest positions set up at one table in the middle of the book fair, facing a small audience. The guests and hosts would use headphone microphones. There was a PA (public address system) set up for the benefit of a small audience. During the live show I would sit at a separate table with my mixing console and the producer and associate producer at my side. There would be a talkback set up for the producer and the host to be able to communicate with one another. An ISDN unit would transmit the show to the Broadcast Centre and live to air.

Tech Stores had something called a McCurdy Turret System for exactly this kind of remote. Carlos and I decided to give it a try. The only problem was neither of us had ever used it before, and we had only the barest idea how it worked. There were no instructions and we didn't have access to anyone else who knew how it worked, if such a person existed. The only way to figure it out was to plug it all together in various permutations until it finally worked. I would say that it was a completely unintuitive system except that I know people who used to work for McCurdy and I wouldn't want to hurt anyone's feelings.

For some reason that eludes me now, but that I'm sure made perfect sense at the time, we didn't start trying to figure it out until the day of the remote. There were moments I didn't think we'd ever get the bloody thing working. But we did, and I will be eternally grateful to Carlos for his help—without him I'd probably still be staring at it cross-eyed.

Once I understood how the McCurdy Turret System worked, I began to use it on all my remotes. One day another tech watched me set it up. The connectivity was so bizarre that he couldn't believe it worked that way.

"You must be doing it wrong," he insisted.

"You try," I challenged him.

He tried. He failed.

During that first *Salon du livres* there were many long moments where nothing worked properly, during which I seriously entertained the notion that we wouldn't make it to air. There is a moment like that on every remote. That moment can last seconds or it can last hours, but it's always there. Sometimes it's dead simple: you have a microphone set to line instead of to mic on the console (which is more straightforward than it sounds). Fine. You spot the problem and fix it. Sometimes it's more complicated than that, and you have to troubleshoot your entire setup to find the answer, maybe a bad cable or a faulty mixer, and there are no maintenance techs around to help you (well, sometimes there are, on big music remotes, but there never was for me). I had a rule of thumb that served me well: it's never the cable. And it never was. Except for once, when it was.

Sometimes the problem will have nothing to do with your equipment. Once, during a setup for a remote in Welland, I couldn't establish continuity with Master Control. I wasn't too concerned; it was an hour before airtime. Forty-five minutes later it still wasn't working. I was certain the problem wasn't anything on my end. Nor was the problem in Master Control. Turned out it was in between, with Bell. A Bell tech fixed it ten minutes before air time—someone had patched a cable wrong.

Remotes were usually pretty straightforward once you got everything working. Once I had to deal with a bit of feedback from a PA (relatively simple), and another time a dirty turret developed a click whenever the host toggled the microphone on or off (a more complicated problem). But these were relatively minor problems compared to the most nerve-wracking remote I ever endured, which took place in Niagara-on-the-Lake. I was working for the radio drama department at the time. We did multiple remote pickups every summer at the Shaw Festival for the Bell Canada Reading Series. They were usually a lot of fun. Sometimes another engineer would tag along; sometimes it would just be you and a producer. On this particular day I was flying solo.

Because I had to be there early, I packed up my gear the night before and drove the CBC van home to Whitby where I was living at the time. Proud to work for the CBC and proud to be seen working for the CBC, I always liked driving a CBC-branded van (yes, I'm aware that pride cometh before a fall, or at least a near fail). I got up at five in the morning the day of and made the two-and-a-half-hour drive from Whitby to the Royal George Theatre in Niagara-on-the-Lake. Someone let me into the theatre and I set up. I don't remember what reading I was recording on this particular day. It might have been an adaptation of the French novel *Le Grand Meaulnes*, or it could have been something about Emily Carr. Whatever it was, it involved eight or so actors lined up in a row on stage reading from scripts on music stands. I typically used AKG 414s on the actors, plugged into a snake, fed to a Sony MXP61 mixing console. We recorded straight to DAT (digital audio tape) in those days. I had two decks: one master and one backup.

I've always hated DATs.

When I first started doing remotes, I only brought as much equipment as I thought I needed. I mistakenly thought that sort of economy constituted good planning. And maybe it would if you were travelling to the North Pole. But it didn't take me long to figure out that it was much smarter to bring as much as I could cram into the van. Extras of everything. Two consoles instead of one. Extra microphones, stands, snakes, whatever I could get away with. But sometimes even that wasn't enough.

There is no air conditioning in the Royal George Theatre (at least there wasn't then), and it was unbelievably hot that day. I wondered if it might be too hot for the DAT decks. I was parked right outside the theatre. I considered moving the DAT machines into the back of the van and turning on the vehicle's air conditioning. We'd done that once before. But it was getting a little too close to show time, so I left the setup the way it was.

Patrons filed into the theatre. Soon the place was packed. With all those people it got even hotter. The show started. My top deck was a Panasonic. The bottom deck was a Sony. About ten minutes into the show the Panasonic deck stopped recording. No problem. I still had the Sony. I got the Panasonic going again. A few minutes later the Sony froze. Uh oh. What if they both froze at the same time? It went on like this for the entire hour it took to record the reading. First one deck locking up and then the other. I was sweating bullets, but not because of the heat.

Once the recordings were finished, I tested playback. The Sony would play back but the recording was spotty. The Panasonic wouldn't play back at all. This wasn't good. It was a long drive back to the Broadcast Centre. I had screwed up the entire remote. How would I break the news to the producer, Barbara Worthy? I had never seen Babs angry before. Well, there was always a first time.

Usually, I headed back to the Broadcast Centre, unloaded all my gear, returned the van, and headed home on the GO Train. This time I unloaded all my gear as fast as I could and made a beeline for the edit suites. I needed to know if I could get anything off the DAT tapes or if in fact the remote was a complete failure.

The best way to retrieve material from a DAT tape is to play it back from the same machine it was recorded on. I didn't trust the machines I'd recorded on, so I found the same make of machine in two different studios. Playing back the tapes, I saw that some audio had successfully recorded on each tape. But there were gaping holes in both tapes.

I transferred the contents of each DAT tape into Pro Tools, then lined them up on separate tracks, allowing me to see visually just what was missing from each tape. Although each tape was missing several minutes' worth of material, through some miracle each track compensated for the other. Between the two tapes I had an entire show. What a relief! I resolved to bring seventeen spare DAT machines with me to the next remote. Fortunately, technology is constantly evolving; within a couple of years I was recording these sorts of remotes on MacBook laptops, and I never had to rely solely on DAT tapes again.

Remotes weren't always stressful. Most were fun, at least once you knew all the gear was going to work and the remote wasn't likely to get you fired. One in particular that stands out for me took place at the Blyth Festival in Blyth, Huron County. I'd been invited to the festival along with sound effects engineer Anton Szabo to record a high production reading.

For the recording, Anton and I set up AKG 414s on each of the actors and another one for Anton's sound effects. Anton had a keyboard sampler plugged in for additional effects. I was situated on the stage not far from Anton's setup, well behind the actors, but visible to the audience. I had two DAT machines but, having learned my lesson at the Royal George, they were only for backup. I would do my main recording on Pro Tools on a Mac laptop. The only glitch I encountered on this remote was a 60 hertz buzz on one of the lines, but somebody that worked for the theatre solved that by lifting the ground on an extension cord. We recorded one dress rehearsal, and then the actual performance, but I don't remember much about either recording except that they went well.

What I do remember is that after the performance, James, Anton, myself and several others went for a lovely supper at the Stage Manager's house. I am doing the Stage Manager a great injustice by not remembering her name. She had a house on a hill outside Blyth. Not just any hill—it was a hill from which you could see for miles and miles. A house from which you could see the sun set not into the rooftops of houses halfway up the sky, as in the city, but directly into the horizon, painting half the sky wonderful shades of red. That night, I found myself enveloped in a wonderful sense of fellowship. Directors, stage managers, writers, sound effects engineers, producers, and me. Colleagues, but also friends. I felt as though I belonged. Such a night had snuck up on me unawares.

But it would be many years and career milestones before I would earn such a night.

# XIV

## One Leg at a Time

I've met many well-known people during my time with CBC Radio. Sometimes I didn't know they were "somebodies."

"Did you know that was Joyce Carol Oates sitting beside you in the Media Library?" producer Ann Jansen asked me one day.

I'd had no idea. And that was fine with me. Most of the time meeting famous people I pretended that I didn't know who they were anyway. It was just easier that way. It levelled the playing field. Even if I did happen to know who they were, I didn't necessarily know much about them. We had jazz artist Diana Krall on the show *Q* one day. I hadn't set up any microphones because she wasn't supposed to perform. As we sat in the studio control room just before the interview, one of the show's producers asked if she wanted to perform during the interview.

"Sure," she said.

"Can you set her up?" the producer asked me.

I turned to Diana. "What instrument do you play?"

Everyone looked at me like I'd crawled out of a hole in the ground.

"Piano," Diana said. "I play piano."

I knew the name Diana Krall but I wasn't knowledgeable about her career or music. For all I knew she could have played saxophone (and for all I know she does).

I already had mics on the piano, actually, so it was just a matter of adjusting them. The interview was delightful. The host asked Diana what type of music she enjoyed in her downtime: "If you were to sit down, what's your music?"

"Right now?"

"Yeah."

Diana played a few nondescript notes on the piano. Her twin sons had been born the year before. "Millie the Elephant packed her trunk and sang goodbye to the circus," she sang, and laughed. "That's about where I'm at right now."

What does meeting famous people get you? The ability to name drop (like I'm doing right now). Does anybody like a name dropper? I don't mind writing about the occasional celebrity encounter, but I've rarely felt comfortable talking about them.

The thing is, whatever these people have accomplished, at the end of the day they're human, just like the rest of us. And unless you work with them for a while (and maybe not even then), a brief encounter is not going to make you the best of pals.

Still, all that said, I cannot deny that meeting and occasionally working with celebrities can be interesting and is often entertaining. Meeting artists takes on a special significance when you're a fan of their work. Eric Idle may put his trousers on one leg at a time, but let's face it: he's Eric Idle of Monty Python. Like Diana Krall and so many others, he also appeared on the show *Q*, where he called us all "freeloading bastards" during the show's credits and understood perfectly well just how much we'd all get a kick out of that.

Phil Collins, Tony Banks, and Mike Rutherford of Genesis also appeared on *Q* one day during my time on the show.

"People hate me," Phil told the nation that day. "Because of the songs that you hear all the time, and you just wish that they'd go away sometimes."

Some people, maybe. Not me. The music of Genesis had been the soundtrack of my teenaged years, and I think Phil Collins' debut album *Face Value* is a terrific piece of work.

A few minutes earlier, adjusting Phil's mic, I had said, "Excuse me, guys. I'd just like to take a moment and thank you all for your music. I'm a big fan."

"Oh, thank you," Phil, Tony, and Mike all replied more or less in unison, sounding quite sincere, despite having no doubt heard that a million times over the years.

Eric Idle, Phil Collins, and yes, even Diana Krall are pretty darned famous. But many of the so-called famous people I've met over the years at CBC Radio would be more what you might call "niche" famous. Well known only in certain circles. Like Ra McGuire, the man behind the songs "We're Here for a Good Time (Not A Long Time)," "Raise a Little Hell," and "The Boys in the Bright White Sportscar," to name just a few of Ra's hits with the band Trooper.

McGuire appeared on a show I recorded in 2006 called *The National Playlist*. Unfortunately, Ra was in Vancouver, so I didn't get to meet him in person. We were communicating with him via a "Switched 56," a kind of high-falutin' telephone line. After establishing the line, Ra mentioned that he couldn't hear himself in his headphones. This was odd. I phoned Vancouver Master Control to find out what was going on.

"You have to send his voice back to himself," the tech in Vancouver told me. "That's the only way he'll be able to hear himself in his headphones."

This didn't make any sense to me, as it would mess up the mix/minus, resulting in a distracting echo in Ra's headphones. I told Vancouver as much.

"I know," the tech said. "But there's nothing I can do about it. That's how the booth's wired."

This was a real head scratcher. Why would anybody build a booth that way? (The answer, I learned later from former Vancouver recording engineer Chris Cutress is that they wouldn't, at least not deliberately. Eventually the booth was fixed, just not soon enough for me and Ra). Embarrassed that there seemed to be no way around this problem, I broke the news to Ra, who took it well. He seemed like a decent fellow. In fact, he seemed like such a nice guy that when the opportunity presented itself, I separated him from the mix and spoke to him down the line:

"Hey Ra? It's Joe, the tech in Toronto. I just wanted to tell you how much I love your music, especially "We're Here for a Good Time, Not a Long Time." The song had accompanied me on cassette when I lived in France in 1993 and was inextricably interwoven with my memories of Aix-en-Provence.

"That's nice of you to say," Ra said. "Thanks."

I asked him about the origins of the song. He told me that he'd been stressed about coming up with new material for Trooper's third album. A friend of his—I think he said it was his driver—could see that he was worked up and asked him why. When Ra explained, his friend said, "Try to relax, man. Remember: we're here for a good time, not a long time."

Once Ra had that line, the music came easily.

Most of my encounters with well-known personalities were professional and businesslike, as you would expect in the context of work. Sometimes, though, they were charming and playful, such as the time I ran into Canadian actor Graham Greene outside the old Jarvis Street facility one day. Fellow radio technician Joram Kalfa and I had left the Radio Building out the back way, toward Wood Street, to have lunch somewhere. You had to pass through a security kiosk to get out of the compound. As Joram and I were leaving we met Greene, who was at the CBC that day working on a radio play.

The security kiosk we had to pass through was a small structure, really only big enough for one person to pass through at a time. For some reason Joram and Graham decided they could do it simultaneously. When this proved awkward, Joram conceded the right of way to the pony-tailed actor, who looked at my friend and exclaimed, "Hey, I know you!"

Joram said, "No, I don't think so."

"No, no," Graham said, "We've worked together before, I'm sure of it."

"No, we haven't," Joram insisted. "Honest, I'd know."

"You're sure?"

"Oh yeah," chuckled my friend.

Past the kiosk onto Wood Street now, Greene briefly considered this. Then he said, "Well, didn't we work on that one thing together?"

Joram said, for the last time, no.

"Oh," said Greene. "Well, neither did I. Must have been two other guys."

I always appreciated guests who went out of their way to acknowledge my existence. After recording an interview for *Q*, Canadian recording artists Tegan and Sara marched around the audio console to vigorously shake my hand. It made a lasting positive impression.

Several years earlier Joni Mitchell had visited the Toronto Broadcast Centre to pre-record an interview for *Morningside* with Peter Gzowski. My friend Trish Thornton recorded Joni performing one of her songs. I was booked in the studio immediately afterward to record the actual interview with Gzowski during Trish's lunch break.

Afterward, leaning on the doorframe to the control room, I watched Gzowski escort Joni out into the hall. It wasn't necessary to pass by the control room to leave. As I watched them go, Joni deliberately broke free of Gzowski and marched back up the hall toward me. Seeing her approach, I straightened up.

"Thank you, it was nice to meet you," she said.

"It was nice to meet you, too," I said.

And we smiled at one other.

Like two human beings.

# XV
## French Radio: CJBC

In 1993 I asked for a leave of absence from the CBC to study French in France. I'd grown up amongst French Acadians in Prince Edward Island and had wanted to learn French ever since. My boss at the time, Kel Lack, applauded the idea and was only too happy to accommodate me.

Before going to France, I seriously overestimated my proficiency in French. I had studied French in school until Grade Eleven. I don't know what the heck I did in all those classes but it sure wasn't learning French. My first few days in Aix-en-Provence I couldn't understand anyone.

By Christmas, though, I was able to carry on rudimentary conversations. My strategy was to insist on speaking only French. Unfortunately, everyone else wanted to practise their English on me. For example, one banker I did regular business with insisted on speaking to me in English while I spoke French. Few things are more ridiculous than speaking French as a second language to someone intent on speaking English as a second language. The loser was whoever was forced to switch to their native tongue first. I always lost, until the end of my time in France, when during our final encounter she ran head-long into a word she didn't know and was forced to switch back to French first. *La victoire était douce* (victory was sweet).

I also resorted to one particular trick to prevent people from speaking English to me. If I spoke French and they responded in English, I replied in French with "Je suis désolé, mais je ne parle pas l'anglais. Je suis suédois" (I'm sorry, but I don't speak English. I'm Swedish). I'd even jabber a few nonsensical phrases in Swedish to prove it: "Kan jag prata med Eva tack? En hund. Och en annan hund. Sex sardiner i en sardin tenn" (Can I speak to Eva please? A dog. Hey, another dog. Six sardines in a sardine tin.) I had plenty of Swedish friends in France who enjoyed teaching me nonsense.

By the time I returned home and to the CBC in August 1994, my French had improved dramatically (my Swedish not so much).

My boss, Kel Lack, had retired, and Charlie Cheffins had taken his place. Charlie was a pleasant fellow with a gentle British accent who up until recently had been an ordinary tech like the rest of us. When I first met him, he had been doing the early morning sports shift in Studio A. Then almost overnight he was running the place (or at least the radio operations part of the place), which is what happens sometimes when people discover you're secretly capable— like Charlie was. Charlie thought it was brilliant that I'd gone to France and learned some French. It meant that he'd be able to place me in the French department. I agreed, and so began four and a half years of working almost exclusively for CJBC.

Just about everyone I worked with at CJBC was bilingual to one degree or another. My French was still very much a work in progress. I continued to improve, but at a much slower pace. My enthusiasm for speaking French had waned somewhat now that I was living my life in English once again. And I was having a bit of trouble with francophone accents in Canada. Not hearing one or two words in a sentence correctly can be enough to make the meaning of an entire sentence suspect. Making matters worse, almost everyone at CJBC was as bad about speaking French to me as the folks in France had been. Just like my banker frenemy, when I spoke French, they replied in English (there were a couple of exceptions). Still, with all the French floating around CJBC, I couldn't help but improve my French just by keeping my ears open.

Most days at CJBC began in the control room of Studio 522. I would break the day in gently with a telephone interview or two for journalists such as Pascale Turbide (later of Radio-Canada's *Enquête*) or Brigitte Bureau. In between interviews, CJBC's communications manager, Diane Belhumeur, might arrive loaded up with what she called, "les choses plats" (boring stuff).

"Les choses plat" consisted mostly of recording and mixing station IDs. Although the work was boring, it was always fun chatting with Diane as we did it. She frequently spoke to me in French. It was while doing *les choses plat* that I made my first successful French pun. I was dubbing audio for Diane one day when Pascale stuck her head in the door and asked me what I was doing.

"Dubbing," I told her. "Comme D'dubitude." (A play on "comme d'habitude," which means "as usual." I was rather proud of that one. Not sure Pascale was quite as impressed.)

In between jobs, I would often select Studio 521 on my console's router and listen to music that the morning show tech, Steve Starchev, was playing through his console next door. Steve, a philosophical soul with a great love of music, had a vast personal collection of CDs and records from all over the world that he liked to listen to in between shows. He once took all that neat music and turned it into a pilot for a radio show. Sadly, he only managed to get one episode on the air. Steve himself was a terrific musician, playing guitar, bagpipes, and hurdy-gurdy (and probably more).

Steve liked to crack jokes and tell funny stories. One of his favourite anecdotes was about explaining preservatives to a Frenchman. Steve didn't know the French word for "preservative" so he guessed that it was the same in French as in English, like so many English words. But when Steve explained that North American food contains a lot of preservatives, the Frenchman got a funny look on his face. Only later did Steve find out that, for the French, "les préservatifs" are condoms.

One day Steve asked me how my writing was going (I'm always writing one thing or another). I told him that it wasn't going all that well because I was feeling a bit stressed.

"Brahma says breathe in, breathe out," he told me, and repeated the phrase a couple of times, like a mantra. "You need to take in air before you can expel air. You can't always be producing. Every now and then you have to stop and draw a breath."

Since then I have followed Steve's advice, to good effect.

(Tragically, Steve died way too young, in 2006, at the age of 51. Ever since I have missed him and his wise counsel.)

Afternoons at CJBC I moved across the hall to Studio 521 to operate a simple half-hour phone show called *Les Petites Annonces*, basically classified ads on radio. *Les Petites Annonces* was followed by *De A à X*, with host Francois X, produced by the lovely Esther Ste-Croix. It was followed by *CJBC Express*, a fast-paced current affairs show for the afternoon drive slot, produced by Daniel Martineaux, ably assisted by Brigitte Egan.

Sometimes I operated the Saturday morning show as well, *Sameplait*, hosted by Claudette Gravel. The first time I did *Sameplait* was back in Studio Z on Carleton Street. The show started just after six am. Decidedly not a morning person, I was quite grumpy at having to get up early to do the show.

My mood persisted when I got to the studio and met the producer, Simone Fadel, a francophone from Egypt. I wasn't surly, exactly, but nor was I friendly. Until Simone toasted me up a bagel and offered me a cup of coffee and it became simply impossible to maintain a sour mood in the face of someone radiating such good cheer. Once I thawed, I confessed to Simone that I'd started the show a bit grumpy.

"Grumpy?" she said in her inimitable French–Egyptian accent. "What is grumpy?"

I explained the meaning of the word. I believe the entire concept of grumpiness might have been alien to Simone, but she loved the word "grumpy." Whenever I worked with her from that point on, she would ask me, again in that charming accent, "Are you grumpy today, Joe?"

Simone, as I mentioned, was from Egypt, a part of la Francophonie. La Francophonie is a group of fifty-seven states and governments where French is mostly spoken and where most of the population are Francophones. It includes obvious places like France, Switzerland, Belgium, and Canada. Quebec and New Brunswick are singled out as member states. The Congo, Egypt, Vietnam, and Ghana are also a part of la Francophonie. So (I suspect many would be surprised to discover) are Bulgaria, Lebanon, Madagascar, Romania, and Vanuatu, and plenty more.

Working for CJBC, I was fortunate to meet people from all around la Francophonie. People like Simone, and others like author/broadcaster Didier Kabagema. Didier was of Rwandan descent and spent most of his childhood in Congo and Gagon before moving to

Canada, where he worked as a journalist with CJBC. Didier was an inspiration. He published his first novel during my final months at CJBC and has since published many others (writing under the nom de plume Didier Leclair), putting my feeble attempts to become an author completely to shame. His first novel, *Toronto, je t'aime*, won the Trillium Book Award.

I've mentioned before that radio techs threw the best Christmas parties. This was true right up until we moved from Jarvis Street to the Toronto Broadcast Centre, where we tried holding the parties in a windowless lounge on the third floor. It just wasn't the same, and nobody ever came up with a better solution, so tech Christmas parties came to an abrupt and ignominious end.

The French, on the other hand, knew better than to have their parties in claustrophobic rooms with no soul. They booked private rooms at restaurants, and those became the best Christmas parties, but they were by invitation only. Fortunately, working for CJBC, I got invited. The food was terrific, the music great, and the atmosphere was always a lot of fun.

After four and a half years of working with CJBC and all its wonderful people, I was offered a chance to join the radio drama department. It was an opportunity I couldn't pass up. I did my last *Les Petites Annonces*, my final *De A à X*, mon dernier *CJBC Express*. They wouldn't be my final French productions, though. In the years to come French producer Gabriel Dube would produce several radio plays in French, which I would engineer.

"Mais c'est un autre histoire" (but that's another story).

# XVI

## Four Days Chez Margaret Atwood

In March 1995, after having worked at CJBC for about half a year, it was my privilege to do a special series of recordings for Radio Canada. Accompanied by a radio producer from Rimouski, Quebec, I spent four days recording Margaret Atwood at her home in downtown Toronto.

When first asked to do the assignment, I wasn't all that enthusiastic about the idea, not feeling quite at the top of my game in the technical realm after my recent leave of absence. The fact that the remote involved Margaret Atwood increased my apprehension. Though I had never read her work I was well aware that she is considered the First Lady of Canadian Literature, and if I was going to fall on my face, I didn't want her to be a part of it.

The recordings were to consist of Atwood being interviewed in French by one Victor-Lévy Beaulieu. Such was my lack of sophistication that I assumed Beaulieu to be a CBC staff announcer out of Rimouski. Producer Doris Dumais had requested a DAT recorder, a cassette recorder, a console, two microphone table stands, and two AKG 414 microphones.

I spoke with Doris by telephone a few days before the remote. She spoke slowly because the production assistant who arranged the call had told her I was just learning French. We discussed everything I could think of that might present a problem. She assured me that she did these sorts of remotes often. I asked her why she had selected 414s for voice recording and she indicated that I could choose other microphones if I preferred but didn't sound all that convincing about it. I knew from experience that producers like to get exactly what they ask for, so I decided to stick with the 414s. (This was several years before I'd regularly employ 414s to record the Bell Canada Reading Series at the Shaw Festival. My near disaster recording on DATs at the Shaw was also well in the future; in 1995 DATs seemed a perfectly acceptable option.) Doris sounded pleasant and I suspected that she would be easy to get along with. We had understood each other's French, and after our conversation I felt optimistic about the remote.

An announcer from Quebec who was a friend of mine got terribly excited hearing that I would be working with Victor-Lévy Beaulieu. Beaulieu, it turned out, was a major literary figure in Quebec, on a par, perhaps, with Atwood. My friend informed me that Beaulieu not only wrote books but wrote for television as well. His most recent project had been a revisionist book on Voltaire.

At a quarter to one on the first day of the remote—a bright, sunny day—I stood on the curb outside Atwood's home in Toronto's Annex, my equipment at my feet. A cab pulled up at one o'clock sharp. A woman with short curly red hair and glasses emerged and cheerfully introduced herself as Doris Dumais. Victor-Lévy Beaulieu accompanied her. Sporting a broad-brimmed black hat and a frizzy white beard that obscured most of his face, he offered to help me carry my equipment up to the front door. I told him, "C'est mon boulot. (It's my job.)" But I was impressed that he had offered.

Margaret Atwood's friendly young assistant Sarah Cooper answered the door. She made the introductions, and Ms. Atwood and I exchanged greetings in French. I put on the best accent I could, which wasn't that good, sadly, but just the same I fancied that Atwood's initial impression of me was that I was a francophone. (In retrospect, however, considering both my accent and my last name, this is highly unlikely.)

Sarah led me to the room where we would be recording. I was to sit at the foot of a massive oak table with Doris on my right, Atwood opposite me at the table's head, and Beaulieu close by on her left. As I set up, I listened to the others talk in the adjacent room. I had been wondering how good Atwood's French was. I realized that her active vocabulary was quite a bit more extensive than mine.

I called Atwood and Beaulieu in to do some voice tests. When Doris entered and saw my equipment, she wrinkled her nose. She didn't like the look of my console. I hadn't felt the need to bring a large console because the recording consisted of only two microphones, so I had chosen a tiny Shure mixer. Evidently Doris had never seen a Shure mixer before. The smallness of it seemed to concern her. It featured rotary pots instead of faders that went up and down. She asked me lots of questions about it, chiefly, why didn't it have faders that went up and down? The last time she did a remote like this, she informed me, the technician had brought a large console with proper faders. I assured her that it would be fine, and she relented. I know that she was nervous. So was I.

We started recording and I began to regret using the 414 microphones. Atwood sounded just fine, leaning in close and hardly budging an inch from one day to the next. But for the movement of her lips she might have been carved in stone. Beaulieu, on the other hand, changed his position constantly. Often, he wound up about as far away from the microphone as it was possible for him to get without leaving his chair. To compensate I jacked up his level and urged him to get closer to the microphone, and he obliged readily, but it was never long before he got wrapped up in the interview again and started sounding as if he were broadcasting from a cave.

Atwood was unfailingly friendly throughout the four days of recording. We spoke to one another only in French and addressed one another using the formal "vous." At one point she inquired if I found recording interviews such as this one boring. "Pas si c'est quelque chose d'interessant (not if it's something interesting)," I told her, grateful to have found the words in French. Everyone chuckled and expressed the hope that this interview was indeed interesting. I assured them that I thought it was, though truth be told I didn't understand much of Beaulieu's French.

Each day was interspersed with several coffee breaks. Atwood made coffee for everyone, which we drank in her kitchen. I usually remained quiet as the others spoke in rapid French. Sometimes I stayed with the equipment to fret over the recordings. Once Atwood's assistant Sarah dug out a copy of Atwood's *Good Bones* for me, calling it an "Introductory Volume for Men." At Sarah's request Atwood signed it for me, writing on the inside cover, "Good luck, Joe—Margaret Atwood."

After we finished recording on the second day, Atwood asked me to show our Quebecois guests the way to a bookstore located nearby in the Annex and to do any necessary translating for them. Having been informed by Atwood that we were coming, the owner of the store received us with open arms. Feeling insecure about my French, I felt a bit like a fraud translating, though I managed okay.

The evening of the third day Atwood took us all out to dinner at Thai Magic on Yonge Street. I was the second to arrive. Atwood was the first. Seeing her seated alone in a booth just beyond the entrance, I thought, I don't want to go in there and be alone with the First Lady of Canadian Literature. I was afraid she would insist on speaking French and I wouldn't acquit myself well. Or worse, we would speak English and I wouldn't acquit myself well. But it was Margaret Atwood, for God's sake—it wasn't every day you were granted a private audience with someone like that. I went in and she welcomed me with a smile and we spoke to one another in English for the first time. Among other things, I asked her how well she understood Beaulieu's French. She confessed that he had a quirk of speaking several phrases of more or less incomprehensible French and then summing up his question in one crystal clear phrase. It had saved her more than once.

Adrienne Clarkson joined us. She speaks French quite well, and when Doris Dumais and Victor-Lévy Beaulieu showed up, it was Clarkson who dominated the conversation. At the end of the night Atwood insisted on treating. When we parted, everyone went his or her own way. Atwood returned home alone in the dark. Afterward I thought perhaps I should have offered to accompany her. It might have been chivalrous to do so, but the idea didn't sit right with me. I felt it might be interpreted as just wanting to spend more time in the company of a famous person. I had the impression that Atwood preferred to walk home alone anyway.

After we finished recording on the final day it took me a while to gather up my equipment, and I was the last to leave. Atwood saw me off at the door, accompanied by her cat and Sarah Cooper. As I left, she wished me "good luck."

Doris Dumais took the DAT tapes with her back to Rimouski before I had a chance to listen to them in a proper studio. I thought I might never know exactly how the recordings turned out. Half a year later, however, a colleague heard the show broadcast and assured me that the sound quality had been fine. I was relieved. Shortly after that I received internal CBC mail from Doris. On one of our coffee breaks she had snapped a photo of Margaret Atwood, Sarah Cooper, Victor-Lévy Beaulieu and me. She sent me a copy of the photo and brief note that told me that everyone in Rimouski thought I looked like Paul McCartney. I was pleased. Not because everyone in Rimouski thought I looked like one of the Beatles, but because I figured Doris wouldn't have sent me the picture if she hadn't been satisfied with my work.

Eventually the interviews were translated by Phyllis Aronoff and Howard Scott and published by McClelland & Stewart Inc. in a book entitled, like the radio broadcast it is based on, *Two Solicitudes: Conversations*. I still haven't read it. One day I must, if only to see what Victor-Lévy Beaulieu actually said.

# XVII

## A Dramatic Turn of Events

In 1996, I auditioned for a play called *Anybody for Murder*, staged by the Milton Players Theatre Group. Hoping for a supporting role, I landed the lead. Not trying to brag here; the director just typecast me as a conniving, murderous bastard.

It was a challenging role. Scads of dialogue on every page, all to be delivered in a pompous British accent. Having been weaned on Monty Python as a kid I didn't think the accent would be a problem. I trotted forth my best British accent for the read-through.

Susan Cranford, the director, happened to be from Liverpool. She stopped me after a couple of pages: "Do you think you could do even a tiny bit of a British accent?"

Intensive accent training followed. Half the battle, Susan told me, was simply to enunciate every word. She reserved special coaching for words like "water" and "theatre" ("WOO-tah" and "thee-EH-tuh." Or something like that). Fortunately, I didn't have to ad lib in a British accent. I just had a select vocabulary that needed to sound British. If I got it wrong, Susan corrected me. I don't expect I even came close to nailing it, but after one performance, someone told me I sounded like Cary Grant, known for his "transatlantic" accent. Not exactly what I'd been going for, but it could have been worse.

Susan's other wish was that I sport a moustache. I had largely given up on moustaches after an ill-advised attempt to grow one in my late teens, but no sacrifice was too great for my art, so I dutifully grew a prim and proper affair that elicited shudders from family and friends.

Performing in *Anybody for Murder* under Susan's direction was a great experience. I wish I could have participated in more such productions. Still, that single experience was enough to have a pro-found impact on my career at the CBC.

Soon after my moustache firmly established itself on my upper lip, I ran into CBC recording engineer John McCarthy at the St. Andrew subway station in Toronto. Although both of us were techs for CBC Radio, we didn't really know one another. There were about eighty radio technicians working for the CBC at the time and we didn't all run in the same circles. John was ten years older than I was, and he was a high-end recording engineer working in radio drama. I was a Group 4 Radio Technician doing a stint for the French services. Until that day we'd barely spoken, and had it not been for the moustache, it might have remained that way.

Spotting me on the subway platform, John approached me, peered at the hair on my lip, and said, "What—is—that—THING—underneath your nose?"

Okay, he didn't say that. But he did make some crack about the moustache.

Slightly embarrassed, I said, "It's for a play I'm in."

This immediately piqued John's interest. "You're into the theatre?"

I confessed that I was.

Unbeknownst to me, John was on the look-out for a new radio drama recording engineer. Had it not been for the moustache, I might never have mentioned the play. Had I not mentioned the play, John might never have invited me to join the radio drama department, and the rest of my life might have unspooled completely differently.

As it turned out though, the journey from that subway platform in 1996 to actually joining the radio drama department was any-thing but straightforward. In fact, it took me another three years.

My friend Greg DeClute was already a recording engineer for radio drama, along with John McCarthy, Janice Bayer, Drago Grandic, John Marynowicz, and sound effects engineers Anton Szabo, Joe Hill, John Stewart, Bill Robinson, and Matt Willcott.

I remember Greg DeClute in particular in our early days as radio technicians. Greg was always reading manuals. He spent as much time as he could in Studio G, the drama studio on Jarvis Street. Greg was obviously going places. Janice Bayer, too. Myself, I didn't aspire to be a high-end recording engineer. I had other plans. I was going to leave the CBC and become a full-time writer or film director or something. I was never quite clear on exactly how or when this was going to happen, but I had no doubt that it would happen (it hasn't happened yet).

Also, I didn't self-identify as a tech the same way that Greg and Janice did. To me, the gear was a means to an end. True techs, it seemed to me, fawned over gear like lovers. They liked it for its own sake. I wasn't interested in reading manuals from cover to cover, back then. I just wanted to know as much as I needed to know to make the gear do what I needed it to do.

I would come to change my mind about that.

Shortly after my encounter with John McCarthy, Operations Manager Charlie Cheffins mentioned that drama was looking for someone to replace Janice, who was leaving the CBC. Would I be interested in throwing my hat in the ring?

I said no.

I wasn't looking for change just then. I'd recently gotten married and didn't want to have to learn a new job. Radio drama seemed like a high-pressure environment. I wasn't sure I wanted to be a part of all that. I just wanted to park my brain at the door for a while.

My friend Wayne Richards got the job instead.

(To be clear, he might have gotten it anyway even if I had thrown my hat in the ring.)

Fast forward three years to 1999.

I'd come to regard CJBC as a trap. The work had become quite boring; I couldn't imagine doing it for the rest of my career. I approached Charlie Cheffins about a new gig. There were a few possibilities. I could go back to the tech pool. I could join Radio Music as a music recording engineer. Or...

"What about radio drama?" Charlie asked me.

"Nah," I said. "I hear they're kind of snooty."

Looking back, I'm amazed I said that. I don't think I actually felt that way for more than the few seconds it took me to say it. I think the truth is I was afraid they wouldn't have me.

I wasn't the only one with concerns. After I'd worked in the radio drama department for a while, Greg DeClute confessed to me that he'd had reservations. He'd been afraid that I got bored too easily. He knew that I'd taken a year off to live in France and he didn't want to invest a lot of time training me only to have me take off again. There had already been too much turnover in radio drama. He wanted someone he could count on to stick around.

But Greg came around, and so did I.

And John McCarthy hadn't forgotten my moustache, and our conversation on the subway platform.

One day in late 1999, while working for CJBC in Studio 522, the phone rang. It was John.

"How'd you like to come and work for the radio drama department?" he asked.

"You bet!" I told him.

I couldn't wait to start.

A few weeks later I moved to 2F100 with the rest of the radio drama recording and sound effects engineers, where I began my career in radio drama. Despite Greg's concerns, I would remain there until just before they shut the place down.

# XVIII
## Tools of the Trade

I felt as though I'd been tailor-made for radio drama. It was as though all my experience in radio from the age of sixteen, all the writing I'd ever done, my stint in community theatre, my interest in music, all of it had conspired to prepare me for making radio plays. I had even written and produced a radio play before, as a student at Ryerson Polytechnical Institute.

Still, I had an awful lot to learn.

John McCarthy set about teaching me.

Up until this point, John had been an enigmatic figure to me, part of what I imagined to be an elite cadre of high-end recording engineers, well beyond anything I could ever aspire to be. Tall, bearded and bespectacled, from a distance he appeared aloof and serious. As I got to know him, I realized that he certainly wasn't aloof, and although the jobs he occupied demanded a certain degree of seriousness and thoughtfulness—qualities that come naturally to John—you could not have a conversation with him without plenty of laughter.

There is something about John that has always put me in mind of a certain wizard. Give him a staff in one hand and a conical hat and he would not be entirely out of place in a Tolkien novel. It is his bearing, his comportment. Like Gandalf, John is a counsellor, an advisor, a mentor. He was responsible for the two most pivotal moments of my career: inviting me into the radio drama department, and (a decade later) promoting me into management. Although he has never performed any actual magic that I'm aware of, I'm fairly certain that he could kick Sauron's ass.

On my first day in the drama department, John sat me down in a suite called Dialogue Edit and launched a piece of audio editing software called Sonic Solutions. I had used similar software before:

D-Cart, also used by the Australian Broadcasting Corporation; and Dalet, a version of which we still used twenty years later (called DaletPlus). Sonic Solutions was considerably more powerful than either of those.

John showed me the basics, and then made a special point of showing me hot keys—keystroke combinations that I could use instead of a mouse. He told me cautionary tales of people who relied on "mousing" only to wind up with carpal tunnel syndrome. I heeded his words and learned every possible hot-key combination. Not only did this make me a fast editor, I never suffered from carpal tunnel syndrome.

John gave me an edit of a radio play to practise on, an adaptation of *Alias Grace* by Margaret Atwood. I spent several hours replacing the existing sound effects with completely ludicrous ones, turning a serious dramatic work into something ridiculous. I was quite proud of the result.

"What have you done to my beautiful radio play?" John exclaimed in mock outrage when I played it back for him.

Once I was up to speed on Sonic Solutions, it was time to tackle the Neve Capricorn console in Studio 212. This was a rather more daunting task.

Recording engineer Greg DeClute spent several days teaching the console to me and a handful of my colleagues. On the morning of the first day, to get our attention and let us know we weren't in Kansas anymore, Greg challenged us to get tone up on the board. The purpose of tone, you might recall, is to line up audio equipment and establish continuity. Getting tone up on the board is the first thing I always do when confronted with a new console. I had never failed to get tone up on a board before. It's pretty easy to get tone up on analog consoles.

None of us could get tone up on the Capricorn. On a digital console like the Capricorn it's not exactly an intuitive process. After showing us how, Greg told us about a producer who was asked by a writer what would happen if everyone showed up to a recording session except the recording engineer. Would the producer be able to operate the Capricorn and record the show?

"Of course," the producer told the writer confidently.

He was wrong. He wouldn't have stood a chance. With all due respect to the producer in question, without training, he wouldn't even have been able to get tone up.

I wasn't sure I was up to the task myself. Was I smart enough to understand something as complicated as a Neve Capricorn in an environment as complex as Studio 212?

This was 1999, the year before my twin daughters were born. After taking Greg's course, I had the freedom to come in on weekends to experiment. My goal was to make sure that I was able to record from every possible source, play it back through Sonic Solutions, route tracks through the various outboard processing gear, and mix it all using the Capricorn's automation. This was the bare minimum I needed to know to make a radio play.

During his course, Greg had encouraged us to learn more than the bare minimum. "Be super-users," he told us. "Seek to understand as much as possible about the gear you're using. Don't run to someone else for help every time you run into trouble. Figure it out for yourselves. Be the one that other people run to."

Those were his exact words.

(No, they're not. It was a long time ago. I don't think I've ever heard Greg start a sentence with the word "seek." But that was the gist of it.)

I also needed to master Studio 212 itself. I needed to understand how to accurately translate the written word into sonic reality, how to get the most out of the acoustic spaces available to me. Doing so wasn't necessarily straightforward.

On a conventional radio show, you position a microphone in front of the host and guests and make sure their levels are good. Sometimes it's a little more involved, such as when you want to have a band in the studio or someone wants to cook something or practise Tai Chi live on air. Everything has to sound "on mic" all the time. This is presentational radio, where radio shows present content to listeners in a straightforward, unambiguous manner.

Radio drama, on the other hand, is representational. Much of what goes into a radio play represents something other than what it actually is. The trick is convincing listeners to accept the reality that is being represented. Actors represent characters that they're not. Sounds represent noises that they're not—for instance, squeezing a box of corn starch wrapped in duct tape to represent a character walking on snow.

Few people I know think in terms of presentational versus representational radio. It's not necessary to be conscious of the distinction unless you happen to be mixing the two, in which case you risk confusing your listeners, the way Orson Welles inadvertently did with his live broadcast of *War of the Worlds*. When you move into the realm of representational radio, it's usually a good idea to let your listeners know that you're doing so, though if done responsibly it can be fun to blur the line. The show *This is That* which once aired on CBC Radio is a good example of this.

The challenge for those working in representational radio is how to make listeners believe that what they're hearing is what you want them to think they're hearing. For instance, consider a radio play about the French Revolution and the sound of a nobleman getting his head chopped off by a guillotine. How would you create that sound without actually chopping off someone's head? Which you would obviously not want to do. Even if you did chop off someone's head in the studio listeners almost certainly wouldn't understand what they were hearing without actually seeing it happen, as they would on television or film. In such an instance it becomes necessary to produce a sound that conveys the idea of someone getting their head chopped off that sounds even more like someone getting their head chopped off than what that would actually sound like, if you see what I mean.

I once recorded a scene from *Romeo and Juliet* with a novice director. Juliet was supposed to be on the balcony with Romeo on the ground. The director suggested that we place Juliet on a chair to convey that she was higher than Romeo. I explained to the director that height doesn't "read" on the radio. Placing Juliet on a chair wouldn't convey to the listening audience that she was on a balcony. Listeners at home wouldn't be able to see her on the chair, so placing her on the chair accomplishes nothing.

What we needed to do was record the scene from Romeo's point of view, with that actor close to the microphone, and place the actor playing Juliet an appropriate distance away from the microphone. Not so far away that the actor couldn't be heard, but far enough away to convey the idea that the two characters were a fair distance apart. That Juliet was on a balcony would be clear from the context of the play. We just needed to nudge listeners' perceptions toward perceiving the relative distance. "Theatre of the mind" would do the rest.

I don't mean to suggest that any of this is rocket science.

But I did need to understand it all before I could get to work.

# XIX

## *Cherry Docs*

My first official sound effects gig in the radio drama department was on a radio play called *Cherry Docs*, written by David Gow, directed by Damir Andrei. *Cherry Docs* was originally a stage play. It's about a liberal Jewish lawyer defending a neo-Nazi skinhead from a murder charge. Or rather, it's about the journey these two men take together as they confront one another's prejudices and their own. Or rather, it was about me learning how to make sound effects for a radio play.

I remember virtually nothing about *Cherry Docs* itself. I had to look up the plot. This has nothing to do with the quality of the play, which is quite well regarded. It's because we recorded it a long time ago, and as we were making it, I wasn't thinking about the story. I was thinking about how sound effects could help tell that story.

I had been schooled in the basics of the craft. I knew to comb the script to figure out what sound effects were required. I knew to divvy them up into three categories: sound effects that I would perform live with the actors, sound effects that I would create and record separately, and sound effects that I would source from CDs.

On the first day of recording with the cast, my first sound effect was lighting a match for the main character, a foul-mouthed and violent racist played by actor Randy Hughson. Hughson's character was supposed to be smoking a cigarette.

Why was I required to light the match? Couldn't Randy have lit the match himself? For that matter, couldn't Randy have performed all the sound effects himself? It's true, Randy could have lit the match. But he probably wouldn't have known where to light the match in proximity to the microphone. Lighting the match too close or too far away could have ruined a perfectly good take.

Also, lighting a match is simple, but it's just one example. Sound effects sequences could be a lot more complex. Sometimes several sound effects were required during a single take. We preferred actors to concentrate on their performances rather than having to clink glasses, light matches, pretend to tromp around on snow, and so on.

And then there was the business of how to create the sound effect to begin with. It wasn't always an intuitive process. Lighting a match is pretty straightforward. Lots of other sound effects aren't. There are tricks, such as waving a thin stick in front of a mic to create the whoosh of an arrow or touching a damp rag to a hot surface to create the sound of frying. We had an entire room full of bizarre contraptions and knick-knacks capable of making all sorts of weird sounds. Devices for making wind, doorbells, screen doors, or the sound of someone getting hanged. It was useful to have someone around who knew where all these contraptions were, and how to make them work.

Anyway, there I was, the alleged sound effects specialist about to perform my first professional sound effect. On the first take, at the appropriate point in the script, I lit the match, and promptly dropped the lit match in Randy's hair. Fortunately, I was able to blow the match out before any damage could be done, but I was mortified. Thank God Randy wasn't actually the scary character he so effectively portrayed!

During that same day of recording for *Cherry Docs*, the fire alarm in the Broadcast Centre went off. This was a complete coincidence, having nothing to do with my incident with the match. Standing on John Street alongside the rest of the occupants of the Broadcast Centre waiting to get back inside, Randy turned to me.

"So, how long have you been doing sound effects?" he asked.

I looked at my watch. "About fifteen minutes."

Back in the studio, I recorded as many sound effects as I could with Randy and the rest of the cast. Recording sound effects at the same time as the actors deliver their lines (as opposed to on their own later) is usually a good idea. Not only does it ensure that the sound effects are recorded in the right ambient space, it enhances performances as actors respond to the sound effects in the moment. It also makes for less work in post.

Still, it wasn't something I really enjoyed. I always felt slightly embarrassed doing sound effects with actors. Sometimes the sound effects felt silly, such as using a knife and fork to eat an invisible breakfast on an empty plate. Or I'd make a stupid mistake, like performing a sound effect at the wrong time. We had two dedicated sound effects specialists on staff, Matt Willcott and Anton Szabo, guys who actually knew what they were doing. Me, I was just a dilettante. I never forgot that. Still, whenever called upon to perform live sound effects, I always did the best that I could.

Once I was finished with the cast, I turned my attention to recording wild sound effects. This process is called "foley" after Jack Donovan Foley, a pioneer in the field of film sound effects. Foley is the process of recording sound effects in isolation. They're mixed into sound tracks afterwards. I was a lot more comfortable doing foley than performing sound effects with actors.

Foley can be recorded anywhere. I recorded most of the sound effects I needed for *Cherry Docs* on the floor of Studio 212. Over the years my colleagues and I recorded car doors, squeaky doors, jail cells, elevators, breaking plates, baths, showers, sword fights, fist fights, even gunshots in various parts of 212. For *Cherry Docs*, some of the action took place in a car, so I spent one afternoon recording myself driving my wife's Pontiac Sunbird, speeding up, slowing down, turning, using the windshield wipers, buckling the seatbelt, and so on. We often talked about preserving and cataloguing the sound effects we created ourselves, to save time on future productions, and eventually started using a system called Soundminer to do exactly that.

Any sound effects that I didn't record with the cast or as foley, I sourced from CD. We had quite an elaborate sound effects collection. Over seventy-three thousand sound effects, collections from Canada, Britain, the US, with names like Sounds of a Different Realm, Evil FX, Hollywood Edge, Top Secret, Wacky World of Robots, Widgets and Gizmos, Star Trek, Sound Ideas, and so on. Despite the breadth of our collection, it didn't have everything, which is why we often had to create our own sound effects.

While I was busy recording and gathering sound effects, Greg DeClute created the dialogue edit, choosing all the best performances from the actors and making a single continuous dialogue track. When he finished this to the director's satisfaction, he handed it over to me to do the sound effects assembly.

Whenever it came time for me to do a sound effects assembly, I was always grateful that I'd already recorded as many sound effects as possible with the actors. Anything that I hadn't recorded (the foley sound effects and those sourced from CD) needed to be loaded into my workstation (in those days a Mac G4) and then placed on separate tracks using our digital audio editing software, Sonic Solutions (we would move to Pro Tools a few years later). The sound effects usually took up a lot of tracks, layered on top of one another. A scene with characters arguing in a car might include a track of them arguing, another track with the sound of their car, yet another of passing traffic, several spot tracks of blinkers, wipers, seatbelts, and so on, and maybe a music track as well.

Once I finished the sound effects assembly, and after Greg recorded a music track for the show one studio over in Studio 211, it was time to mix the show. In those days we almost always mixed big shows in Studio 212 with the cast long gone and the studio floor mostly empty. *Cherry Docs* was no exception. Greg sat on the left and I sat on the right before the Neve Capricorn console in the control room. Damir, the director, sat behind us.

Mixes were usually a collaborative process, although that depended on the director. For *Cherry Docs*, we followed Damir's direction, but everybody provided input into what sounded best. As the mix progressed, we moved dialogue, sound effects and music around that weren't quite in the right places. We added electronic processing where required (i.e., if a little reverb was required here and there). Greg equalized the dialogue track of a character who was supposed to sound like he was on a telephone. The Capricorn console remembered every move we made on the various faders and dials and played it all back afterward just the way we mixed it.

Once we were happy with the mix, it was time to print it. We turned down the lights, launched the CD burner and DAT backups, pressed play on the console, sat back in our chairs and listened, hoping to God that we hadn't made any mistakes. If we did, we stopped, fixed them, and started the print over again with a fresh CD.

I loved the Neve Capricorn, but it wasn't perfect. Every now and then one of us would notice that it had fallen out of automation. When it did, we leapt out of our chairs cussing and swearing, trying to re-engage the automation before it missed any of our carefully programmed moves. If we caught it in time, we were fine. Usually, though, it was too late, and we were forced to start the print all over again.

Once the show was successfully printed, we turned up the lights and handed the finished CD and backup DATS to Damir, who (hopefully) checked it one more time before presenting the finished product for broadcast.

And Greg and I moved on to our next projects.

# XX
## Requiem for a Studio

I loved working in Studio 212.

Studio 212 was our dream studio. It was the radio drama studio in the Toronto Broadcast Centre, the successor to Studio G on Jarvis Street. It was a one-of-a-kind facility, built for the express purpose of producing theatre-of-the-mind, painstakingly designed to provide creative teams the ability to replicate acoustic environments with maximum flexibility.

I spent most of my time in Studio 212's control room sitting behind a Neve Capricorn recording console (later, a Euphonix System 5). Typically, a recording engineer and a sound effects engineer would sit behind the console looking out over the production floor. There was a credenza behind them, beneath which sat patch bays and outboard processing gear such as effects and reverb units. Directors, writers, and associate producers would sit behind the credenza during recording and mix sessions, ordering the engineers around.

Behind the control room was an equipment room. It housed the brains of the recording console and doubled as a shortcut from the east side of the building to the west for those of us in the know.

The control room of Studio 212 was a hub, surrounded by several other rooms which served as different acoustic spaces in which to record actors. The main studio floor sat in front of the control room. It was the largest and arguably most impressive space. The studio floor was deep and wide and two storeys high. There were different materials on the floor to approximate different walking surfaces, among them wood, marble, and concrete. Two staircases led to a balcony. The staircase on the right (looking out from the control room) had two different surfaces (a good idea in theory, but in practice there wasn't much difference between them acoustically).

The winding staircase on the left, constructed of metal, was perfect for approximating the sounds of stairs on ships and in prisons.

There were baffles on the studio floor that you could wheel around to create smaller acoustic spaces. Each baffle had two sides: a soft, sound-absorbing surface, and a hard, reflective surface. Which side you used depended on what kind of acoustic environment you wished to replicate. A small closet? Place an actor and your microphone inside three baffles and allow the actor's voice to reflect off the hard surfaces. A living room? Four or five baffles with soft surfaces underneath the balcony. A castle, church, or gymnasium? Use the entire space augmented by a couple of mics on the balcony and maybe a *soupçon* of electronic reverb (which I always called "schmoo," as in, "a little schmoo on that will help," because that's what fellow CBC recording engineer Doug Doctor called it).

At the far end of the main studio floor was a combination kitchen/bathroom. It had a working stove, fridge, and bathtub. There were tons of dishes, pots, and pans in the cupboards. It's said that they were originally going to put a working toilet in there but they were afraid that people would use it, and it wouldn't get cleaned, and it would just get ugly. They were probably right. This space was relatively small and covered in ceramic tiles. It was excellent for recording kitchens and bathrooms (obviously) but served equally well for jail cells and locker rooms—any small, acoustically live environment.

To the immediate right of the control room was a room we called the Neutral Room because it sounded, well, neutral.

Behind the control room, to the left of the equipment room, lay a room we called the Office. I'll leave it to the discerning reader to determine what sorts of scenes we recorded in there.

To the right of the main studio floor was a tiny closet of a room with a sliding glass door. We called this the Acoustic Chamber. It became the default room for recording actors who were supposed to be in cars. Once I rented a car with a big trunk to do a remote in Niagara-on-the-Lake. Associate Producer Tracy Rideout came with me (Tracy later became Executive Producer of CBC Radio Comedy). On the way back, as Tracy and I were talking, it occurred to me that our voices sounded exactly like actors recorded in the Acoustic Chamber. So it certainly worked as a double for at least one make of car: a Toyota Echo Hatchback.

Left of the main studio floor, through an acoustically re-inforced door, was a long hallway that ended in a small chamber. Every surface in this space except for the floor was covered with Sonex Acoustical Foam, a sound-absorbing material. The idea was that if you spoke in this room, your voice would not reflect off any surfaces. It would sound the way your voice sounds outside in the real world, theoretically. If you shouted down the hallway, which was over nine meters (thirty feet) long, you would sound as though you were shouting across a large pond or a football field. If you spoke in the chamber at the end of the hall, you might sound the way you would on the beach. We called this room the Dead Room. Matt Willcott, one of our sound effects engineers, told me that he wanted to write a memoir called "Live Effects in a Dead Room." He's long since retired and should have it mostly written by now.

The floor of the corridor in the Dead Room consisted of shallow boxes. If you lifted the covers off these boxes, you would find several different types of surfaces: small rocks, pebbles, sand. Not often, but every now and then, we asked our actors or sound effects engineers to walk on these to simulate walking on different surfaces. Rather less sophisticated, but no less effective, we also kept a medium-sized cardboard box in the Dead Room. It was filled with old quarter-inch audio tape that had been liberated from its reels. When actors walked on this old audiotape, it sounded like they were walking on dead leaves.

All our outdoor scenes (well, the ones not actually record-ed outdoors) were recorded in the Dead Room. Properly done, it worked well, especially after you added outdoor ambiances to the voice tracks, such as wind or rain or automobiles or ocean surf. If you tried to fake it by recording outdoor scenes in one of the other spaces—spaces meant for interior recording—listeners might not realize what you had done, but psycho-acoustically they would register that something wasn't quite right.

You had to be careful though. Not every spot in the Dead Room worked well. If you placed your microphone too close to a wall, even with Sonex Acoustical Foam lining the walls, the actors' voices reflected back and sounded boxy. As a result, they might sound like they were at the beach, but inside a wooden crate.

Of course, outside in the real world, there are many opportunities for sound to reflect off various surfaces. Often when I was recording outside on location, I found myself up against a brick wall or a wooden house or some other place that flavoured my recordings with odd reflections and other unique characteristics. Although the Dead Room provided an excellent approximation of outdoor environments and allowed engineers a lot more control than might have been possible recording outdoors, nothing beats actually recording outdoors. Also, actors sometimes found it hard to be cooped up in the Dead Room for too long—they'd start to feel a bit peculiar in there after a while. This could be why one day not long after the Dead Room was built, one actor carved her initials in the acoustical foam. It was never repaired, and she was never invited back.

It could be said that Studio 212 was ever-so-slightly over-engineered. I've already mentioned the staircase with the two surfaces that weren't that much different from one another acoustically. If you really wanted to get fancy, you could place your microphone underneath an array of baffles permanently affixed to the ceiling (called the Cloud). You could flip those baffles to either hard or soft surfaces using a long pole that we kept attached to a nearby wall. When I first started working in 212, I dutifully flipped the Cloud baffles depending on my acoustic requirements, but it didn't take long for me to realize that it didn't have much of an impact. Rarely was an actor's mouth directed toward the heavens. Some of the floor surfaces were equally ineffective. They differed from one another so subtly that you couldn't hear any difference between them, especially with actors wearing sneakers. (We rarely used footsteps anyway—start putting footsteps in your radio plays and the next thing you know it's all about the footsteps. You'll drive yourself nuts. Just put them in where you absolutely need to.)

But far be it from me to nitpick about such a unique studio. I'll never see its like again.

# XXI
## 2F100

When I wasn't learning how to make radio plays, I had a desk in 2F100, a cavernous room I shared with the rest of the radio drama technical gang, which, around Christmas 1999, consisted of me, recording engineers Greg DeClute, Wayne Richards, Drago Grandic, and sound effects engineers Matt Willcott and Anton Szabo. There was also another technician, but he left the department weeks after I joined the department. I've always felt a little bad about him. He wanted to be a part of the drama department, but it didn't work out, and I took his place. My desk in 2F100 had actually been his desk.

As he was leaving on his last day, carrying a box with his stuff in one hand and a lamp in the other, I said, "Would you mind, uh, leaving the lamp?"

He looked like a dog that didn't understand why someone had just kicked it.

"Okay," he said, and handed me the lamp.

Last I heard, he was working in Los Angeles, where it typically averages eighteen degrees year round and they get less rain in a year than Canadians get snow on an average Monday in November. I expect he's having the last laugh.

2F100 was dark and dingy. There were windows all along one side facing the atrium. We kept the blinds drawn to prevent sunlight from striking our skin, lest it burn us, as though we were a nest of vampires.

We shared 2F100 with huge metallic shelves containing old 78-rpm sound effects records, none of which had been used in years. One day Drago Grandic moved the shelves to create a room within a room. He placed a long leather couch inside and created a curtain out of old magnetic tape to serve as a door. It was a perfect little hideaway, which came in handy after my twin girls were born two months premature, and my wife and I had to feed them every three hours day and night for weeks on end. I came to work each day utterly exhausted. During lunch I used Drago's room to catch a few sorely needed Zzzzs. Afterward I splashed my face with cold water and staggered back to work.

Around this time, I became addicted to chewing gum. I'm chewing it now, as I write this, twenty-one years later. I'd read that Hollywood writer William Goldman chewed gum to stay awake watching movies when he was on the jury at Cannes. I figured if it kept him awake maybe it would keep me awake, too.

Eventually John McCarthy ordered us to throw all the old 78s out. Drago lost his room and I lost my little hideaway. It wasn't so bad for me because by then my daughters Keira and Erin were sleeping through the night, but it was a bit of a loss for the corporation. The 78s contained intriguing one-of-a-kind sound effects, including sound that appeared to have been recorded during World War II. But there was no budget to transfer them to another medium, and it was a little too early technologically to digitize them (slow transfer speeds, not enough storage capacity, and no funding to do it anyway). And there was no will to store them elsewhere, so they were all destroyed. We had a bunch of sound effects on cart, too, which we also threw out. I don't think anybody missed those, though. Never once did I hear anybody say, "Gee, too bad we don't have those old carts anymore."

For the first eleven years I worked at the CBC I had no desk, phone, or computer. All I had was a locker and a tiny little mailbox. Now, for the first time ever, I had a desk, my own phone, and a computer. I also had my own CBC email address, though I couldn't check it on my Seanix computer because at first my Seanix wasn't connected to the BAN (Building Area Network). All I used the Seanix for was creating sound effects lists and doing "network testing."

We called it network testing but really it was just playing a computer game called Need for Speed II, for which we'd created our own private network in 2F100. Sometimes as many as five or six of us raced together on our breaks and lunch. Greg DeClute and I became especially proficient at these so-called tests, often racing neck and neck. It was important to keep the door to 2F100 closed during the tests because much like, say, the Manhattan Project, the tests were absolutely top secret, strictly on a need-to-know basis. Just the same, I'm sure our fearless leader John McCarthy knew perfectly well what was going on.

Of course, this activity had nothing to do with our actual jobs other than as a welcome break. The longer I worked in the radio drama department, the busier I seemed to get. If we weren't preparing for casts, or recording casts, or doing post-production, we were supporting the department in other ways. The six of us (five after Drago left) supported shows such as *Sunday Showcase*, *Monday Night Playhouse*, *Monday Playbill*, *Muckraker*, *Between the Covers*, *The Mystery Project*, and *The Vinyl Café*. Some of us—Greg, Wayne and myself, and Drago when he was still there—were loaned out to other shows in the A&E department such as *Writers & Company* and *Definitely Not the Opera (DNTO)*. I always felt like I hit the ground running every morning and was still jogging by the end of the day. There was the odd slow day but mostly we worked our butts off. That is, right up until somebody got the bright idea that we should all go out on strike.

# XXII

## Strike!

For my first few years at CBC Radio it was easy to forget that I was in a union. A series of unions, actually—three of them from the time I joined the CBC in 1988 until I became a manager in 2007.

At first, I was only dimly aware of the existence of these unions. They collected their pound of flesh from my paycheques and that was it. Every now and then, though, they made their presence felt in other ways.

One day, for example, the CBC asked me to be present at a recording session at Manta Sound. Not because they needed me to do any actual work, but to honour their collective agreement with NABET (the National Association of Broadcast Employees and Technicians).

The radio show *Sunday Morning* was recording a new theme package of music for their show. According to the collective agreement, the CBC was supposed to use one of their own recording engineers (there were many experienced, talented engineers to choose from), but either the people doing the sessions preferred someone else, or none of our recording engineers was available. I was working as a Group 4 Radio Technician at this time, so I was not qualified to do the work (it would be several more years before I became a recording engineer).

Because the collective agreement required that someone from NABET be present, and it didn't matter who, they sent me. Outside the context of the collective agreement, it was kind of dumb. My job was simply to be there. All I did the entire session was watch. I didn't mind—it was a fascinating session. The two guys leading the session were Matt Zimbel from the Canadian Jazz Fusion group Manteca and Doug Wilde, who would join Manteca later as co-leader of the group with Matt.

There was a bit of drama during the session. One of the session players wasn't quite delivering the goods. Apparently she was playing a bit out of tune. I couldn't hear it myself, but it was a big deal to the professional musicians in the room. Zimbel and Wilde did their best to get what they needed without making her explicitly aware that there was a problem. There was much discussion in the control room about how to deal with the situation. The musician was young and talented with a terrific reputation. She was just having a bad day. Ultimately Zimbel and Wilde placed her in an isolation booth, where they were able to tweak her playing with subtle direction and multiple retakes without affecting the work of the other musicians. She responded enthusiastically. In the end, Zimbel and Wilde got what they needed.

I was impressed. Lesser men might have attempted to bully or humiliate the musician, which almost certainly would have resulted in tears and an inferior product. Not Zimbel and Wilde. Watching them was like attending a masterclass in tact. It was worth the price of admission. Except, I hadn't paid any admission—I was getting paid for being there. For doing pretty much nothing, other than observe.

I understood that my presence was meant to discourage the CBC from hiring outside the union. Otherwise, theoretically, the CBC could just start hiring whomever they wanted whenever they wanted, paying them whatever they wanted. Still, I couldn't help but feel that it was all a bit silly. Why, I asked myself, was a union even necessary? Couldn't we all just play nice together? Couldn't the CBC just be counted upon to do the right thing?

I was of the mind that although I belonged to a union, it didn't really apply to me. Unions were for dock workers, not people like me. I considered myself a white-collar worker, whatever that was. I worked according to my work ethic, not because someone told me how long or how hard to work. When older technicians insisted on taking every single break and made sure to claim every red cent of overtime, turnaround, and night differential owed to them, I shook my head and told myself, "That's not me, and never will be."

In time, however, some of the benefits of belonging to a union gradually dawned on me. For instance, I got paid more. It was harder to lay me off. There were such things as overtime, turn-around, and night differential. I got paid for sick days, moving, bereavement, et cetera, all of which might not have existed were it not for the strength in numbers provided by belonging to one union or another. I still thought it was unfortunate that we lived in a world where we didn't just do right by one another, but over time, as I grew more aware of humanity's resistance to doing the right thing of its own accord, I concluded that unions were a regrettable necessity.

In the spring of 1996 one serious impact of belonging to a union became apparent. I was single and not earning that much as a Group 4 Radio Technician, living paycheque to paycheque, as so many of us do. I was engaged to be married on July 20. That spring, though, it looked like my union, CEP at this time (the Communications, Energy and Paperworkers Union of Canada) couldn't come to terms with CBC management. One summer day, I went home to my one-bedroom apartment in High Park certain that I would be on strike the following morning.

Going on strike would have been disastrous for me. My fiancé Lynda was about to quit her job in Prince Edward Island and move up to Toronto to be with me. She wouldn't have a job and I wouldn't be getting paid. I knew little about strike pay; I assumed it wouldn't be enough to tide us over. We wouldn't be able to pay rent, wouldn't be able to afford to fly to PEI where the wedding was to take place, and certainly wouldn't be able to take a decent honeymoon.

The deadline for negotiations was midnight. Apprehensive, I stayed up late to watch the news. During the midnight local CBLT newscast, it was reported that CBC and CEP were extending negotiating until past midnight. Both sides finally came to an agreement around 1:30am. Entering the Broadcast Centre the next morning, I felt like I'd dodged a bullet.

I was able to forget about belonging to a union until shortly after I joined the radio drama department in 1999, when we got word that negotiations weren't going well. Job security and wages were a sticking point. We had been without a contract since June. It was now February. I was in a better position financially because my wife was now working but I still wasn't keen on the idea of a strike.

The membership of CEP was asked to vote on whether to give the union a strike mandate. In Toronto, we did so across Front Street in a small boardroom in the Metro Convention Centre. I did not want to vote yes, because I did not want to be on strike, but I felt like I had no choice. If we didn't give the union a strike mandate, they would have no clout with management and we would be forced to accept whatever terms they offered. I felt like a pawn.

(Afterward, my friends at CBLFT-TV interviewed me briefly on the subject. I was reluctant to be interviewed in French because I didn't think my French was television-worthy, but they convinced me, so I provided a short blurb. I still have a copy on VHS tape. I watched it recently. My French is acceptable but undermined by a nervous laugh at the end.)

Negotiations completely broke down the evening of February 17, 1999, setting the stage for the first strike by technicians since 1981. Over the next couple of weeks, CBC remained on the air but with pared-down newscasts and repeat programming. Most local content was cancelled. We stopped production on popular shows. Ratings for *The National* plummeted fifteen percent and ratings overall went down twenty percent. *The National* reduced their show from one hour to twenty minutes. Reruns ran instead of live programming on *Newsworld*.

I hadn't believed it would happen. I went to bed Tuesday night certain the union and CBC management would sort it all out by midnight and the following morning it would be business as usual. Confident that saner heads would prevail, I hit the sack well before the strike deadline of midnight with my clock radio set to wake me up at 6:30am. I expected to wake up to the sound of Anubha Parray reading the CBC regional news as usual, evidence that a strike had been averted. On-air personnel belonged to the Canadian Media

Guild but the CEP had asked the Guild membership not to cross our picket lines in the event of a strike. I figured that if CEP walked, Anubha wouldn't be broadcasting.

When I awoke and heard Parray's voice, I assumed we weren't on strike. A part of me was even disappointed because, I thought, it would have been nice to be able to sleep in. Half a minute later, however, Parray announced that CEP was indeed on strike. I could not hear any on-air impact; apparently a manager who knew what he or she was doing was operating the console. My immediate reaction was, oh no! It really happened. My second reaction was to wonder what Parray was doing on the air. My final reaction was, well, to sleep in.

I was truthfully a little worried. I had no idea how long the strike would last. I had just bought a new house, my first. How would we pay the mortgage and all the other bills? Fortunately, my wife Lynda was a pharmacist, working in a franchise drugstore in small-town Ontario, so we had some income.

This was a Wednesday. My union steward had scheduled me to picket the following Monday and Tuesday, if we went out. He scheduled me to picket two ten-hour days because I lived far from the downtown core. I phoned the union office to see what was going on and was told they wouldn't mind support that first day on the picket line. I decided that the least I could get out of this bad situation was a day off, so I didn't bother.

I wandered around in a daze that day, trying to sort out the ramifications of being on strike. I thought that I should do up our finances to see if we would be all right, but I didn't have the courage. I was fairly certain that we wouldn't be able to make all our payments. I kept one eye on the news all day and was surprised to see that there was very little coverage of the strike.

I drove my wife Lynda to work, then visited the bank to see what would happen if we missed a mortgage payment or two. I spoke with the bank manager, who was friendly, and he told me that I would have to default on three payments in a row before the situation would get serious. I left somewhat reassured.

The following day my curiosity got the better of me. I went into Toronto to see how things were on the picket line, wearing the clothes that I usually wore in nice warm studios. I felt a little guilty for not having been there the first day. I arrived expecting to see a great ring of picketers surrounding the Broadcast Center, but there were only enough to cover the three main entrances. The picketers walked in small circles in front of these entrances. There was an RV belonging to CEP parked on John Street. I greeted people I knew. Someone pointed me to a sign-in sheet. I wrote my time of arrival beside my name. Someone else pointed me to a pile of white cardboard picket signs. I found a picket sign reading "CBC Techs on Strike" and "How about dinner and a movie first?" and slung it around my neck. Conversation on the line revolved around how long we all thought we would be out (the consensus was a long time).

That first day I picketed four hours, four of the twenty I was expected to do each week. Having not dressed warmly enough I shivered through most of it. To make it through the rest of the strike without frostbite I would have to learn to dress properly. My boots weren't comfortable on the concrete, and after four hours my back was killing me. I spent most of the time standing around talking to people, many of them colleagues I knew from the Guild. They were crossing our picket line, but most of them were doing so respectfully, waiting several minutes and then requesting a management escort.

Ignorant people did appear who barged through the picket line. We were fairly vigilant those first few days, catching many of these people, holding them back (verbally, not physically) and insisting that they wait for the management escort. If we caught them early enough they usually complied, but there were those who gave us the tin ear. These ones received some verbal abuse, and we vowed to remember them after the strike.

I spent the first three days in shock. That was how long it took me to get up the nerve to do our finances. On Friday I finally hunkered down and added everything up. To my surprise, I discovered that we could pay all our bills and the mortgage on Lynda's salary alone. Together with what I would make on the picket line (one hundred dollars the first week, one hundred and fifty the second week, and two hundred each subsequent week, for twenty hours of walking the picket line a week) we would wind up (just barely) in the clear with a little extra money in the bank to tide us over for a while. It would be tight, but we would manage.

Picketing is fine if you've recently had a lobotomy, but otherwise it's a tedious activity. Maybe once or twice a shift something interesting happened to prod my brain into consciousness. Recording engineer Doug Doctor reported one day that while standing outside the Union office wearing his picket sign, a well-dressed fellow gave him twenty bucks to buy the guys on the line coffee and donuts. One night a gentleman by the name of Leroy from CBC sales bought thirty of us Swiss Chalet dinners. Such acts of generosity were heartening in sub-zero temperatures after hours of mindless slogging it.

One day as I was picketing before the Wellington Street entrance of the Toronto Broadcast Centre I spotted Alex Frame, the Vice President of CBC Radio. He'd emerged to have a smoke. I approached him and introduced myself as a radio technician. I asked him if he had any news about the negotiations. He had nothing to report, and we chatted for a while. Before he went back inside, he asked me if there was anything we needed on the line. Having been asked this several times I had a stock response ready. "A little twelve-year-old scotch would warm things up nicely."

Frame laughed and left. He returned five minutes later with a large CBC Radio 2 mug full of twelve-year-old Glenlivit.

"I stole it from Harold's old desk," he told me. He meant the former Vice President of Radio, Harold Redekopp (later VP of Television). "Share it with the radio people."

The scotch went down well, and I got to keep the mug. As instructed, I shared it with the radio people, one of whom said, "Wow. Alex Frame did that? That's a nice thing for him to have done." Barbara Budd, the co-host of *As It Happens*, who happened to be present, mentioned that she thought Frame himself was a teetotaller.

The first few days of picketing just about killed me—I was not a fan of the cold—but I got tough soon enough. Before the strike, it had been my habit to disembark from the GO Train and follow enclosed pedestrian spaces as much as I could before darting out onto the street as close as possible to the Workman's Compensation building. Then I would go underground for the final two-minute walk into the Broadcast Centre. During the strike I got off the GO Train and spent the next seven to eight hours outside. I learned to dress warmly: track pants under my jeans, two pairs of socks, a T-shirt, a long-sleeved shirt, a sweater or sweatshirt, a warm green fuzzy, and on top of all that my canvas Australian Outback coat. A scarf, warm gloves and either earmuffs or a warm hat, depending on just how cold it was, completed the ensemble. I wore sneakers because they were warm enough with the two pairs of socks, and I liked them for trudging around the building on the concrete.

Over the next few weeks, I picketed my requisite twenty hours a week, signing in and out of each shift. I volunteered to picket overnight, when our ranks were thin and needed to be bolstered. We were soon told that our strike pay would increase to two hundred and fifty bucks for twenty hours of picketing, which made the picketing just that much more bearable.

We had oil barrels set up at strategic locations around the building. We burned wood in them—creosote-soaked wood, someone told me. One night I went on a wood-hunting mission with fellow radio technician Chuck Jutras. This was a lot more fun than picketing, especially because Chuck is easily the funniest guy I've known at the corporation (which is saying a lot considering all the professional comedians I've worked with over the years). We found a bunch of discarded pallets at a factory, loaded them into the back of Chuck's truck, and brought them back for the oil barrels. I tried not to stand around the barrels, though—I didn't want to smell like smoke or breathe the fumes, though some nights it was so cold I couldn't resist. Most nights, though, I marched quickly around the building to keep warm. There were grates in front of the building along Wellington Street that vented warm air, providing some relief. When we couldn't stand it anymore, we'd take a short break someplace warm—a coffee shop, or under Metro Hall across the street, or sometimes in the CEP RV.

Rumors swirled of people signing in and then no one seeing them again until it was time to sign out, off drinking coffee someplace warm or seeing a movie up the street. Others chose not to walk the picket line at all, forgoing strike pay, opting instead to pick up jobs elsewhere, such as delivering pizza. Yet others stayed at home.

We heard stories of colleagues who went to other CBC locations to work as scabs, helping to keep those places on the air. I know people who to this day have not forgiven them for that.

Several staff were made supervisors immediately before the strike to help keep the CBC on the air. They usually became a part of a body called APS (the Association of Professional Supervisors). Except as a strategy to keep the CBC on the air, it didn't always make sense to make them supervisors. They usually didn't have staff reporting to them. After the job actions it made little sense having them in these positions. However, nobody that I'm aware of held it against these people for accepting and benefitting from these positions.

A few days into the strike my hometown newspaper, the *Summerside Journal-Pioneer*, wrote an editorial coming down heavily on the side of management against the union. It was filled with what I perceived as factual errors and misperceptions. Outraged, I was stirred to write a rebuttal, which they published.

During the strike, I don't recall a single person ever calling to see how my wife and I were doing. Although I registered this fact, I didn't blame anyone for it. Certainly, I myself have fallen short in this regard. Some folk probably didn't need to check in because we'd already covered it in casual conversation, usually after, "How are you?" "Well, we're on strike, you know." "How's that going?" "Oh, we're surviving," kind of thing. It is, perhaps, a bit of a commentary on modern life. We're all caught up in our own lives, with little thought to give to anyone else, really.

And the truth was Lynda and I were doing fine. We had turned off the financial spigots, ceased buying unnecessary stuff. I bought cheap soup for lunch on the picket line, or ate what people donated, such as donuts and pizza. I received strike pay, which wasn't as much as I ordinarily would have been paid, but it was not taxed.

And in the end, I was somewhat astonished to see that I finished the strike with more money in the bank than I'd started with. Others were not so lucky. There were several instances of both husband and wife working for the CBC, both of whom were on strike. No doubt they found the situation rather more difficult than Lynda and I did.

At this time, winter 1999, about ten thousand people worked for the CBC. About eighteen hundred of us technical types were on strike. That meant that most of the CBC wasn't on strike. Schedulers, for instance, were represented by CUPE (Canadian Union of Public Employees). CUPE themselves had struck briefly in 1989 (I remember my friends in that union escorting me across the picket line). Reporters, journalists, on-air talent, and so on were represented by the Canadian Media Guild. Eventually we would all be represented by the Canadian Media Guild, but that was still a few years away. For now, both CUPE and CMG had to be escorted across our picket lines to get to work.

I slowly began to resent those who were still working. There was a stereotype of the manager or producer who would approach you on the picket line to ask, "How's it going? Have you heard anything?" And then go inside to do their best to keep the place on the air while the rest of us continued to picket out in the freezing cold.

One radio producer in particular appeared to support us on the line, making all the right sympathetic noises. Inside, he worked hard to make the best radio possible. One of his colleagues suggested that maybe they shouldn't be working so hard to create programming that appeared to be unaffected by the strike. Shouldn't they be seeking a means to support their colleagues out on the street instead? The producer didn't seem to get it.

After the strike, I met this producer in the hall. We spoke briefly about the job action. I'm rather ashamed of this conversation. Perhaps you have to go through such moments and reflect on them afterwards to be able to grow as a person.

"I know you guys were doing your best to support us in your way," I told him disingenuously, deliberately trying to make him feel guilty.

He hung his head down low and didn't meet my eyes. "Of course, of course," he mumbled.

I may have succeeded in making him feel guilty, but I immediately felt guilty myself. Two wrongs don't make a right. He wasn't a bad guy. He was just trying to make good radio. And I'm a hypocrite. The truth is, if he had been on strike and I had been charged with making radio in his place, I probably would have seized the opportunity to prove that I could make radio every bit as good as he could.

I did not reserve my resentment for individuals alone. I saved a healthy amount for unions, too. Unions who didn't appear to lift a finger to support us, such as the CMG (Canadian Media Guild) and the APS. I have since softened my stance toward both because it's all water under the bridge and we all need to get along.

All told, we were off the job for seven weeks. We settled for 10 to 11% wage increases over 37 months and improvements regarding job security.

The strike had been a fairly innocuous event in the grand scheme of things, but it placed divisions in the hearts of some, pitting us against one another, technicians versus management, picketer versus scab, disingenuous picketer versus disingenuous producer. It was quite an education.

Almost two years later, in December 2001, we had another job action. The union considered it a lockout as opposed to a strike, and it only lasted two weeks, but otherwise the experience was pretty much the same as in 1999.

Four years later, in August 2005, we experienced yet another job action.

But it wasn't at all the same and requires a completely separate chapter.

# Photos

*The staff of CBC Radio (including the author) circa 1989.*
*(CBC Archives)*

*Gerry Samson in Studio Z*
*(Photo courtesy of Elizabeth Osti)*

*Andrew Moodie in Studio Q, Jarvis Street*
*(Photo courtesy of Andrew Moodie)*

*Joram Kalfa, Joe Mahoney and Peter Chin in the old Radio Master Control on Jarvis Street*
*(Photo courtesy of Claire de Visme)*

*Larry Alder putting up tape in the Jarvis Street Radio Master Control*
*(Photo courtesy of Larry Alder)*

*Systems Technologist Paul Cutler in Jarvis Street Radio Master Control*
*(Photo courtesy of Larry Alder)*

*Sarah Cooper, Joe Mahoney, Victor-Levy-Beaulieu, Margaret-Atwood, Chez Margaret Atwood*
*(Photo by Doris Dumais)*

*Studio 212 Main Floor, Toronto Broadcast Centre*
*(Photo by John McCarthy)*

*Recording Engineer Greg DeClute in control room of Studio 212*
*(Photo by Joe Mahoney)*

*The Dead Room in the Toronto Broadcast Centre's Studio 212
(Photo by John McCarthy)*

*Andrew Gillies and Joe Mahoney recording the radio play Birth*
*(Photo from the author's personal collection)*

*Joe Mahoney directing the radio play* Birth *with Rosie Fernandez and Michael Lennick (Photo from the author's personal collection)*

*Floyd Favel, Edna Rain, Thomas King and Tara Beagan recording*
The Dead Dog Café *in Studio 212*
*(Photo by Joe Mahoney)*

*Joe Mahoney performing sound effects in Studio 212 for the radio play* Faint Hope
*(Photo by Greg DeClute)*

*The author's favourite editing studio, SFX 3*
*(Photo by John McCarthy)*

# XXIII
## Hybrids

When I first joined the radio drama department, I was still a Group 4 Radio Technician. Greg DeClute, Wayne Richards and Drago Grandic, on the other hand, were all Group 6 Recording Engineers, a classification that John McCarthy had fought to have created several years earlier. That classification was about to go away.

Not long after we got back inside after the strike of 1999, the CBC announced some pretty big cuts. Some thought this was to make up for the wage increases we'd just won. No doubt there were many factors, including the advent of desktop radio. In the past, radio technicians like me did almost all the recording and much of the editing on quarter-inch tape in radio studios. Now a lot of the editing could be done on computers. Technologists Deraj Ramnares and John Baldwin had begun installing a network-wide desktop editing system for CBC Radio called D-Cart in 1993, which went into production in 1994. It was supplanted by a more sophisticated system called Dalet in 1996. (Desktop television was still a few years away.)

With the advent of these desktop editing systems, a lot of the work traditionally done in the studios could now be done at producers' desks. This did not bode well for radio technicians. Some technicians saw the writing on the wall. Pianist Glenn Gould's favourite technician, Lorne Tulk, took me aside one day to warn me that there was no future in my line of work. Soon, he said, CBC would be purchasing shows produced outside the CBC. He was not entirely wrong. *Vinyl Café with Stuart McLean* and *The Age of Persuasion* by Terry O'Reilly eventually followed this model, though as of this writing most shows are still produced in-house.

Before joining CBC Radio, I had been an announcer at a couple of private radio stations where I operated my own shows. In fact,

I was usually the only one in the radio stations when I worked. When I joined CBC Radio, I didn't really understand why it took so many people to make a radio show. Still, I didn't quite see eye to eye with CBC management in that I didn't think it was necessary to have the producer replace the technician. I wondered why the technician couldn't replace the producer.

Of course, it wasn't quite as simple as that. Most producers didn't possess the knowledge required to replace a qualified radio technician. Nor did most technicians possess the full range of skills necessary to be a successful producer. In time, though, with the proper training and experience, individuals from both camps acquired the skills to both produce and operate radio shows. Many people who had started as technicians, such as Kent Hoffman, Tom Shipton, Bryan Hill, and Dean Ples, to name a few, went on to become successful producers. And producers such as Tracy Rideout went on to both produce and tech various comedy shows for years.

It's absurd to suggest that a human being is only capable of a single skill set, that a CBC employee must either be only a technician or a producer. I was always interested in many aspects of production. At the CBC, I resented being limited to a single skill set, pigeonholed into one specific group of tasks. I was always trying to bust out of that. Sometimes I was successful; usually I was not.

On the other hand, when you try to force someone to do something they're not really interested in, results vary. I have seen producers forced to be technicians who clearly considered it a demotion, and who, as a consequence, did the bare minimum to get their show on the air, with no interest in understanding the finer points of audio engineering. Barely comprehending proper metering, zero interest in compression or equalization. The kind of person who relies on chalk marks to know where to set levels. People who fancied themselves true audio engineers refer to people like the ones I've just described above as "operators." It's not a compliment.

Likewise, I've also known many technicians with little interest in producing who were nevertheless forced to incorporate some producing functions (such as editing podcasts) into their work.

The upshot of all this is that one day in 1999, Manager Larry Alder plucked me out of Room 2F100 to escort me to Plant Manager Charlie Cheffins' office, where Charlie rather apologetically handed me a redundancy notice. A redundancy notice meant that they were laying me off from my current position. According to the collective agreement, though, I had bumping rights. If it was determined that I was qualified for another, lower position elsewhere, I could bump whoever was doing that job out of their job and take his or her place.

Larry Alder escorted many technicians to Charlie's office that grim day. I didn't blame either Larry or Charlie. I know they both felt terrible about it. In fact, Charlie quit the CBC shortly afterward. It's my understanding that he quit so that he wouldn't have to do that sort of thing anymore.

I was quite taken aback by this turn of events. I'd already worked at CBC Radio for eleven years. I thought I'd been there long enough and was high enough in seniority to be safe, but I wasn't. Wayne Richards and I were the only ones in the radio drama department to get notices of redundancy, as we were lowest on the seniority list.

But that didn't mean that the other technical types in the drama department—Greg DeClute, Matt Willcott, Anton Szabo and Drago Grandic—weren't at risk. Word was recording engineers on the television side of the operation were threatening to bump into radio, which would threaten Greg and Dragos' positions. Everybody was a little uneasy.

One day Anton Szabo, in his capacity as union rep, accompanied me to a meeting with Mark Kingston, a manager in the TV Presentation Group. Mark, I would learn later in my career, is a true gentleman. The purpose of the meeting was to see if I could bump into one of the positions reporting to Mark. (If I bumped one of Mark's employees, that person could, in turn, bump someone else. Eventually, though, someone would get bumped right out of the corporation). I believe the position Mark had in mind for me was overnight video tape recorder (VTR) technician. That Mark would have been a nice guy to work for, I have no doubt. But that position did not sound at all attractive to me.

Two months after Wayne and I received notices of redundancy, we received actual lay-off letters. This was standard procedure as stated in the collective agreement. I started to get concerned that this was actually going to happen.

One day Greg, Wayne and I ran into Charlie Cheffins down in the food court. He assured us that wheels were in motion to save most of us. He was referring to a scheme by radio management to turn our jobs into "hybrid" positions—Associate Producer/ Technician jobs that the TV recording engineers wouldn't qualify for. This was a bit of dirty pool, as it was subverting the bumping process laid out in the collective agreement, but in the end they got away with it (years later the same kind of dirty pool would prevent Greg DeClute from bumping into television).

There were several pros and cons to this approach. On the plus side, it meant that I had a shot at one of these positions. If I got it, I wouldn't have to bump into overnight VTR, or worse, wind up on the street. It meant that nobody from television would be able to bump into one of these positions.

The new jobs were classified as Band 7 Associate Producer/Technician positions. This was higher than the Group 4 Radio Technician position I currently occupied, and slightly higher than the Group 6 Recording Engineer positions the other guys occupied. So if we did get the jobs, it would constitute a promotion with a corresponding increase in salary for each of us. And the title included the word "producer," which I liked, as I was just as interested in producing as I was in recording. However, they were only creating six positions, and there were seven of us, so one of us was going to get turfed. It also meant that all of us were essentially being forced to apply for our own jobs (albeit slightly better jobs, especially for me).

Also, the work that we were all doing in radio drama was that of recording engineers, not associate producer/technicians. The associate producer/technician (sometimes called AP Techs) job title would not reflect what we were actually doing. Worse, a recording engineer under the new job classifications was actually a Band 10, not a Band 7, so even though we would still be getting paid more than we currently were, we would still not be getting paid what we should be.

In the meantime, the mechanics of redundancy chugged on. One day I got a call at home from Bea Guttman, who worked in HR. The call was to review what compensation I would receive when I got laid off. I was a little testy with her.

"If they actually lay me off they're even stupider than I think," I told her, in a classic case of "beat up the messenger." Bea didn't have to take that tone from me, and nor did she. She ended the call shortly after my remark. (I apologized to her several years later. She had no memory of the incident.)

In my defense, I was feeling the stress. Within the space of a single year I'd started a new job, been on strike, become a father to two-month premature twins, and now was about to be laid off. Greg DeClute's wife Sandy remarked during all this, "What are they trying to do? Kill Joe?"

Management arranged interviews so we could all apply for these new "hybrid" technical/producer positions. The CBC refers to such interviews as "Boards," which usually consist of three or four management types grilling you for up to an hour. I was comfortable with all the managers on my Board and felt like it went well.

Still, there weren't enough positions for everyone. One of us had to go. Drago Grandic saved management the trouble of choosing between us by quitting. He'd been offered a great opportunity at the CNIB where he would work on their digital audio library project. During an exit interview with a CBC HR rep he cited his reasons for leaving as the resentment and loss of trust following the 1999 strike and the toxic politics between management and unions.

"The constant anxiety about who's going to be terminated next make it difficult to focus on our beautiful craft," he told the HR rep. "It isn't fun anymore."

I've always felt that if Drago hadn't quit, I would have wound up working overnight VTR. So, thanks, Drago.

Ultimately, I was hired as a Band 7 Associate Producer/Technician. Instead of getting fired, I got a promotion and continued to work alongside Anton, Matt, Greg and Wayne, who also kept their jobs under the same "hybrid" title.

We weren't the only ones who had to apply for our own jobs. Many others went through the same process, including one radio technician, who, a few months after being made to apply for his own job, took his own life. I'm not suggesting that the stress and existential absurdity of the restructuring process made him commit suicide. I am saying that it can't have helped.

As far as I know, no radio technicians actually got fired during this period. Most were redeployed to television. It was the end of an era for radio, which had to make do with one heck of a lot fewer radio technicians from that point on.

Over time the discrepancy in what we should have been paid as Band 7 Associate Producer/Technicians versus Band 10 Recording Engineers would amount to several thousand dollars and would be addressed eight years later when the CBC, cooperating with the CMG, reviewed every single job in the corporation. My colleagues and I made the case that that our core function all along was making radio plays, and that the only job category for recording and mixing radio plays was a Band 10 Recording Engineer. There was, in fact, no mention of recording and mixing radio plays in the Associate Producer/Technician job description. I would record over one hundred full cast radio plays over my career and was credited as a recording engineer in every single one. We won the job evaluation challenge and were compensated several thousands of dollars in back pay.

# XXIV
## *Muckraker*

The first radio drama series that I worked on regularly was a weekly half-hour sketch comedy called *Muckraker*. *Muckraker* aired every Saturday morning at 11:30am and promised to "take you behind the headlines for the real story on the latest news."

*Muckraker* was a fictional online newspaper staffed by five intrepid reporters, a device that allowed us to set up actual news stories from the previous week. Once the stories were set up, the show segued into comedy sketches about those stories, with the cast assuming the roles of various colourful characters poking fun at Canadian and international news.

*Muckraker* was created by a fellow by the name of Gary Pearson. I never actually met Gary. I knew who he was because I'd once seen him perform an excellent impression of Captain Kirk in a live comedy sketch show, but I don't remember ever seeing him set foot in the studio. (Memory is a funny thing. It's entirely possible that the man I saw perform Captain Kirk so effectively that night long ago was someone else entirely. However, I am absolutely certain that Gary created *Muckraker*.)

Not remembering seeing Gary while we recorded *Muckraker* doesn't mean that he was never there. Nor is it a bad thing, as the writing team was ably represented by head writer Jerry Schaefer (whom you might remember as Possum Lake animal control officer Ed Frid on *The Red Green Show*). A fellow by the name of Chris Earle also wrote for the show, but I never met him either. The Executive Producer of *Muckraker* was Anton Leo. Anton also directed most episodes.

I took turns recording and mixing episodes of *Muckraker* with Wayne Richards, alternating weeks. Anton Szabo (not to be confused with Anton Leo) did the sound effects for most, if not all, shows.

The *Muckraker* cast was a talented bunch. I liked them all. Peter Oldring (also featured in the satirical CBC radio show *This is That*) did an old man voice that is the funniest old man voice I've ever heard. It should be considered a national treasure. Every now and then I would get him to do it just for me. I don't know why he doesn't talk in that voice all the time. I enjoyed Richard (Rick) Waugh's performances so much that I wrote a part for him in a pet project I did a few years later. You know Rick, you just don't know it—you've heard him many times doing commercials on private radio. You've also seen him on *Designated Survivor*, *The Umbrella Academy*, and *The Queen's Gambit* (among others) in supporting roles.

Mag Ruffman, who enjoyed a successful television and film career appearing in such **projects as *Anne of Green Gables* and *Alias Grace***, was a pleasure to work with. Deann Degruijter, known for her work in theatre as well as *PAW Patrol, Creative Galaxy*, **and more, was a ball of energy and a lot of fun to be around.** Glen Gaston, also a positive presence, has appeared in both movies and theatrical productions since *Muckraker*.

Taping comedy shows over the years, I often thought that it was too bad that audiences didn't get to hear the bits we cut out. You get some of the funniest people in the country in the same room and it's not long before we're all laughing just as hard between takes as during them.

We packaged *Muckraker* on a pretty tight schedule. The writers produced scripts for us late Thursday afternoons just in time for recording sessions Thursday evenings. While the cast read through the script a couple of rooms over, I'd peruse my own copy to determine the best way to block each scene. By blocking, I mean arranging how the actors moved through the scene with respect to one another and the microphone.

Sometimes, as I've written elsewhere, the blocking was as simple as having the actors stand next to one another facing the microphone. Other times it was more complicated. I've also written about that, but it won't hurt to provide another example:

A mother is shouting out her window at her son, who's climbing a tree outside on the front lawn. She's afraid he might fall out of the tree and break his neck. How do you make a scene like that sound convincing on the radio without recording it on location? (We didn't have time to visit all the locations in our script. Even if we did, they might not have sounded convincing. In the world of audio, with no pictures to help your brain figure out what you're hearing, stuff doesn't always sound like what it actually is.)

In Studio 212, I might have placed the son inside the Dead Room (no hard surfaces for his voice to reflect off, simulating an outdoor environment), and his mother in the main studio within some artfully placed soft-sided baffles. There was a window between the Dead Room and the main studio to allow interaction between the actors. By tweaking the actors' proximity to the microphone and one another, and by adding the appropriate ambiance in post, I could make a scene like that sound pretty convincing. Studio 212 really was brilliantly conceived, designed to give production teams maximum flexibility to recreate just about any environment, internal or external, that they could think of.

It was arguably the director's job to do this kind of blocking, but not every director had sufficient experience or interest. Wayne and I usually helped Anton Leo block the scenes. This is not a slight against Anton: his expertise was comedy, not blocking radio plays. Directors such as Gregory J. Sinclair, James Roy, Bill Lane, and Bill Howell, on the other hand, who were profoundly interested in the medium of radio drama, were constantly pushing the boundaries. They often surprised me with their innovative blocking. Most of what I know about the craft of making radio plays I learned from them.

Despite assisting with the blocking, I was still pretty green when I was working on *Muckraker*. And I was pretty much flying without a net. Recording during the evening, there was no one around to help me if things went south, apart from Anton Szabo, who, though resourceful, had not been trained on the Neve Capricorn at that time.

I was so green, in fact, that I didn't even know how to hard reboot the Mac Computers if they froze.

"Press the power button for five seconds until it restarts," John McCarthy told me shortly before my first evening shift, courteously refraining from rolling his eyes.

In my defense, this was 2002. It was my first exposure to Apple computers. I didn't like Macs at all back then. I'd been a hardcore PC guy since I'd bought my first IBM XT 286 back in 1991. I knew the PC operating system. I was familiar with DOS. I didn't know anything about Macs. There was a lot about them that drove me nuts.

For example, on the Mac Quads we used to run our editing software, it was not possible to eject the CD tray from the Mac computer itself. You had to do it through a button on the keyboard. The problem with this was that the computer was not located in the control room with us. Because the computer was noisy (not good when you're working with sound), it was housed in a completely different room down the hall, connected to the monitor, keyboard and mouse in the control room via extremely long cables amplified by range extenders. I'd go to the Mac in the other room to insert or remove a CD only to discover that I'd forgotten to eject the tray from the keyboard, forcing me to go back to the control room to hit eject.

Then there was the spinning wheel of death. When a Mac computer hung, it hung real good. It displayed a colourful little wheel on your monitor that spun forever and ever, and God help you if you forgot to save your work before the Spinning Wheel of Death showed up.

Back to *Muckraker*. During each take, I sat in the control room, hunched over the console, listening closely. I was listening to make sure there were no issues with the sound, but I was also listening to see if I could help make the scene funnier. Sadly, the *Muckraker* team wasn't the least bit interested in my input. Only once did they ever accept a suggestion from me. It was for a sketch that concerned an incident with Jean Chrétien. Back in August 2000, then Prime Minister Jean Chrétien was touring an agricultural show in Prince Edward Island when a twenty-three-year-old protestor shoved a pie in his face.

"You have developed a funny way of serving pies these days," Chrétien told supporters later. "I'm not that hungry."

This sort of thing was right up *Muckraker*'s alley. The resulting sketch related the broad details of the incident: the Prime Minister getting pied in the face, and the protestor getting arrested. There was a line: "I'm taking you into custody."

I suggested we change the line to, "I'm taking you into custardy. Uh, custody."

Hey, I'm not saying it's the funniest line ever. But of all my suggestions during my time with *Muckraker*, that's the one they took. It was Rick Waugh who agreed to deliver the line. Thanks, Rick.

We usually finished recording the cast around eleven pm, at which time the cast and crew bailed, leaving Anton Szabo and me to clean up. Afterward, I raced home as quickly as possible to hit the sack because I needed to be back in bright and early the next morning to edit, assemble, and mix the show. Neither Wayne Richards nor I were particularly fond of this quick turn-around. Once, rushing home on Highway 401, I got stopped by a cop for speeding.

"Do you know how fast you were going?" he asked me.

"No," I told him honestly.

"There are jets that fly slower than you," he said.

Keen to get home, I'd been doing over 140 km/hour without realizing it. Luckily, I was only fined fifty bucks and didn't lose any points. Except with my wife, that is.

During our Thursday night recording sessions, Tracy Rideout (at that time an Associate Producer) kept track of the good takes. Friday mornings when I came into edit and assemble the show, we worked off Tracy's notes.

Fridays were as annoying as Thursday evenings were fun. It was a pretty intense day. For a while, the show aired on Friday nights as well as Saturday mornings, so there was a lot of pressure to finish mixing by eight pm.

The mixing process was essentially the same as any radio play except that instead of mixing it in Studio 212, where it had been recorded the previous night, we mixed it in Studio 213, otherwise known as Sound Effects 3, or SFX 3. SFX 3 quickly became my favourite studio. Mixing in SFX 3, I had access to Pro Tools, a Digidesign Pro Tools Control 24 mixing board, one piece of outboard gear (a Harmonizer), and the Waves Gold Plug-in Bundle. Plugins are software effects processors that allow you to manipulate sound in all sorts of fancy ways.

On a conventional radio play the recording engineer edited the voice tracks and then handed the project over to the sound effects engineer to assemble the sound effects, and together they mixed the show under the supervision of the director.

On *Muckraker*, Anton Szabo always prepared his sound effects before the recording session, recording many of them live into the sketches. The rest of the sound effects he loaded up in the hard drive, readily accessible. Having the sound effects already recorded and pre-loaded greatly reduced the time needed to mix the show. This was critical, because it still took a damned long time. Anton (Szabo) usually didn't participate in the Friday mix sessions. SFX 3 was a smaller studio. It was easier and more comfortable just to have one engineer working with the director and associate producer.

I can't speak for Wayne (who, you might recall, engineered the show every second week), but the way I mixed the show was scene by scene, editing the dialogue first, then fleshing out the sound effects (and music, if there was any). Ideally, we took the best single take of each sketch based on Tracy's notes. Unfortunately, it never worked out that way. Anton Leo always insisted on listening to every bloody take. Then he took bits from several takes to create a composite take. All this futzing around slowed down the process and drove Wayne and I nuts (I can safely speak for Wayne on that point).

"Why doesn't he just follow the damned notes?" we asked ourselves.

Of course, he was trying to get the funniest bits into the show. Ironically, years later, when Greg DeClute and I started directing, editing and mixing our own radio plays, we were infinitely fussier than any of the directors we ever worked with, including Anton.

Creating each episode was a painstaking process, but it was also pretty rewarding as the show came alive. It was quite an education, too. I learned how to make dialogue pop. I made crazy edits that

I never thought would work but that did anyway. I manipulated sound in crazy ways, using all the tools at my disposal, bending sound to my will, mwa ha ha.

At first, levels drove me crazy. You want the volume of the show to be consistent throughout, within a certain dynamic range, peaking at about -20 dBfs (decibels relative to Full Scale). I came from live radio where I managed levels on the fly. Maintaining consistent levels in the digital domain was trickier. I worked off two meters, a standalone dBfs meter on my left and a similar meter on the DAT machine to my right. The meter on my left also showed me whether my content was in or out of phase (which you can hear if you're not wearing headphones, but it's nice to have visual confirmation. More on phase later. Brace yourself).

There's a phenomenon called "threshold shift." You probably experience this in your car when you're listening to the radio. When you first get in the car, you set your car stereo to a certain level, then you get driving and the road noise is loud so you crank the radio up. You get out on the highway and it's even louder so you jack the radio up even more. At the grocery store, you get out and buy your groceries. When you get back in your car and turn it on, you can't believe how loud your radio is. You're a victim of threshold shift.

I also experienced threshold shift mixing radio shows, but it was more about ear fatigue. As the day wore on, my ears got tired, and as my ears got tired, I gradually made everything louder, forcing me to revisit parts of my mix to make the levels consistent. Eventually, I acquired the discipline to do this as I went along, constantly checking levels on both meters to ensure consistency. And I tried not to vary the volume of the studio monitors, a lesson John Johnston had taught me a decade earlier.

They were long days, mixing *Muckraker*. Twelve, thirteen hour days followed by the long commute home. Once we finished mixing the show, we still had to print it in real time onto DAT tapes (later we burned it onto CDs). If there was a mistake, we had to stop, fix it, and start again (we didn't usually make mistakes; we didn't have time to). Once printed, Anton Leo grabbed the tapes and ran them up to the third floor to Radio Master Control for broadcast. More than once we weren't entirely sure we'd make it in time—but we always did.

After a while they stopped the Friday night broadcast, so we only had Saturday to worry about. This bought us more time, but it also meant that we could tweak even later into the night. And when we switched from capturing the show on DAT tapes to burning it onto CDs, it didn't really save us any time. In fact, it sometimes added time. To make a CD, we had to "bounce" the show into a two-track (stereo) version in Pro Tools, and then use a program called Toast to burn the CD.

This was usually pretty straightforward, if we set the bounce up properly. But there was one stretch of several weeks when the Mac Superdrive wouldn't burn the CD properly. If we couldn't burn the CD, then we couldn't get it to Master Control for broadcast. When we burnt a CD that didn't work, and that we couldn't reuse, we called it "burning a coaster" as that's all the CD was good for. I burnt a lot of coasters during that period. Eventually Audio Systems (which is what radio maintenance was called back then) fixed the Superdrive for me.

That wasn't the only technical problem I experienced. One Saturday night I was at home watching a movie with my wife when the phone rang. *Muckraker* was on the air, but I wasn't listening to it. Having recorded and mixed the thing, I'd heard it enough already. It was Director/Exec Producer Anton Leo on the phone.

"They all sound like ghosts," he complained.

He was talking about the cast.

Reluctantly, I turned on the radio. Sure enough, half the cast sounded barely present. They sounded like I'd recorded them from the next room over. Anton told me that the cast sounded that way in most of the country. Curiously, they sounded fine in parts of Alberta. Although he was too polite to come right out and say it, Anton clearly wanted to know how the hell I'd wrecked his show.

Immediately I suspected that the cast sounded this way because the show was being broadcast out of phase.

What does that mean exactly?

It means that the show's audio, in particular the voices of the actors, was cancelling itself out.

How could this happen?

Sound travels through the air in waves. Saying that sound travels in waves can be misleading though. Many people think of sound as looking like the surface of water, with peaks and troughs, because the motion of sound is often represented visually as a sine wave. This is just a convenient way to illustrate what's going on. The truth is sound waves travel through air as longitudinal waves. Longitudinal waves don't have peaks and troughs. What's actually happening is that as sound passes through a pocket of air, it displaces particles of air before and after that pocket as the energy of the sound wave passes through it.

Without going too far down this rabbit hole, consider that when an object creates a sound wave that passes through air (such as a human voice), it creates high- and low-pressure areas in the air around it—areas where the air particles are bunched up, and areas where the air particles are spread apart. These are called compressions and rarefactions, respectively. They are not literally peaks and troughs of waves; they are different concentrations of air particles moving through space, pushing and pulling, creating pressure fluctuations.

How does phase come into this?

When two compressions come together (two areas where the air particles are bunched up) and are followed by two rarefactions (areas where air particles are less concentrated) the sound waves reinforce one another. This is called constructive interference and results in louder sound. If, on the other hand, a rarefaction meets a compression (a low-pressure area meets a high-pressure area) then the longitudinal waves cancel one another out. If they cancel one another out completely, the air particles behave as though they are at rest, with no interference at all. This is called destructive interference, and results in no sound.

The interaction of longitudinal waves in a medium such as air is rarely straightforward, especially when enclosed within reflective boundaries such as walls, with other reflective objects such as furniture scattered throughout. In the real world it's unlikely that sound waves would completely cancel one another out. They can, however, do a lot of damage to one another, and that's what I thought was happening to *Muckraker* that night. I thought that I must have done something during either the recording or the packaging process that resulted in that particular show being out of phase.

Sound can wind up out of phase for several reasons, though. It can happen at the recording stage. An actor might stand in the wrong spot relative to the microphone. Recording using a style called MS stereo (I'll spare you the details of that), we kept a close eye on the phase meter when we had several actors ranged around our MS stereo microphone. If an actor wandered in behind the microphone, he got recorded out of phase. I was pretty sure I hadn't let that happen.

There is an issue closely related to phase called "polarity." They are often confused because both polarity and phase manifest themselves in similar cancellation and interference issues. They are not the same, though. Phase has to do with timing and signal delay. Polarity is when you have two possible choices that are mutually exclusive, such as a fan blowing air or a vacuum drawing air in, or flipping a coin either heads or tails, or observing positive or negative when you insert a battery, or deciding whether to be good or evil. When you're talking about sound, polarity is a question of direction of flow of electrical current.

Polarity issues can arise from bad or incorrectly used cables, microphones, and loudspeakers. On the home front, for example, a listener might have audio issues because their stereo speakers are wired up wrong. Many people do this without even realizing it. If you accidentally reverse the polarity of one channel on one of your speakers—putting the black (negative) speaker wire where the red (positive) one is supposed to go, then you will mess up your speaker drivers, which work by rocking back and forth. If you reverse the polarity of a speaker, one speaker cone will behave opposite of what it's supposed to, going forward when it's supposed to be going backward, the opposite of the cone in the other speaker (assuming the other speaker's wired correctly). When this happens, the longitudinal sound waves from the two speakers partially cancel one another out, resulting in weak bass and weird stereo imaging, which you don't want.

Here's a trick: Take your two stereo speakers and place them about a foot apart facing one another. Turn the stereo up. If it sounds big and juicy, the polarity is likely fine and all is well. If it sounds thin and tinny, the speakers might be wired incorrectly. Try reversing the wires in the back of one speaker. You should hear a significant difference in the quality of sound. You want it sounding big and juicy, with full bass. (Note that if you reverse the polarity of both speakers, you'll be fine, because then the speakers won't be cancelling one another out.)

The odds of everybody in Canada except those in parts of Alberta having all their stereos wired up incorrectly were inconceivably slim. So that probably wasn't the issue.

I worried about it all weekend. When I got to work on Monday I immediately brought it up with the guys. Nobody could figure out what I might have done.

I'm afraid the answer to the puzzle is a bit anti-climactic. Within a day or so, transmission techs discovered that the problem had been a bad patch in the CN Tower. Either a cable had been patched wrong or the cable itself had been wired incorrectly, reversing the polarity. The reason the show sounded fine in Alberta was because Alberta received the show via a different means of transmission.

It was good to know I hadn't done anything wrong. Not that it mattered if I had; I would have just had to own up to it and learn from it. Which some poor transmitter tech no doubt had to do this time round.

# XXV

## The Handmaid's Tale

No, not the book. Or the TV series. Or the stage play. Or the opera.

The radio play.

No, not the BBC version, the CBC version.

In 2002 CBC Radio commissioned Michael O'Brien to adapt Margaret Atwood's *The Handmaid's Tale* for radio. Michael had already written several radio plays for us and knew how to write them properly, for the medium of radio. Ann Jansen directed and produced it.

Ann had only recently gotten into directing radio plays. I'd previously worked with her on an adaptation of Jane Urquhart's *Away*, adapted by Beverly Cooper, my first actual gig as a recording engineer. (Beverly Cooper also knows how to write radio plays.) The first time I ever worked with Ann, I made a terrible mistake. I'd voice tracked an actor to DAT. Unbeknownst to me someone had set the DAT to 32 kbps instead of the standard 44.1. I hadn't noticed. I had to break the news to Ann that we needed to bring the actor back in to re-record them. Never having met Ann before, I had no idea how she'd react. She not only took the news well but took pains to make me feel better about it, like a decent human being. This became the basis of a good friendship. I came to think of Ann as a (slightly) older sister.

My pals Wayne Richards and Matt Willcott did the sound effects for *The Handmaid's Tale*. Michael White scored and performed the original music. I was the recording engineer. My other pal Sandra Jeffries was the Associate Producer.

Sandra and I were big fans of the TV show *The X-Files* at the time. An iconic character on that show was known only as "Cigarette Smoking Man," played by William B. Davis. One day in Studio 212 Sandra and I looked up to find Cigarette Smoking Man in the studio with us. He was there to play the Commander, alongside Emma Campbell as Offred and Donna Goodhand as the Commander's barren wife Serena Joy.

Having Cigarette Smoking Man from *The X-Files* appear in the studio with us was surreal. But it didn't hold a candle to what came next. Truly one of the most bizarre moments of my entire recording career was recording William B. Davis feigning an orgasm before me, simulating having sex with the character of Offred to impregnate her. Nobody said much as we recorded a few takes of this. You would have thought that it was just another day at the office, and that we recorded that sort of thing every day (we did not).

Shirley Douglas played Aunt Lydia. Shirley was married to Donald Sutherland. Keifer Sutherland is her son. She was a lot of fun. Occasionally, Shirley took exception to Ann's direction. Once I happened to be on the studio floor adjusting a mic when Ann spoke up from the control room, her voice booming through the studio floor speakers.

Shirley narrowed her eyes and cocked her head. "Joe," she declaimed. "What is that mad woman in the control room trying to tell me?"

I did my best to translate.

Kim Campbell played Aunt Elizabeth. Yes, that Kim Campbell, the only woman ever to have Prime Ministered this fine country (so far). Having Kim Campbell in the studio was an occasion. Ann arranged an impromptu photo session on the studio floor. Everyone gathered around to have their picture taken with the former Prime Minister. Well, not everyone. Wayne Richards and I were in the control room getting things ready for the next scene. Wayne happened to look up as this was happening.

"What are they doing?" he asked me.

"Looks like they're taking a group photo with Kim Campbell," I observed.

"Why didn't they ask us to be a part of it?" Wayne demanded to know. "We're only the ones who do all the goddamned work!"

We never let Ann live that one down.

# XXVI
## Stuart McLean

*The Vinyl Café with Stuart McLean* may not have been big, but it was small.

(That was the show's motto.)

*The Vinyl Café* debuted in 1994. I was a fan from the beginning. It was a great show. How do I know it was a great show? Because it would trap me in my car long after I'd reached my destination. I just couldn't stop listening. That was always happening to me with *The Vinyl Café*. Stuart McLean was one of the biggest celebrities CBC Radio had to offer, and *The Vinyl Café* one of the best shows. I never let Stuart know I felt that way. Maybe I should have.

Stuart had been a long-time journalist with CBC Radio. He came to fame with his seven-year stint contributing to *Morningside*. He created radio magic with host Peter Gzowski. Before that he'd contributed documentaries to *Sunday Morning*. He won an AC-TRA award for Best Radio Documentary for contributing to that show's coverage of the Jonestown massacre. Over time he became a best-selling author and the celebrity host of *The Vinyl Café*. He won the Stephen Leacock Memorial Medal for Humour three times, was appointed an Officer of the Order of Canada, was a professor emeritus at Ryerson University in Toronto and well, you get the idea. But I knew him as the host of *The Vinyl Café*, both from listening to the show on the air and by working with him in the studio, at least when he wasn't touring the show around Canada and the United States.

Our first day working together I wasn't quite sure what to expect. Although I liked his show, I knew nothing about the man. Would he be full of himself? Have a bad temper? Treat me like a piece of the equipment? I was optimistic but prepared for the worst.

Stuart arrived in SFX 3, we greeted one another, and I directed him to the announce booth. He took a seat before the mic. I'd set up a vintage Neumann U-87 microphone for him, one of the best you can get, they go for about $3500 new. Stuart started talking. Then he stopped. He got a funny look on his face. He picked up a pencil and dropped it. The mic picked up the sound of the pencil dropping with exceptional clarity. It was an especially good mic.

I got a bad feeling.

"It sounds weird," Stuart said. "There's something wrong with the sound."

I thought, oh, here we go. This guy has a hit show. He's famous. Famous enough to be a pain in the ass.

Stuart messed with the mic some more, having fun with the sound, dropping pencils, making funny noises, just generally being playful, having a good time. Finally, he accepted the sound of the microphone, and we got down to the business of recording an episode of *The Vinyl Café*. He wasn't a pain in the ass, and he never turned into one.

The producer of *The Vinyl Café* at this time was David Amer. Stuart had created the show with David, and David worked on it for ten years before handing the reins over to Jess Milton. Stuart continued to credit David as the Founding Producer of *The Vinyl Café* for the rest of the show's run.

David and I often chatted while editing the show. During one such chat he asked me, "How would you like to go out on the road with us? To record the show and do our music pickups?"

"You'd be better off with Greg DeClute for that," I told him.

That was probably pretty stupid of me. I lacked confidence in my ability to record music at the time. Later, as the recording engineer for *Q*, I would record on average three bands a week. Still, I don't regret telling David that. He did approach Greg. Recording music was Greg's passion. He'd been properly trained for it. He had tons of experience and he was good at it. Greg was the right choice. He accompanied *The Vinyl Café* on the road for years. His music pickups sounded terrific. Greg told me afterward that going on the road with *The Vinyl Café* had been one of highlights of his career.

But I still got to package the show in the studio.

When David Amer retired and it became necessary to appoint a new producer to the show, I believed that it should be either me, Greg, or Wayne Richards. We'd been champing at the bit to become producers. Why not save time, money and bother by just getting us to both record and produce the shows we worked on? When I found out that someone by the name of Jess Milton would become the new producer of *The Vinyl Café*, I was disappointed. Here we go again, I thought. Probably have to teach her everything from the ground up.

I met Jess one evening during a studio taping session. To my dismay, I liked her immediately. Nobody had to teach her anything. She was smart and capable and a perfect production partner for Stuart. She became an instrumental part of the show. For example, on the road, Stuart performed the same live show over and over in multiple towns and cities. This provided Stuart and Jess ample opportunity to refine the show before it was taped for broadcast. Each performance, Jess sat in the audience to track the audience's responses, noting which of Stuart's lines elicited the best laughs and which didn't. Afterward they tweaked the show accordingly and recorded the refined version for broadcast.

Stuart and Jess were an unbeatable combination. They were a pleasure to work with and generous to a fault. One night my mother flew up from Prince Edward Island to visit me for a few days. I couldn't pick her up at the airport because I had to work. I had to voice track Stuart. My mother was a big fan of show. I mentioned all this to Jess as we began to work. She got on the talkback and told Stuart.

"What's your phone number?" Stuart asked me.

Later, when we were pretty sure that my mother had arrived at my place, Stuart called my number. Mom answered.

"Hi, Mrs. Mahoney? It's Stuart McLean. I just wanted to thank you for loaning us your son tonight."

They had a great chat. My mother was tickled pink.

She got to meet Stuart in person, too, when *The Vinyl Café* played Summerside. Jess arranged tickets for my folks. Jess and

Stuart were generous with their tickets. They always offered my wife and I (and Greg and Wayne and Anton and their families) tickets for the live Christmas shows in Toronto.

So yes, Stuart was a nice guy. He wasn't without sass, though.

One day he arrived in the studio dressed to the nines.

I checked out his sharp new suit, looked down at my ragged jeans with holes in the knees, and said, "Gee, I didn't know I was supposed to dress up for this gig."

"Well, you were, asshole," he told me.

(He was joking, of course.)

Stuart passed away February 15, 2017, at age 68. It was a blow not just to those of us who knew him, but to everyone who had ever listened to Stuart's special brand of radio whimsy. It was a privilege to have been able to work with such a man.

# XXVII

## *Faster Than Light*

O nce upon a time I made my own radio show.
I mean one that was actually mine, as opposed to someone else's.

I only ever made one of these that actually aired. You might well ask, what's the big deal? So you made one lousy radio show. Other people make their own radio shows all the time. What's so special about this one?

Nothing, really. Except to me, and maybe those who helped me make it.

It was a science fiction radio show. It was a radio show about science fiction, featuring science fiction, hosted by a science fiction writer, and, on a meta-level, was science fiction itself. I still think it's a cool idea.

You see, I've loved science fiction ever since I was six years old. I've loved it since I stumbled upon this crazy low-budget television show from Japan called *Johnny Sokko and His Giant Robot*. Johnny Sokko was extremely low budget and super cheesy, but it didn't matter. What kid doesn't want a giant robot as a best friend? Especially one that can fly and clobber alien villains. Once I could read, it was Robert A. Heinlein's juveniles (*Have Space Suit Will Travel; Rocket Ship Galileo*) and James Blish's adaptations of the original *Star Trek* scripts (unlike most people, I read most of the original *Star Trek* television episodes before ever seeing one on TV), and then Isaac Asimov's robot stories, and Cordwainer Smith (*The Ballad of Lost C'Mell*) and A. E. Van Vogt (*Slan*), and David Brin (*The Postman*), and on and on and on.

It so happens that the CBC has produced some excellent science fiction and fantasy over the years. Sound effects guru Matt Willcott, with whom I would make many radio plays, often regaled me with stories of crafting sound effects for the space opera *Johnny Chase: Secret Agent of Space*, broadcast on CBC Radio for two seasons between 1978 and 1981. Produced by **Don Ferguson** (of *The Royal Canadian Air Farce* fame) and Henry Sobodka, it was about a secret agent traversing the galaxy on behalf of the Earth Empire. It featured music by the Canadian Progressive Rock band FM and is remembered fondly to this day by those who were lucky enough to have heard it broadcast. There was also *Vanishing Point*, a science fiction anthology series produced by Bill Lane, and *Nightfall*, a supernatural/horror anthology series created and produced (for the first two seasons, at least) by Bill Howell.

Working for the radio drama department, I aspired to join this select club. One day I mentioned this to producer Barbara Worthy, who doubles as a ball of enthusiasm. She promptly suggested we pitch a science fiction show, so off the top of my head I suggested a show based on science fiction magazines such as *Analog*, *Asimov's*, and *The Magazine of Science Fiction & Fantasy*. I thought it would be fun to produce full-cast radio adaptations of classic science fiction stories interspersed with interviews of science fiction luminaries and other fun, fantastical elements. Never dreaming that anything would come of it.

James Roy happened to be Deputy Head of the radio drama department at the time. Shortly after our conversation, Barbara marched into his office and pitched the idea. To my astonishment, he gave us a greenlight, providing a budget and a broadcast slot for a pilot.

Barbara and I got right to work. The first order of business was finding a host for the show. Years earlier, I had worked on a couple of episodes of *Ideas* about science fiction produced by a young freelancer by the name of Rob Sawyer. Rob and I had a lot in common. We both loved science fiction and we were both interested in writing. We were both graduates of Ryerson's Radio and Television Arts program. Rob told me that he had a novel coming out soon called *Golden Fleece*. I told him I'd keep an eye out for it.

Secretly, I thought that Rob Sawyer would vanish into the ether like so many other freelancers I'd met and never heard tell of again.

After all, I was going to be the famous author, not him. But in the time it took me to write one novel (*A Time and a Place*, published October, 2017, thanks for asking), Robert J. Sawyer wrote twenty-three novels. He also won many (if not all) of the field's major awards, such as the Hugo, the Nebula, and the John W. Campbell Memorial Award. In short, Rob became one of the most successful writers on the planet (of any genre, let alone science fiction).

I read *Golden Fleece*, along with many of Rob's other novels, and watched his growing success from afar with something akin to amazement. From time to time I sent him notes of congratulations. Rob always responded warmly. Once, he suggested I call him to chat, but he was already pretty famous by then, and I was kind of shy, so I didn't. Until it became time to produce a science fiction radio show.

"You know who would be the perfect host?" I told Barbara. "Rob Sawyer."

"Call him," she said.

I was still kind of shy. I emailed him instead.

Rob was interested.

Rob, Barbara and I met to talk about it. We agreed that it would be modelled after classic science fiction magazines. That Rob would host. That it would include one adaptation and an original drama, and that the latter would be the first part of a potential serial. I would write and adapt the dramas and Rob would contribute an essay. Rob would also interview a science fiction personality still to be determined. Rob was enthusiastic and perfectly willing to collaborate.

I wrote what I thought was a fun opening involving Rob taking off in a spaceship of his own to launch the show (this was the meta-science fictional component, which grew more elaborate in subsequent pilots). We picked Canadian science fiction author Nalo Hopkinson (*Brown Girl in the Ring; Midnight Robber*) to interview in between the two radio plays. Once we had part one of the original drama (*Captain's Away!*) and the adaptation (Tom Godwin's "*The Cold Equations*") in the can (more on them in separate chapters) we recorded all the other bits, including SF poetry by Rob's wife Carolyn Clink (read by Barbara Worthy) and Rob's intros and extros. I also included a brief station ID recorded by William B. Davis, aka "Cigarette Smoking Man" on *The X-Files*. I had asked Davis to record the station ID when we worked together on Margaret Atwood's *The Handmaid's Tale*.

I had some corrections for Rob's essay. I feared this was rather presumptuous of me, considering Rob's track record of having written several award-winning, best-selling novels versus my track-record of having (at that point) sold a mere short story or two.

I apologized as I gave him the corrections. "Who am I to correct your work?"

"You're the producer," he reassured me. "If it needs correcting it needs correcting!"

We needed a name for the show. Early on I considered "All in a Dream," a lyric from a favourite Neil Young song. I even wrote a draft of the script using that name. But now, two decades later, I cringe at the thought. Fortunately, somebody—probably Rob—suggested *Faster Than Light*, which, in three simple words, perfectly encapsulated what we were up to. You could shorten it to *FTL* and literate fans would still know what we were talking about. We all loved it instantly.

Creating *Faster Than Light* was the most fun I've ever had making radio. I loved every single second of it. All the fussy producers I've ever worked with—and I've worked with some damned fussy producers—didn't hold a candle to me on this show. Everything—every line, every level, every edit—had to be absolutely perfect.

*Faster Than Light* broadcast on September 22, 2002 as part of *Sunday Showcase* (in mono) and again on September 23 on *Monday Night Playhouse* (in stereo). We had a listening party at my home. Barbara Worthy, Rob Sawyer, Rob's wife Carolyn, my family and several friends attended. It was great fun, though I have one regret. I happened to be watching my pennies at the time (public broadcasting, remember) so I purchased flimsy four-ounce hamburgers to barbecue instead of nice plump five-ounce burgers. What a cheapskate! Nobody complained, but I still wince every time I think about it. On the plus side, the show was well received by Rob and my friends.

The response from our listeners was even more positive. *Faster Than Light* did pretty good for itself. It was named a finalist for the Prix Aurora Awards 2003 for the Best in Canadian SF and Fantasy. One of its elements, *The Cold Equations*, a full-cast adaptation, was selected by CBC's internal jury for the New York Awards. The show received an unprecedented response for the drama department. Many listeners wrote to convey unbridled enthusiasm for the show. Particularly gratifying was feedback from as far away as California and Australia, from listeners who tuned in over the Internet. James Roy informed me that it was the biggest response any *Sunday Showcase* show had ever received.

I would like to think that the response was a consequence of the effort we'd put into the show, and I'm sure that was indeed a factor, but I know it also had a lot to do with Rob Sawyer's role in the production. *Faster Than Light* had been quite well promoted by Rob and his fans before the broadcast. I suspect that many of those who wrote in were already fans of Rob's work. Still, the feedback bode well. Everyone wanted more.

Adrian Mills was the Executive Director of Programming at the time. A former children's TV programmer for the BBC, he invited me into his office to talk about the show.

"What do you think of it?" he asked.

"It's the best work I've ever done in my life on anything," I told him honestly.

I was inordinately proud of it. I still am.

We were asked to make a second pilot, and then a third, and even a fourth, but with each pilot the concept seemed to stray further and further from its original conception. In the end, I'm afraid the stars never quite aligned for *Faster Than Light*. I was told later that Adrian Mills had rejected it on the grounds that, "if you put a show like that on the air you'll never get it off."

I treasure the experience just the same. I became friends with Rob Sawyer and his wife Carolyn Clink. I learned how to adapt a short story into another medium. I got to write, mix, and broadcast an original drama of my own. I discovered that directing was a lot harder than it looked watching from behind a console. And I acquired a modicum of empathy for fussy producers.

In a sense, *Faster Than Light* lives on. In the fictional universe of Robert J. Sawyer's novel *Rollback*, published a few years later, *Faster Than Light* did become a regular series on CBC Radio. Where, for all I know, it continues to be broadcast to this day.

# XXVIII

## The Cold Equations

"*T*he Cold Equations*" is a short story by Tom Godwin, first
published in *Astounding Magazine* in August 1954. You might
want to read it before we go any further. I wouldn't want to spoil
anything for you.

The spoilers begin here.

The story is about a teenaged girl named Marilyn Lee Cross
who stows away on an emergency space shuttle with disastrous
results. I chose it as one of the two radio plays we included in our
science fiction radio pilot *Faster Than Light*.

I chose it because it was dark and sombre. I'm partial to humour, but I wanted something with a little gravitas, something that
I thought people would take seriously. I wasn't the first to adapt
"*The Cold Equations*" for radio. It had been adapted twice before, for
an episode of the radio program *X Minus One* in 1955, and for the
radio program *Exploring Tomorrow* in 1958.

In the story, Marilyn just wants to visit her brother on a nearby
planet. The emergency shuttle is delivering critical medical supplies
to sick miners on that planet. Unbeknownst to Marilyn, the shuttle
is designed with a strict set of parameters: it has just enough fuel to
carry its sole pilot and his critical cargo to the planet. With Marilyn on board, the shuttle will run out of fuel, the mission will fail,
and the miners will die.

Critics of the story point out that the writer, Tom Godwin, un-
necessarily stacked the deck against the girl. Why was it necessary to
design the shuttle with such a slim margin of error? Godwin might
argue that fuel would be a precious resource in space; you wouldn't
want to use any more than was absolutely necessary. Of course, the
real reason is that Godwin needed to create a very specific set of

circumstances for the story to work. But consider the plane crash in Colombia that tragically killed most of the Brazilian Chapecoense Real football team. The plane ran out of fuel because the company that owned the plane skimped on fuel to save money, with horrific consequences. Godwin's plot may not be so unrealistic after all.

Realistic or not, in the universe of the story the girl must be jettisoned from the shuttle into deep space for the mission to succeed. Not exactly a Hollywood ending. My story editor, Dave Carley, felt that Marilyn learns the consequences of her ill-fated decision to stow away too quickly. She spends the rest of the story waiting to die, while the shuttle pilot reflects on the cold, harsh reality of the universe. There is no hope and therefore no real tension.

I didn't necessarily agree, at least initially. I'd originally come across the story in an English class in high school in one of our textbooks. I began reading it during class, during the teacher's lecture, and quickly forgot about the lecture. I found the story utterly gripping. This was long before cold-blooded authors like George R. R. Martin began killing off our favourite novel and television characters with impunity. I didn't believe that the girl was going to die. I kept waiting for her to be saved and was utterly gobsmacked when she was finally jettisoned from the space shuttle. Reading the story as a teenager, I had never encountered such a brutal ending before. It left quite an impact.

But Dave felt strongly that we needed more tension, more suspense, so for my version of the story I concocted a storyline where there was some slim hope that another ship (the Stardust) would catch up with the emergency shuttle and rescue Marilyn. I made other changes as well. In the original story, Marilyn was older, in her late teens. I reduced her age to thirteen to make it more believable that she would do something so ill-considered as to sneak onto an emergency shuttle without understanding the consequences. This also injected a little more pathos into the story. Because it was radio, I needed her to speak at the beginning of the story to help illuminate to the listener what was going on. (You can't just have a character say, "I'm sneaking into the shuttle now," and so on. Well, you can, but that would be narration, and I didn't want a narrator.) I had Marilyn sneak into the shuttle while talking to her cat, Chloe, which happened to be the name of one of my cats at the time (named, in turn, after the Elton John song "Chloe").

Writing the adaptation, I felt like I was writing yet another draft of Tom Godwin's story. This may be horribly presumptuous, and my apologies to Tom Godwin, but I felt like it was an opportunity to correct some of the story's flaws. For one thing, the original story was quite wordy. I cut an awful lot out of it. Now, I have a lot more respect for Tom Godwin than some, such as magazine editor Algis Budrys, who reportedly once said that *"The Cold Equations"* was "the best short story that Godwin ever wrote and he didn't write it" — referring to the fact that editor John W. Campbell sent the story back to Godwin three times before Godwin finally got it right, that is, before Godwin stopped coming up with ingenious means of saving the girl. Oh, and also referring to allegations that Godwin borrowed the idea from a story published in EC Comics' Weird Science #13.

Anyway, Campbell recognized the true power of the story: the idea that the universe is impartial. It doesn't care whether you live or die. Reading it in high school, I had glimpsed, perhaps for the first time in my life, a sense of the implacability of the universe. You play by its rules or you die. The stowaway is done in by cold, hard facts. For others to live, she had to die.

Several drafts into my version of the story, I was happy with everything except the ending. Something was missing. It didn't feel complete, somehow. Endings don't always come easy for me. I work hard at them because I consider them extremely important. Getting the ending wrong can ruin an entire story. Getting it right can elevate all that came before.

I discussed it with my wife Lynda. Something she said (unfortunately, I don't remember what) made me realize that the pilot didn't need to talk or think after ejecting Marilyn from the shuttle. He needed to acknowledge what he'd just been through. He needed to cry. It was an epiphany for me. It allowed me to cut a bunch of extraneous explanatory dialogue and get on with the emotion of the scene.

Later, one of my colleagues suggested that if you allow a character to cry, you are depriving the audience of the chance to cry themselves, because you're doing it for them. I felt differently. Making the pilot cry felt like what would actually happen. I know that truth doesn't necessarily equate to good fiction—the truth is deeper than that—but sometimes it does. My pilot cried, and it felt right and true to me.

Once the script was complete, we held auditions for the cast. An embarrassing number of actors showed up for the casting call (we auditioned for both radio plays included in *Faster Than Light* at the same time, *The Cold Equations* and *Captain's Away!*). Ultimately, we cast Canadian actor Matthew MacFadzean (not to be confused with British actor Matthew Macfadyen) in the role of the shuttle pilot, and Vivian Endicott-Douglas as the young stowaway Marilyn. Shawn Smyth played the stowaway's brother Gerry Cross. Andrew Gillies played Commander Delhart of the Stardust. Sergio Dizio played the Clerk, and Jennifer Dean, one of the surveyors. Julia Tait was our casting director (replacing regular radio drama Casting Director Linda Grearson, who, I believe, was subbing for Deputy Head James Roy at the time).

Barbara Worthy directed *The Cold Equations* while I sat behind the Neve Capricorn console recording the show. Matt Willcott performed all the live sound effects. I was extremely happy with the work of our actors. I have to single out Vivian, though, who was extraordinary. She nailed every single take of every single scene. We could have used any of her lines in any take.

We did have trouble with one lengthy scene during which the pilot must stoically accept Marilyn's fate. Matthew couldn't quite nail the pilot's tone and neither Barbara nor I could figure out what direction to give Matthew to make it work. We did four takes and were running out of time—we only had the actors for so long. We were forced to move on and record other scenes. Just before production wrapped for the day we came back to that problematic scene and did two more takes. Matthew finally nailed the tone, sounding troubled, yet resolute.

It didn't take me long to edit *The Cold Equations*, probably a couple of hours. I used most of the scenes we recorded in their entirety, which was unusual. Usually we scavenged lines from other takes of the same scene. I mixed the twenty-five-minute-long play in a single day in SFX 3.

I didn't have the budget for much original music, but I was able to use an original piece of music for the opening called "Snowfire Reprize" by Rod Crocker. I used a couple of Manheim Steamroller pieces from *Fresh Air 1* for a couple of tiny music bridges. At the end, I had Mozart's "Lacrimosa" swell up underneath the pilot's tears. At first I thought it might be too much, a little too heavy, but after listening to the completed mix in the studio I was convinced that the pathos of the piece supported it.

*The Cold Equations* may not be the most accomplished or sonically interesting radio play I've ever worked on, but I'm pretty darned happy with it.

# XXIX
## *Captain's Away!*

Once I finished producing *The Cold Equations* for our science fiction radio show pilot *Faster Than Light*, I turned my attention to the second radio play in the show, an original called *Captain's Away!* (I always wrote *Captain's Away!* with an exclamation mark in the title because I liked the look of it. According to Goodreads there are 758 books with exclamation marks in the title, most of which are kids' books, including a bunch by Dr. Suess.)

I didn't intend *Captain's Away!* just for kids but it was something I thought kids would enjoy. It was based on an idea I'd had several years earlier that had stuck with me. Roy Orbison once said if you had to write an idea down to remember it, it probably wasn't worth remembering. I'd written the idea for *Captain's Away!* down somewhere but I hadn't needed to. It was an idea that had definitely stuck with me over the years.

The premise was pretty straightforward. A waitress is approached by a crackpot who refers to her as "Captain" and implores her to return to her ship in space to lead her crew on a dangerous mission. Except that the stranger isn't actually a crackpot and there really is a spaceship, and circumstances force our hero to assume the identity of the captain with no idea what she's doing. All the while the questions linger: is she the captain or isn't she? And if so, why can't she remember being the captain?

Intending the piece to be a serial to be aired in ten-minute chapters during each instance of *Faster Than Light*, I set out to write just the first episode. I wound up writing the first three episodes, but we only ever produced the first one. I wrote it as a light, comic piece with plenty of opportunities for cool sound effects.

I got into a bit of trouble during the writing of it. When I gave what I considered to be the final draft to James Roy, he pointed out that this was not the way it was done. I was supposed to have written an outline and then a first draft and then a second draft and then a third draft and a polish, with feedback at every stage to inform the next stage. I don't think I knew that. I was used to writing fiction on my own. Writing with the input of others was a foreign concept to me. But James was right. I was stomping all over the way things were supposed to be done. He accepted the piece just the same, though.

We cast the actors for both *The Cold Equations* and *Captain's Away!* at the same time. Casting, I discovered, is quite difficult. It was difficult to make up our minds. There were so many great actors to choose from. I really liked a fellow by the name of Julian Richings for the part of the crackpot stranger named Choki. Julian has a wonderful British accent that I thought would work nicely (I was delighted to see him turn up in *Orphan Black*, *The Expanse, and The Umbrella Academy* years later), but we opted for Sergio Dizio instead (whom we also cast in *The Cold Equations*), after Sergio wowed us with a faux Italian accent. Later, after hearing Sergio's comic Italian accent in the production, Damiano Pietropaolo, Director of CBC Radio Arts & Entertainment at the time, of obvious Italian descent, expressed dismay. Until he brought it up, it hadn't occurred to me that giving the character a comic accent based on an Italian accent might be considered offensive. That certainly wasn't my intention.

We cast Kristina Nicoll as the lead and Richard (Rick) Waugh (whom you might remember from my chapter on *Muckraker*) as her boss (Rick also doubled as a bus driver for a couple of lines). Both were terrific.

I contracted Wayne Richards to contribute original theme music and he came up with a fabulous piece that I called "The Ah Oooh Song" (I don't know if it has an actual name). I finished the play with another original piece of music by Rod Crocker called "Turn-around," which I also love.

Making *Captain's Away!* was a lot of fun and I was disappoint-ed we didn't get to make any more. To make up for it, I'm hard at work on my second novel, working title "*Captain's Away*" (this time without the exclamation mark). It's not quite the same story as the radio play version—it's a lot less silly and there's much more to it—but it has the same spirit.

And maybe one day we'll make a radio version of it.

# XXX
## *Barney's Version*

In March 2003, I recorded a radio play called *Barney's Version*, based on Canadian author Mordecai Richler's last book of the same name. In the book, Barney Panofsky relates his life story, concentrating on his three marriages and the disappearance of his best friend, Bernard "Boogie" Moscovitch. The play was adapted for radio by Howard Wiseman, and directed by Greg Sinclair, or Gregory J. Sinclair, as he was always known in the credits. (Once, when one of Greg's dramas went long and had to be cut for time, I suggested we save a second or two by cutting the "ory J" out of the credits.)

Matt Willcott, a year away from retirement but still giving it his all, performed sound effects. The glue in this massive production (and by radio drama standards *Barney's Version* was definitely a massive production) was Associate Producer Colleen Woods.

There were many fine actors in this production, including Denis O'Conner (whose credits include the theatrical production *The Dragonfly of Chicoutimi*, and over 300 radio plays for CBC/ Radio Canada), Kathy Greenwood (*Whose Line Is It, Anyway?* and *The Wind At My Back*), acclaimed actor, director and critic David Gardner, and Wendy Crewson (*The Santa Claus* movies, in which she played Tim Allen's ex-wife, and *Air Force One*, in which she played Harrison Ford's wife), among others.

Greg had briefly considered the American actor Richard Dreyfuss in the role of Barney, but ultimately decided on German-born Canadian actor Saul Rubinek. Rubinek had enjoyed big parts in major Hollywood productions. He'd been working as an actor since he was a kid, on the stage, television, radio and film. He had also written, directed, and produced.

How do you get someone of Saul Rubinek's stature to star in a Canadian radio play? Our casting director, Linda Grearson, put a call into his agent. Not only was Saul available, he was interested. This wouldn't be his first gig for the CBC. He'd cut his teeth working on CBC television and radio productions. Saul lives in L.A. with his wife and two kids, so Greg flew him in.

I'd first heard of Saul Rubinek at school at Ryerson, when a teacher had screened a copy of a film about a Russian named Igor Sergeyevich Gouzenko.

Igor who?

Good question.

In 1945, three days after World War Two, a Russian by the name of Igor Sergeyevich Gouzenko defected to Canada carrying one hundred and nine documents proving that the Russians were trying to steal atomic secrets. Gouzenko's defection (among other things) sparked the Cold War, as the West used the evidence of espionage to end their alliance with the Russians. Gouzenko, fearing for his life, was given a new identity (and became known for wearing a sack on his head during public appearances). But he lived a middle-class life in the Toronto suburb of Clarkson and died of a heart attack in 1982 at the age of sixty-three.

Curiously, the film about Gouzenko, which was written by well-known Canadian journalist and writer Rick Salutin, doesn't appear on Saul Rubinek's extensive filmography on IMDb. Nor is it mentioned in a Wikipedia article about Gouzenko. It's no doubt buried in the CBC's television archives and may never see the light of day again.

Since seeing Saul's portrayal of Gouzenko, I'd seen him in the films *The Unforgiven* with Clint Eastwood, *The Family Man* with Nicholas Cage, and *True Romance* with Christian Slater. He was an accomplished, well-regarded character actor. Rick Salutin called him "very funny." Greg Sinclair believed that Saul, along with fellow lead Wendy Crewson, were among the best in the business.

When I first learned that Saul Rubinek was going to star in one of our plays, I thought that a guy like that might be a bit full of himself. Probably used to being coddled with craft services, limos, trailers and the like. We didn't have stuff like that in the radio drama department.

Saul showed up on the first day, all business. Okay, what's happening, what are we doing, what page are we on? Short (5'7", the same height as Tom Cruise) and plump (not fat), with big bushy eyebrows, he looked more like an accountant than a leading man. He could convincingly play Eugene Levy's brother.

He insisted on wearing headphones during the first scene. I was not happy to hear this. I wasn't keen on actors wearing headphones. There was the problem of headphone leakage, limited mobility for the actors (the headphones weren't wireless), and actors becoming too conscious of their voices. In my view, the actors needed to perform their scenes without worrying about what they sounded like. Also, there were a lot of scenes in this play, with many different setups. It would be troublesome to have to run headphones for Saul in every different scene. I was afraid this might be just the tip of the iceberg, the first of many such demands.

I set up the headphones for him.

Immediately after asking for headphones, Saul asked for a table to set his script and other assorted paraphernalia on. I hauled out an old desk that we used as a sound effects prop. Saul set all his stuff on it. Matt pointed out that the table I had selected, which was on wheels, was missing a wheel. It was liable to tip over. Oh. No worries—I found three or four old books to prop it up. But when I lifted it up to shove the books under the problematic corner, the table promptly flipped over, tossing all Saul's papers onto the floor in a jumbled mess.

I braced myself for an outburst. None came. Without saying a word, Saul leaned over and picked up all his papers without complaint while I finished stabilizing the table.

This was a good sign (although why I didn't just find another table with four legs would be a darned good question).

We got through several scenes in a brisk, efficient manner, with Saul completely focused on the task at hand.

For one scene he needed to be sitting, so I found him a chair (with the appropriate number of legs). He sat down before the microphone. We'd gotten rid of the desk, so I thought maybe he might like a music stand to put his script on.

"Wanna stand?" I asked him, holding up a music stand in one hand.

"I'm sitting," he said.

Greg, Matt and I laughed, thinking that he was joking.

Brandishing the music stand, I repeated, "No, do you wanna stand?"

"Can't you just lower the mic?" he asked.

I realized that he wasn't joking, that he had misunderstood.

I repeated as clearly as I could, "Would you like a stand?" but by then he was talking to Greg about some plot point, so I left the music stand in front of him and returned to the control room.

Shortly after that Saul began pestering me about being heard in the control room. Whenever we finished recording a scene and my presence was required on the studio floor, I muted the microphones, effectively turning them off. You don't want to have microphones on if you think you might have to handle or move them. Also, when I was on the floor I wanted to be able to speak to the actors and sound effects engineer candidly, without anyone in the control room hearing me. Several times early on Saul tried to talk to the director in the control room after I had muted the microphones, and when he was unsuccessful he didn't get angry per se, but he was visibly irritated:

"Why can't he hear me? Can't you set something up, you know, some kind of permanent mic on the floor which just automatically switches on at the end of every scene so I can talk to the director?"

I told him, "Saul, that might be a good idea with you, but to tell you the truth, other actors, we just don't want to hear what they have to say," which earned a laugh from Greg, Matt, and Wendy, and even Saul laughed.

"I'll tell you what," I told him. "I'll suggest it to the other engineers, but it probably won't go over very well."

"Why don't you just build it with a switch so you can turn it off whenever you want?" Saul suggested. "And remember: if you create such a system, you must call it the "Rubinek" system."

So he was obviously not without a sense of humour about the whole thing.

Still, I tried to be much more diligent about leaving the mic on so that Saul could be heard in the control room, and any time I had to turn it off, I warned Saul that we wouldn't be able to hear him for a couple of minutes. I continued to set up headphones for him in every scene. By the third day of recording, I felt that Saul had adapted to the pace of radio drama recording. He'd warmed up considerably (or maybe I had warmed up to him). He was calmer, more relaxed.

There was an old grand piano in the studio. Between takes Saul would sit down and play. He always played the same piece, "Gnossienne 1," by French composer Erik Satie.

I was impressed to hear Saul play this piece (and play it well) because I happened to love it. My sister Susan had played it when she was studying piano in high school, inspiring me to memorize it myself. Other than my immediate family, I didn't know anyone else who even knew of the piece, let alone how to play it.

During another break, Saul told us about working with Clint Eastwood on the set of *Unforgiven*. Saul had a major role in that film as a journalist by the name of W. W. Beauchamp. He told us that Clint always did two takes of every scene: one take and a safety. To block the big fight scene at the end, Clint came in and said to everyone, "Okay, you figure it out, I'm going for a coffee." Then he went away, came back a couple of hours later and asked, "You got it all worked out?" And then shot the scene.

After getting the master shot and the safety in the can, the cast and crew spent three days shooting extra coverage of the scene, getting all the little cutaways and close ups.

"If you watch that scene," Saul told us, "you'll see just one person sitting, and that's me, because I knew they would take three days to shoot the coverage and I didn't want to be standing the whole time."

Saul was himself just getting into directing at that time. He spent a lot of time with Clint learning about directing and has since directed several television features. The impulse to direct was strong in him. He couldn't resist the temptation to direct other actors during the recording of *Barney's Version*.

"No, you have to say, 'the Twelve year old!' very aggressively, not mildly," he instructed David Gardner, who played Barney's lawyer, referring to Barney's favourite scotch. Gardner, an accomplished director himself, didn't appear to mind. It was obvious that Saul's intent was to make the scene as effective as possible.

Another time Saul burst into the control room to ask Greg to tell an actor something he felt strongly she needed to know, presumably not telling her himself out of fear of offending her. Greg took this all in stride. In fact, the partnership between Saul and Greg was a potent one as they constantly challenged the limitations of the medium.

One obvious limitation of radio is that you can't see what's going on. For this reason you have to exercise considerable caution when conveying action in a radio play, especially when attempting travelling shots. A travelling shot is a shot in television, film or radio in which the camera/microphone follows characters on the move. Think Xander on his skateboard in the opening shot of the very first episode of *Buffy the Vampire Slayer*, skating down the street and into his high school. Another famous example is the seven minute and forty-seven-second-long tracking shot that opens Robert Altman's *The Player*. Imagine how confusing that shot would be without pictures.

Travelling shots can be tricky in any medium. Joss Whedon, creator of *Buffy the Vampire Slayer* and director of the pilot episode, reportedly regretted the time it took to set up and execute the travelling shot with Xander. He was used to film. In film, you can take more time to get a shot, unlike television with its stricter shooting schedules.

In radio, writers often write travelling shots accidentally. They don't even realize they've done it until they get to that scene in the studio and the recording engineer exclaims, what the heck? This is a travelling shot! You do realize how difficult travelling shots are to convey on radio, don't you? To which the writer responds, why are you surprised? Didn't you read the script before getting here? To which the engineer grumbles, well, the director should have caught it, at which point the director jerks awake in his chair and asks, what scene are we on?

Travelling shots are tough to present on the radio because the listener can't see movement. If you fail to convey the fact that the characters are moving via the only two options available—dialogue and sound effects—then the listener won't understand what's going on and your production will suffer.

However, it can be done if you know what you're doing. There was a scene in *Barney's Version* in which Barney runs back and forth between his living room and his kitchen trying to remember the word for "colander." When I first read this scene in the script, I immediately considered it a mistake and began contemplating how it might be rewritten so that it wouldn't be a travelling shot. I thought it would be tough to make the listener understand that Barney was moving back and forth between a living room and a kitchen.

Greg and Saul begged to differ. We were blessed with a terrific studio (Studio 212) in which multiple setups were possible. Greg instructed me to set up a living room acoustic space directly adjacent to our built-in working kitchen. The kitchen acoustic was completely different than the living room acoustic. Listening to dialogue spoken in one, you could not mistake it for the other. This was critical.

To make the travelling shot work, we set up two stereo microphones, one in front of Barney's chair in the living room, and another covering the kitchen. We kept both microphones live, so that when Barney (Saul) moved from the kitchen to the living room and back again you could clearly hear the change in acoustic. Saul made lots of noise while moving back and forth so that the listener could clearly track his movements.

By this point in the show we had completely established the living room as a distinct acoustic environment, by (among other things) consistently using the same sound props (leather chair, glass of scotch, tape recorder). This, together with liberal use of obvious kitchen props (cutlery drawer, dishes etc.), made it abundantly clear to the listener exactly where Barney was at all times.

When I wasn't setting up neat travelling shots for Greg, he kept me and Matt Willcott busy lugging stuff around, couches, chairs, tables, from one setup to another. Matt and I hardly ever did this kind of thing. It was radio, after all. It wasn't like anyone was going to see the furniture. In most radio plays, we just imagined the chairs and tables were there, unless we really needed to hear them somehow, and even then we just used a stool to double as a table or to create the squeak of a chair being drawn back. But Greg was going out of his way to make the actors—Saul in particular—comfortable. Many of our actors were experienced film and television actors who preferred to perform their actions with real props.

From time to time, as we lugged one piece of furniture or another, Matt would grumble, "Who's gonna see the table on the radio?" That's when he wasn't saying, "Tippet and Richardson: you tip it and I'll rip it!" (Tippet Richardson being a well-known moving company in Toronto.)

"You know, I'm a recording engineer, not a mover," I told Greg. "I'm supposed to be more of a white-collar worker."

Wendy Crewson overheard me. "Well, you're an engineer, right? There's all kinds of engineers. Sanitation engineers, for instance. Don't they move things?"

"I think whether I'm a sanitation engineer or a recording engineer depends on the drama I'm recording," I told her.

Later, I asked Wendy what it was like working with Harrison Ford.

"He's a wonderful person," she told me. "Not at all like he comes across in interviews. He's a party boy, a lot of fun. He used to zoom up to my trailer on his motorcycle and bang on the trailer. Come on, let's go! he would shout, and then with me on the back of his motorcycle, smoking a big doobie and thinking, if only they could see me now! we'd zoom off for Thai food."

When she told me that Harrison was a nice guy, I told her I'd ask Harrison the same thing about her.

"You know what I think he'd say? The exact same thing I said about him," she said, and laughed.

All of the actors in *Barney's Version* were superb. This is not surprising. Casting Director Linda Grearson never let us down. We had no trouble attracting top-notch talent. Actors seemed to like making radio plays with us. The atmosphere in Studio 212 was always pleasant. And when you're performing for radio you don't even have to memorize your lines: you have the script right in front of you.

Two performances stand out. Kathy Greenwood was sincere and touching as Barney Panofsky's ill-treated second wife. Kathy brought an endearing quality to the role that made Panofsky look like a fool for not loving her properly. And Saul as Barney Panofsky was a revelation to me. It wasn't Method, I don't think—when not in character, Saul was himself—but when he sat in Barney's chair and drank Barney's scotch and tried in vain to remember what a colander was called, Saul Rubinek inhabited Barney Panofsky. He didn't just lift the words off the page. He strapped Saturn 5 rockets to them, achieved escape velocity, and placed them in orbit. As I recorded him, I tried to figure out how he was doing it.

For one thing, he knew the script cold. He may have memorized much of it. If not, he'd clearly gone over it many times. He was not one hundred percent married to the script. If he felt the need to change a line slightly to make it sound more natural, he changed it. Subtle changes here and there. He was not afraid to grunt and clear his throat and fart and burp and inject whatever other flourishes he felt were required to bring Barney Panofsky to life. Nobody objected.

I don't expect I'll ever fully understand the alchemy involved.

Saul's work was illuminating in other ways, too. Looking back, I see that in a few short years I had become lazy, conservative, and rigid in my thinking. Saul was operating on a whole different level. His energy, enthusiasm, and professionalism challenged me to open my mind, to think bigger, to do better. His example has informed my work ever since, whatever form that work has taken.

# XXXI
## To the Ships!

Certain projects that I worked on generated "takeaways"—lines that were too good just to forget about. The project might have been good or lousy, it didn't matter. What mattered was the quality of the takeaway. Some takeaways were crude and cannot be repeated in polite company. Others were crude and can perhaps be repeated in polite company. Others were just funny (to me, at least).

For instance, I once worked on a radio play called *Heart of a Dog* (an adaptation of Mikhail Bulgakov's novella, a satire of Bolshevism directed by James Roy), in which a character kept muttering (in a Russian accent) "arsefessor" (don't ask me why) to refer to another character who was a professor. For years afterward I would hear my colleagues muttering from time to time, "Arsefessor!" (Hey, I never said these takeaways were in any way socially beneficial.) The thing is, after working on one of these plays for a month or two (or three), certain words and lines got burned into your brain.

Another takeaway came from an adaptation of the play *Trojan Women* (starring Alison Sealy-Smith and featuring original music by Colin Linden, broadcast on February 15, 1998). The play called for one character to summon the warriors to the ship by calling out, "To the ships!" Sound effects engineer Matt Willcott was called upon to utter these immortal words, as all the actors had left by the time the crew realized that the line hadn't been recorded. Matt was a brilliant sound effects foley artist but a quiet, unassuming man, so when called upon to cry out "To the ships!" he said it as if commenting on the weather, as opposed to summoning an army to battle as the script called for.

On the second take Matt generated enough enthusiasm to make the line sound like he was asking for someone to pass him a jar of peanut butter.

The third take sounded like a question: "To the ships?"

Each take fell woefully short of the necessary vigour but became increasingly hilarious for the crew in the control room. And the line, "To the ships!" became the rallying cry of the radio drama department.

To the ships!

# XXXII

## *Faster Than Light*:
## The Second and Third Pilots

After the success of the *Faster Than Light* pilot, we did not receive a green light to proceed with a series. But that wasn't the end of the story. The Executive Director of Radio Programming, Adrian Mills, did not reject the show outright. The following summer James Roy, now Acting Director of our department, approached me about doing another pilot for a summer run of the show. Presented in a half-hour format, it would be *Faster Than Light* "light." Unfortunately, James had no budget for it.

No problem. We took a radio play directed by Bill Lane from the archives and built a show around it. I wrote a frame for the show about auditioning for a new host. Rob's main competition was a robot called Huey (played by Julian Ford) whose main claim to fame was starring as a robot in the classic science fiction movie *Silent Running* with Bruce Dern. Huey didn't get the job. Linda Spence also acted in this pilot as a fictional Associate Producer.

The summer series didn't pan out, though. James was willing to proceed, but with no funding and very little time to write and produce ten episodes, I didn't think I could do the show justice. Seeing as it appeared we'd have an opportunity to try again later with proper funding and adequate time, I opted to wait.

That fall we did get funding to do another pilot. For this attempt, I brought in Fergus Heywood to co-produce. Fergus had been highly recommended to me by Greg Sinclair. He enthusiastically agreed to help out. We were assigned Alison Moss as Senior Producer, whom I always loved working with. I would eventually work with her on the summer replacement series *Next* with the superb host Nora Young. It was a good team.

Chris Boyce, Head of the Program Development Committee, organized a facilitated session to help us further define the show. Fergus, Alison, Rob Sawyer, Chris Boyce and I all sat down to figure it out. Richard Handler, an experienced Arts producer, was also involved. This third pilot was a serious effort, but the whole spirit was completely different than the first pilot. The show would be half an hour instead of an hour. It would include one full-cast radio play instead of two, and it would not include a continuation of *Captain's Away!*, although I had written several episodes.

Chris had us come up with a mandate:

"To fire the imaginations of Canadians by presenting thought-provoking encounters with masters of science fiction and fantasy along with engaging dramatizations of their work."

When we were finally ready, I hired Wayne Richards to write and record original theme music for the opening of the show. We would use an original composition from Fergus Heywood for the closing. Having decided to make the theme of this pilot "The Other," we secured the services of Cathi Bond, an experienced free-lancer, to produce a short documentary on "the other" in science fiction films throughout history.

I wrote a high production frame for the episode that consisted of three parts. In the opening, a mad scientist creates a host for the show in an homage to Frankenstein, a classic "other" in science fiction. The mad scientist was played by Tony Daniels, who did a brilliant German accent as Dr. Frankenstein. Once the host has been created, he takes over and introduces the show. After the first part of the show, a second interlude or frame features the mad scientist conducting an experiment in which he accidentally transforms himself into a fly (an obvious homage to *The Fly*). Rob the host returns to usher us into the next part of the show, an original adaptation of "*Born of Man and Woman*" by Richard Matheson, adapted and directed by Barry Morgan. The end credits featured Rob as the host along with the mad scientist. Not realizing that the fly trapped in the studio with him is the mad scientist, Rob swats him.

I was attempting to seamlessly mix representational radio with presentational radio. The drama and the high production intro, middle and extro were all representational. You listened to those the way you would watch a movie or television show. They weren't talking directly to the audience. They were meant to be entertaining as opposed to informative. Whereas the bits with Rob talking directly to the audience, and Cathi Bond presenting her short documentary, were presentational. The trick was to guide the audience from one style of radio to another without confusing them.

Ultimately the fate of the show would be determined by the Program Development Committee, a group of several experienced broadcasters assembled by Chris Boyce. I remember one of the members of this group listening to the opening of the show after I had finished mixing it. I was quite proud of it. I thought it was funny, and that the sound effects and mix had achieved what I'd set out to do. This person listened to it, gave me no feedback whatsoever, and left the studio. My impression was that he didn't get it and didn't like it. It did not bode well.

We finished the pilot and submitted it to the Program Development Committee. Representing the committee, veteran broadcaster Bill Stunt phoned me sometime afterward to tell me the bad news. He told me that they weren't going to pick up the show as it stood. The committee just didn't think it worked. More work was required.

I didn't entirely disagree. I didn't think it had worked as well as the original *Faster Than Light* pilot. The original had had room to breathe. It possessed a certain charm. We hadn't overthought it. The elements stood on their own. Rob brought a passion and an authenticity to it. The second pilot for the summer run had itself been a Frankenstein monster. I liked the frame we had created for it. But I had been forced to edit the heck out of the Bill Lane radio play in order to make it fit. Even the audio quality of the radio play hadn't been up to snuff; it had originally been recorded on tape and sounded a few tape generations old. The third, "other"-themed pilot had more going for it. I liked the frame. I liked the opening and closing music. I liked Barry Morgan's Richard Matheson adaptation. I liked Cathi's piece. But somehow the third pilot didn't gel as well as the original.

Nevertheless, the committee still hadn't given us a definitive "no." They offered us a chance to make yet a fourth pilot. By now people in the drama department were calling me Wing Commander Joe, I had so many pilots under me.

So, clinging to a slender thread of hope, Fergus, Rob, Alison and I got together to talk about it. Rob made the point that maybe the show needed to be more serious, that our problem was trying to mix humour with seriousness. Thinking of shows like *M\*A\*S\*H* and the film *Life is Beautiful*, I didn't think that was the issue, though it could well have confused the Program Development Committee. Rob also objected to the CBC's obvious efforts to make the show "stealth" science fiction. They didn't want the show to be overtly about science fiction and fantasy. They wanted it to be something else that happened to include science fiction and fantasy. I agreed with Rob on this point. There seemed to be a bias against radio plays. Against storytelling. Against the representational.

By now I had refined the concept even further. I was thinking that the host should be a sonic sorcerer. He would have the power to do anything, be anywhere. This concept, coupled with effective, liberal use of sound effects, would have several virtues. It would allow us to harness the enormous imaginative potential of radio. If the host wanted to be on the surface of Mars, he could be there in the blink of an eye—faster than light, if you will. If he wanted to lasso a comet by the tail, he could. He could pilot a spaceship, visit Heaven or Hell, single-handedly battle an army of knights, or simply conduct an interview. It solved the conceptual problem of how to veer from the fantastic portions of the show's "frame" to the magazine elements of the show. It could work something like this, for example:

SFX: STATIC

FEMALE VOICE: (TREATED) Incoming vessel. You have three seconds to identify yourself before we open fire.

HOST: (TWO SECOND BEAT) (TREATED) I'm Robert J. Sawyer, commanding *Faster Than Light* on CBC Radio. Be advised that if you open fire, we will respond.

FEMALE VOICE: Acknowledged, Faster Than Light. What, may I ask, will you respond with?

ROB: How about an interview with Canadian Independent author Maaja Wentz?

You see? Playful and imaginative. Veering seamlessly from fantasy to reality. It would itself be science fiction and fantasy while presenting the same to our listeners.

Alas, it never happened. The committee never did say no outright, but the truth is, *Faster Than Light* as we conceived of it in all its iterations never stood much of a chance. What we wanted to do was too much at odds with what the CBC was willing to let us do. Greg Sinclair was head of the drama department at the time but did not represent the Program Development Committee. I felt he was on my side. We discussed the project and mutually decided to pull the plug. To make it work for the CBC, we were going to have to turn it into a show that none of us believed in or wanted to do. Greg informed Rob Sawyer of this.

We never got the green light that I had dreamed about for so long.

Still, I wouldn't have traded the experience for anything. I'm pleased with all three pilots we actually recorded. Later, Rob asked me to read and comment on the third draft of his novel *Rollback* (about a man and a woman in their eighties who agree to undergo a procedure to make them younger. It only works on the man. Of course, this has huge implications on their relationship. It's a great read.) Rob made the protagonist a CBC Recording Engineer/ Producer, which is what I aspired to be. He also featured me as a character in the novel, on page ninety-nine.

I went back to my normal life working on other people's radio shows. That year CBC Radio launched a show called *Wiretap*. I could barely make myself listen to it, out of jealousy, I suppose. Finally listening to an episode one day, I found myself impressed. I wrote the producers of *Wiretap* and told them how much I liked the episode, which had included some science fiction. I used my cbc.ca email address so that they would know that it came from a colleague. Nobody from the show ever responded.

Had I managed to get *Faster Than Light* on the air, I would have personally responded to every single email the show received.

# XXXIII
## Matt Watts

One day in 2005, after grabbing a coffee at Ooh La La's, I stepped into the CBC atrium where I was hailed by Tom Anniko, then Executive Producer of CBC Radio Comedy. He was sitting at a table with a lanky young man of about thirty. Tom introduced the young man as Matt Watts, the writer and star of the next radio play I'd be recording. Matt's claim to fame at that time was as one of the creators of the (soon-to-be) Broadway hit *The Drowsy Chaperone* and one of the stars of the second and third season of Ken Finkleman's *The Newsroom*.

The radio play turned out to be *Steve the First*. It was about a laconic young anti-hero named Steve who has an accident and wakes up many years in the future to find himself in the middle of an apocalypse where everybody's suffering from a disease that makes them "melt" over time. People in the grip of the disease are called "melties." It's up to Steve to save the day, except that he has little interest in doing so. Matt is a brilliant comedy writer, and *Steve the First* was a funny show. As a science fiction comedy, it was right up my alley.

Matt and I hit it off. I told him about my attempt to make a science fiction radio series and gave him a copy of *Faster Than Light* to listen to. In an unusual move, after we finished recording the actors, Tom Anniko didn't ask me to mix the show. Instead, he brought the raw tracks to his base of operations in Winnipeg and asked a local recording engineer there to mix it. This fellow is a talented and well-regarded recording engineer but he specialized in recording and mixing music, not radio plays.

Matt Watts was not pleased with the results. He'd listened to my mix of *Faster Than Light* and approached me about remixing

*Steve the First*. I listened to the Winnipeg recording engineer's mix of it and had to agree: it wasn't quite up to snuff. Several of the sound effects just didn't work and the dialogue was too far back in the mix, among other issues. Matt was quite upset. Would I remix it?

I really wanted to remix it because I was certain I could make it much better, but I didn't want to disrespect my colleague. Matt and I went to Tom and asked him what he thought. Tom agreed to allow me to create an alternate mix. But first I felt I had to talk to the other recording engineer. I went into the conversation thinking it would be a delicate discussion but I needn't have worried. He wasn't precious about his work, readily admitting that he was first and foremost a music recording engineer.

I rolled up my sleeves and got to work, replacing sound effects, bringing the dialogue forward, and taking what I've always thought of as a "leave no stone unturned" approach to mixing radio plays. I'd learned a lot mixing *Faster Than Light* and every other radio play I'd mixed in the five years since I'd joined the radio drama department. I was mixing within a smaller dynamic range, making my waveforms look a lot more like the waveforms you'd see in top forty music on commercial radio, the better to allow my product to compete on that medium. I made my sound effects much louder and punchier than when I'd first started out. I worked alone, or sometimes with Matt, without a producer looking over my shoulder and telling me what to do. Having Matt hang around the studio was a huge bonus, because he was the star of the show, so it featured his voice a lot, and if I thought a line needed to be different, either a completely new line or different delivery, I could ask him to record it then and there and simply incorporate it into the mix. There was never any discussion of paying him extra to do that because, for one thing, I didn't have the authority to do that, and for another, neither of us cared. We just wanted to make the absolute best product that we could.

We were both pretty happy with the way *Steve the First* turned out. And we became fast friends in the process. Never up to that point had I felt so sympatico in a creative collaboration.

The CBC contracted Matt to write three more episodes of *Steve the First*. I was just supposed to be the recording engineer on each of them. But when Matt started writing the second episode, he sent his early drafts not only to Tom Anniko but to me as well. I don't know whether he expected me to comment on it, but because I fancied myself a writer I read it and had some pretty strong opinions. I waited a bit to see whether Tom responded, and maybe he did, but if so he didn't copy me, so I sent Matt my thoughts.

Much later Matt told me that he got my notes and read them and they made him angry. He was so mad that he went outside for a smoke and stomped around a bit. And then he thought, dammit, he's right! And went inside and rewrote some stuff based on my notes.

I'm not relating this story to illustrate what a great story editor I am. It's more evidence that Matt and I were operating on the same wavelength when it came to his material. From that point forward I story edited all his radio plays, both officially and unofficially, and much later a television pilot for Thunderbird Entertainment intended for CBC Television.

Matt and I had a lot of fun making *Steve the First* and *Steve the Second*. I became the de facto producer, at least for the mixes, and I did all the post-production sound effects (Anton Szabo did most of the live-to-tape sound effects). There were some memorable moments. Sometimes Matt and I mixed the episodes during the evening. For one scene we needed the sound of a big jug of water bouncing off the floor. I grabbed a great big spare bottle from a water dispenser and brought it into the studio. We hit record on Pro Tools. Matt and I stood in the booth and dropped the completely full, unopened water bottle. To our surprise it cracked, flooding the booth. The carpet was completely soaked. There was little we could do to mop it up or accelerate the drying process, though we did the best we could with scads of paper towels. The next day I had to tell my boss, John McCarthy, about it. John took it well. I don't think there was any lasting damage other than to the water bottle itself, and maybe a slightly moldy carpet.

After mixing an episode I would burn it to CD and take it home and listen to it in several environments: in the car, in the kitchen, in the living room. I wanted to see what it sounded like in each environment. The car was always the noisiest. If a bit of dialogue or a sound effect didn't cut through in any of those environments, I went back to the studio and remixed it until it did. I was trying to make the shows the most sonically successful work of my career. I was happy with the results, but I didn't entirely succeed. After the shows were broadcast, when it came time to print the shows to CD for sale, the woman in charge of doing so, Patsy Stevens, came to visit me in the studio and we had a friendly conversation about the quality. Reviewing the audio on the CDs, she'd noticed a little glitch or two. I was incredulous. She played them back for me. Sure enough there were a couple of weird audio anomalies. Just fraction-of-a-second things that I'd never noticed in all the times I'd listened, but that she'd caught. Of course, she was married to one of the top CBC music recording engineers at the time, Todd Fraracci, and evidently shared his ears. I was embarrassed. I went back to the original mixes and did what I could to fix them, but due to the nature of the glitches my options were limited. They're still there in the final product, to some extent. But I daresay you would probably need the "golden ears" of Patsy (or her husband Todd) to discern them.

*Steve the First* and, later, *Steve the Second* aired Saturday mornings at 11:30am. I think they went over fairly well, but neither Matt nor I became anywhere near as famous as our radio drama hero Douglas Adams, famous for *The Hitchhiker's Guide to the Galaxy*.

Maybe next time.

# XXXIV

## Arthur J. Vaughan:
## *One Officer's Experiences*

O ne day Damiano Pietropaolo, the Director of the Arts & Entertainment department, came to me with a proposal. He was putting together a series called *"Where is Here? The Drama of Immigration"* for *Monday Playbill*. He had in his hands an unpublished memoir written by a former immigration officer by the name of Arthur J. Vaughan. Damiano wanted me to adapt Arthur's memoir into a kind of a drama and planned to hire Gordon Pinsent to play the part of Arthur.

I was happy to be given the opportunity and immediately set to work adapting the memoir, but I just could not lift it off the page. Before long I came to the conclusion that it wasn't going to work, Gordon Pinsent or no. The best thing, I figured, would be to just get Arthur himself to tell all the stories he'd written about.

The only problem was that all the stories in question took place just after the Second World War. I didn't even know if Arthur was still with us. He would have had to be in his eighties. But I picked up the phone and discovered that not only was Arthur still with us, he was sharp as a tack and enthusiastic about telling his story.

With Damiano's blessing, I booked a studio for Arthur in Halifax and another studio for myself in Toronto, and Arthur and I spoke for about an hour. At this time Arthur was eighty-five years old and only afterward did I realize just how inconsiderate I had been. Once we wrapped up our conversation and said goodbye, Arthur didn't realize that the lines and mics were still open, and I heard him say to the technician in Halifax: "I like to talk, but by the jeez! That was long."

I had many opportunities to correspond with Arthur before and after the interview, and to speak with him on the phone, and I came to really like him. Such a gentleman, warm and smart, all of which I believe is evident on the show that resulted from our conversation. Sadly, shortly after the initial broadcast, Arthur became ill. I phoned him up and asked him how he was doing.

"Miserable," he replied.

It turned out he had leukemia, and I do not believe that Arthur wanted to go gently into that good night. Later, his daughter informed me that when he packed his bags to go into the hospital, among the few possessions that he took with him was a CD copy of the show we'd made together.

Being able to tell his story obviously meant a lot to Arthur, and it means a great deal to me to have been able to make it happen for him in the last year of his life.

Damiano arranged to publish the entire *Where Is Here* series with J. Gordon Shillingford Publishing, under their Scirocco Press imprint, which specializes in drama. The written transcript of my interview with Arthur appeared in *Where Is Here: The Drama of Immigration* (Vol. 2). Years later, a woman by the name of Diana Lobb contacted me for the rights, looking to produce "One Officer's Experiences" for the 2016-2017 season of the Kitchener-Waterloo Little Theatre. I was stunned and delighted to learn that my work with Arthur had been published and made available to theatres for production. After establishing that I owned the underlying literary rights, I was only too happy to grant Kitchener-Waterloo Little Theatre the rights for nine performance dates.

Here's the CBC Radio promotional copy for the show:

"One Officer's Experiences: a memoir in the first person by the late Arthur J. Vaughan. In the years following the Second World War, a huge influx of immigrants arrived at Halifax's Ocean terminal, consisting of Piers 20, 21, 22 and 23. Here, the immigrants were processed for landing in Canada. The customs officials they met were often their first taste of the country they were adopting and Arthur J. Vaughan was there to greet them with compassion and curiosity. The late Mr. Vaughan spoke with Joe Mahoney about his experiences, an account both touching and humorous."

# XXXV
## The Great Radio Drama Submission Call

In late 2004, Damiano Pietropaolo stepped down from his position as Head of Radio Arts & Entertainment. Greg Sinclair took his place. Greg immediately made two significant moves. First, he took me off The Schedule. Second, he put out The Great Radio Drama Submission Call.

Taking me off The Schedule meant that I could no longer be assigned to ordinary technical bookings. I considered this absolutely brilliant. I'd been an audio technician seventeen years and I was sick and tired of The Schedule. My every move was dictated by The Schedule. I had no control over The Schedule. If you wanted to have a meeting with me, you had to talk to the scheduling department, not me. I couldn't plan my days or weeks because if I did, my plans could and would be overwritten by the scheduling department. I would explain this to other people in the CBC and they would have no idea what I was talking about. The Schedule was a phenomenon unique to technicians.

I was also tired of feeling like a second-class citizen. In the studio, producers called the shots. They were the bosses. They weren't really the bosses in that I didn't report to a producer. But in the studio, if a producer said, "Do this," I pretty much had to do it. It didn't matter if I'd been on the job seventeen years and they'd been on the job seventeen days. Taking orders from people with a lot less experience than me was getting old.

I got so fed up with being a tech that one day I decided I didn't want to be credited on air as a technician anymore. I told *Writers & Company* producer Mary Stinson this.

"You don't want to be in the credits anymore?" she asked.

"By all means put me in the credits," I told her. "Just don't call me a tech."

Officially I was a Band 7 Associate Producer/Technician. In my mind, I was a recording engineer. I aspired to be a recording engineer/producer. I asked Mary not to refer to me as anything other than somebody helping put the show together. Of course, the nation didn't care what CBC Radio called Joe Mahoney. Only Joe Mahoney cared. But Mary respected my wishes.

The second thing that Greg Sinclair did was put out The Great Radio Drama Submission Call. He wanted to reinvigorate radio drama by attracting new talent and projects. Between The Great Radio Drama Submission Call and being taken off The Schedule this was an exciting time for me.

The radio drama department received over four hundred submissions for potential projects. We divvied them up amongst the recording engineers and the producers to sift through. Each of us would choose one or two to develop and produce. Finally, I thought. Another shot at producing! One step closer to my dream of becoming a Recording Engineer/Producer.

I enjoyed sorting through the slush pile. As an aspiring writer my short stories had been in enough slush piles over the years. It felt good being on the other side. I loved being able to announce to the Canadian science fiction community that I was looking for their submissions on behalf of CBC Radio. I was pretty puffed up about it.

The actual work of reviewing the submissions turned out to be quite a slog. It was maddeningly difficult to discern the wheat from the chaff. So many submissions were just kind of the same. Average. Very few were obviously terrible. The whole process was so subjective. I could easily have missed projects with potential because I just didn't know any better. Over time, though, certain submissions began to stand out, for different reasons. Sometimes the distinguishing factor was who submitted the proposal. Other times it was the proposal's obvious quality. Yet other times it was because the proposal spoke to me in some way. And sometimes it was a combination of the above.

Rob Sawyer, the science fiction author with whom I'd worked on *Faster Than Light*, submitted a proposal with his friend Michael Lennick for a half-hour radio play called *Birth*. *Birth* explored the accidental emergence of sentience among robots on Mars. It wound up on my final list.

Another proposal that stood out was a play called *Worms for Sale* by Stacy Gardner. *Worms for Sale* was about a witty, bored high school graduate in Newfoundland trying to decide whether to stay or leave while being a friend to her heartbroken mother. It was "a play about who we are and how we survive the elements of place." Stacy's proposal, which included snippets of dialogue, exhibited a fresh charm and an originality of voice that appealed to me. *Worms for Sale* found a home on my list.

Meanwhile, Greg Sinclair received a proposal by Joe Straczynski, otherwise known as J. Michael Straczynski, also known as JMS. Greg was quite excited about telling me about this because he knew that as a science fiction fan I would know who JMS was. He was right; I'd been aware of Joe Straczynski's work for several years. Straczynski had been the main creative force behind the hit science fiction television series *Babylon 5*. He'd written most of the episodes. As far as I was concerned, he was a genius. And now Straczynski had proposed an action adventure fantasy series for CBC Radio.

Sinclair and I had images (sound bites?) of Douglas Adams' *Hitchhiker's Guide to the Galaxy* in our minds. Adams' best-selling books had started life as a hit radio series on the BBC. That was the Holy Grail Sinclair and I sought. Surely a project with the likes of Straczynski would bring science fiction and fantasy fans to our doorsteps in droves, and completely rejuvenate the radio drama department. J. Michael Straczynski's *The Adventures of Apocalypse Al* made the final cut.

I don't know how many radio plays we ultimately selected, but it was a fair amount. The next step was to develop each project. I was excited to get started on my choices, *Worms for Sale* and *Birth*. I contacted Stacy Gardner and Rob Sawyer to tell them the good news and arrange times to meet. (I would wind up producing sound effects for three other projects: *ManRadio, The Thing from Beyond my Closet*, and *The Adventures of Apocalypse Al*.)

Rob arrived at the Toronto Broadcast Centre to discuss *Birth* accompanied by his writing partner Michael Lennick. Michael was the brother of former CBC Radio host David Lennick, who had had a radio show about fifteen years earlier called *Sunny Side Up*. (*Sunny Side Up* had actually been one of the first shows I'd ever engineered as a brand-new CBC Radio tech. Nervous, I'd managed to drop a CD on the floor. Fortunately, it had still played.)

Michael Lennick had his own claims to fame. For CFMT-TV in Toronto he'd co-written *The All-Night Show*, which had featured Chuck the Security Guard, played by Chas Lawther, with whom I also made a couple of radio shows over the years. It's a small world. After that Michael toiled as a visual special effects artist for two decades, working on David Cronenberg's *Videodrome* and *The Dead Zone*, and TV series such as *War of the Worlds* (1988). When I met him, Michael was producing well-regarded science and history documentaries.

The Lennick boys had come from famous stock, too. As a member of Wayne & Shuster's repertory company, their mother, Sylvia Lennick, had famously played Julius Caesar's wife, uttering the immortal line, "I told him, 'Julie, don't go!'"

After meeting Rob and Michael, I met with the author of *Worms for Sale*. Stacy Gardner turned out to be a charismatic young woman originally from Newfoundland, now in Toronto working for Covenant House. *Worms for Sale* was the first time she'd submitted any of her work anywhere.

We brought in experienced story editors, Greg Nelson and Beverly Cooper, to work with our new crop of writers. Greg Nelson drew *Birth* and Beverly Cooper, *Worms for Sale*. Each writer (or team of writers) was contracted to write three drafts and then a final polish of each script. The producers and story editors would make notes on each draft and the final polish. The purpose of the polish was to correct any remaining superficial issues, once all the major problems had been (theoretically) addressed. After all that the plays would be considered ready to record.

First up for me would be *Birth*.

# XXXVI

## *Birth*

We spent a few weeks flinging notes back and forth, refining the script for our radio play *Birth*. A couple of sample notes:

Page 7, Line 3: Does Juan always say "goddamned" bugbots? This is twice in a row. Now, if he says it every single time, that could be funny...

And:

Is there any reason why Dr. Askwith couldn't be a woman? To balance the cast...

(I didn't realize at the time that the character was an homage to producer, writer, interviewer **Mark Askwith** of *Prisoners of Gravity* and Space Channel fame.)

After signing off on the final polish we started getting *Birth* ready for production. Michael Lennick, co-writer of the play with Rob Sawyer, let it be known that he was interested in directing it. Considering his background in television and film production, he would have made out just fine. Where he might have lacked the grammar of radio drama production, I could have easily helped out. But I was producer of the project. As such, I had the right to direct it. Because it would constitute my first opportunity to officially direct a radio play and because I'm a selfish bastard, I wasn't about to pass it up. I hoped it would be a stepping stone to more such projects.

I explained this to Michael. He took it graciously.

It typically takes one day to record a full cast for a half-hour radio play such as *Birth*. On cast day I felt confident. Wayne Richards was my recording engineer. It was good to have a friend at the controls. The ebullient Rosie Fernandez was our Associate Producer. Michael Lennick, Rob Sawyer and I sat with Rosie behind the credenza in Studio 212. I would be able to consult with both Michael and Rob about the script if need be. I had spent several years watching various directors do their thing in this very room. If they could do it, I could do it. Right? How hard could it be?

Harder than I expected.

Wayne opened the mics on the Euphonix System 5 console. He hit record on Pro Tools. We recorded a take of the first scene, which had featured the entire cast. Afterward, I didn't feel we'd gotten what we'd needed.

Casting Director Linda Grearson had landed us some fine players. They included Joseph Ziegler (founding member of Toronto's Soulpepper Theatre), Jean Yoon (*Kim's Convenience*), Andrew Gillies (*Orphan Black*), Brenda Robins (*Heartland*), Jani Lauzon (*Saving Hope*; *A Windigo Tale*), and Philip Akin (*The Sum of All Fears*).

Philip was an imposing presence. He had a black belt in Aikido. As I joined the cast on the studio floor to review the scene, I heard him offer up some martial arts advice: "First thing I'd do is kick my opponent in the thigh. Give them a charley horse. It would hurt like hell, disable them right away."

I happened to be studying Matsubayashi Ryu Karate at the time. Once, at the dojo I attended, a black belt had asked me if I'd ever experienced a charley horse. I told him no.

"You should," he told me. "So you know what it feels like."

Without warning, he kicked me hard in the inner thigh, giving me a charley horse.

"You okay?" he asked afterward.

"Fine," I said. The pain was excruciating. I did my best not to let on.

So, I agreed with Philip on that point. I didn't tell him this, though. I was too busy trying to figure what to tell him and his fellow actors about the scene we'd just recorded.

Philip may not have had any more confidence in me than I had in myself. I'd worked with him once on an episode of Bill Howell's *The Mystery Project*. I'd had an issue with the first scene on that show, too. That time the problem had been technical. Something wrong with the quality of the audio. The actors had all sounded off mic. After confirming that nothing was wrong with the console, I checked out the Dead Room where Philip was waiting in front of the MS stereo microphone.

I saw the problem immediately.

"Did you figure it out?" Philip asked.

"Yes," I said.

"Well, what is it?"

"Someone hung the microphone backwards."

Philip laughed and mimed smoking a cigarette. Not just any cigarette. "Have another toke!" he said in strangled voice.

Now here we were a year or so later. I couldn't seem to get the cast's attention. They were talking loudly amongst themselves.

Philip sized up the situation. "Take control, Joe," he commanded.

Okay.

But how?

I didn't know what to tell Philip and his fellow actors. I knew that something in the scene wasn't working, but I had no idea how to fix it. No clue what instructions to give. I could give the actors line readings (saying the lines the way I thought they ought to be said) but it was my understanding that actors typically resented line readings. Nobody likes to be micromanaged. So I didn't do that.

All those years watching other directors, arrogantly thinking, "I can do that." Every bit as naive as a director thinking they could sit down, roll up their sleeves, and operate the multitrack audio console just because they'd sat in the same room as an engineer for years.

I muddled through.

At lunch, I asked Michael how he thought the session was going.

"It's like being chauffeured in a Rolls Royce," he told me courteously, suggesting it was going smoothly.

Given my obvious lack of experience directing, it couldn't possibly have been true. Michael must surely have been wishing that he was directing the production himself. But he was far too gracious to say so.

I was glad to get the cast recording over with. Once we finished taping I had far more control. I edited and mixed *Birth* in my favourite studio, Sound Effects 3 (SFX 3). As with my previous pet project *Faster Than Light*, I turned over every stone to get it perfect, or at least tried to. I edited the dialogue tracks (picking and choosing from various takes) and laid in the sound effects. Michael showed up to help with the final mix.

Shortly before working on *Birth* I'd convinced my boss John McCarthy to purchase new plug-ins for the Pro Tools in SFX 3 (plug-ins are essentially special effects for audio). The usual plug-ins, the Waves Gold Plug-in Bundle, were good but limited. So, I had some great tools to work with. The only problem was that playing with the plug-ins and trying to get everything just right took me twice as long as it would have on a regular project.

The upshot is that I didn't finish the project in the time allotted. I had to come in on a day off. I worked all day, futzing around with the voice of the killer robots, trying to get it just right. Using my new plug-ins I finally managed to create an original treatment for the robot's voice that I was happy with, that I didn't remember hearing anywhere else.

A few days afterward I had a meeting with one of our departmental managers about something else entirely. I happened to mention that I'd come in on a day off to finish mixing *Birth*. I thought she'd be impressed by my dedication. Au contraire.

"You can't do that," she told me.

"Why not?" I asked. "It's not like it cost the CBC anything."

"It's not fair to your colleagues," she said. "Because you come in on a day off and they don't, your work winds up sounding better than theirs."

I mentioned this conversation to producer Bill Lane. "Talk about a culture of mediocrity," he remarked.

*Birth* premiered on July 8, 2005, at 10:00pm. across Canada on CBC Radio One as a part of a limited anthology series called *Deep Night*, executive produced by Gregory J. Sinclair.

Tragically, Michael Lennick passed away in 2014 at the age of 61. Michael and I had hit it off, working together on *Birth*. Yet I never saw or spoke to him once afterward.

I really wish that had not been the case.

# XXXVII

## Worms for Sale

Set on the rock five years after Newfoundland's Ocean Ranger disaster, Stacy Gardner's *Worms for Sale* is a moving and amusing story of a mother still reeling from loss and dealing with a daughter wanting to leave her small Newfoundland town for Toronto.

"The title came first," Stacy told me. "And then the characters just started popping up."

A colleague at Covenant House in Toronto, where Stacy worked, had told her about a recent CBC Radio Drama submission call for which we ultimately received four hundred submissions. Stacy submitted *Worms for Sale*. I selected *Worms for Sale* because Stacy's dialogue and characters popped right off the page. Stacy hadn't expected anything to come of her submission. She felt fortunate to have been shortlisted, then finally commissioned.

"All of it was just beautiful, an unexpected gift," she said.

Stacy got *Worms for Sale* in shape for production with the support of script editor Beverly Cooper. It didn't take long to complete. No sooner had we got the script finalized, though, than I found myself locked out of the CBC, along with most of my colleagues in yet another labour dispute.

Back inside after two months of pounding the pavement, we decided to produce Stacy's play in St. John's, Newfoundland, with the help of regional producer Glen Tilley. I had great admiration for Glen Tilley's work. Glen radiated Newfoundland charm and had produced the renowned satirical radio play *The Great Eastern* (hosted by Paul Moth, aka Mack Furlong). He was also responsible for influencing the build of their first proper radio drama studio in St. John's, Studio F, which over the years has hosted The Wonderful

Grand Band, Great Big Sea, and more. It was in Studio F that we proposed to record *Worms for Sale*.

One day James Roy sidled up to my workstation. "You'd probably better get going on *Worms for Sale*." He didn't explain why but it was clear that something was up.

Alarmed, I phoned Glen to expedite dates and other arrangements. Stacy, excited about the impending recording, planned to accompany us. I was looking forward to my first trip to Newfoundland, as well as the opportunity to direct another radio play.

And then it all came crashing down.

Before we could board the plane to Newfoundland, the Powers That Be cancelled most of the radio drama projects from our submission call that had not already been produced. That included the half-finished *Worms for Sale*. I never learned exactly why, though no doubt it had to do with money.

I was left wondering, if only I had moved the project along faster, booked the tickets to Newfoundland earlier ... but probably it wouldn't have mattered. I felt terrible for Stacy.

"It was just shitty," she described the experience of having *Worms for Sale* cancelled. "Like being in love with someone and then breaking up unexpectedly."

The decision was, of course, entirely the CBC's prerogative. Still, it was embarrassing for me personally. We had set all these writers up only to pull the rug out from under them.

Stacy didn't give up, though. "I stayed with the script," she said. "I got a Toronto Arts grant for the script to adapt it into a stage play."

In the summer of 2012, Stacy produced *Worms for Sale* for The Alumnae Theatre in Toronto, featuring actors Tajanna Penney, Jennifer Neales, William MacGregor, Deborah Perry, and Bruce Williamson. Janina Kowalski directed it.

"It was a seed," Stacy said. "It didn't grow in the original garden, so I took it and grew it in a different one."

It ran for seven sold out nights at The Alumnae Theatre. I made sure I was there to see it. It was great on stage.

It would have been great on the radio, too.

# XXXVIII
## The Lockout

On August 15, 2005, CBC locked out its unionized workforce of producers, technicians and other support staff, about 5500 workers, including me, after negotiations with the Canadian Media Guild broke down after fourteen months. Arnold Amber, President of the CBC branch of the Canadian Media Guild, said at the time, "The talks are all over, it's going forward. We never reached agreement on any of the main issues and there's still about forty items undone." The main issue boiled down to CBC management's desire to have more flexibility over how it hired its employees, with the union in stark contrast looking for more job security for its members.

I happened to be on vacation at the time, camping with my family. At first CBC management had told us that they'd honour our vacations, which in my case had been arranged long before any hint of a lockout. At the very last moment, they changed their minds. It was too late for me to change my family's vacation plans. This meant forfeiting one week's worth of strike pay, but I didn't care. I figured a week of sun and leisure and canoeing and uninterrupted family time would be a lot more fun than picketing.

I wasn't wrong. Still, this job action would prove quite a bit different in character than the previous two. For one thing, it took place during the summer, when it was warm. That made picketing infinitely more pleasant. But perhaps more importantly for me personally, I decided to blog the entire event. This would have an enormous impact on how I experienced the labour dispute.

By the second week of the lockout I had set up a blog using the free online blogging service Blogger. I chose the pseudonym "CBC Workerbee." I decided to blog anonymously because I had no idea what management would think about my blogging. It seemed prudent to play it safe, though I wasn't great about keeping it a secret. Friend and colleague Laurence Stevenson called CBC Workerbee's identity "the worst kept secret of the lockout."

I came to (almost, sort of) enjoy the 2005 lockout. A part of me looked forward to hitting the picket line and gathering more information to blog about. I picketed, snapped photos, and then returned home to write about what I'd experienced. The words flowed unlike they had ever flowed before. I wasn't the only one blogging about the lockout. Dozens of us across the country put keyboard to screen, with about five blogs in particular posting regularly.

After putting up two posts, I got noticed by the king of the lockout blogs, Tod Maffin, a social media expert and former CBC Radio host and producer. After Maffin linked to CBC Workerbee, I averaged a readership of about five hundred unique readers per post. Blogging became like catnip for me. I had found my voice. Psychologically it was highly therapeutic. What might otherwise have been a very unpleasant summer became at least a little bit fun.

Like the other job actions, the lockout of 2005 turned into a great opportunity to catch up with all my CBC pals. Walking around the Toronto Broadcast Centre in pleasant weather was quite enjoyable. It seemed to me that the Senior Executive Team had made a terrible strategic error locking us out in the summer. We were getting strike pay. We were only working twenty hours a week. I felt as though we could carry on like this forever (or at least until it got cold again).

It was on Tuesday, August 23 that I ventured down to the picket line for the first time. I didn't feel like picketing that day because I had a cold, but I was determined to get my twenty hours in to earn my strike pay. I signed in at 11:45 am on Wellington Street, then picketed counterclockwise around the building, catching up with people I hadn't seen in ages. The mood was good, though I saw that the Guild had a few kinks to work out. There wasn't much food, and the sign-up sheets were handled badly. But I was confident they'd get their act together. Just like CEP had the two times I'd been out with the technicians. "There's no substitute for experience," I noted in my blog.

Everyone had an opinion on the lockout. Many held the Senior Executive Team accountable. SET (as that body is often referred to) consisted, as near as I could figure, of Richard Stursberg (Executive Vice-President), George Smith (Senior Vice-President Human Resources), and Robert Rabinovich (President and Chief Executive Officer). There may have been others, but I had no idea; a vast chasm existed between people like me and people like them in the CBC food chain.

A union rep told me that SET genuinely felt that a lockout was the right thing to do given the dwindling allocation from Ottawa and the impact that inflation was having on the Corporation's financial position. SET genuinely believed (so my union friend said) that contract workers and increased flexibility would save the corporation.

Rumors flew. That the union was in cahoots with management. That they'd worked out an agreement to be locked out for a designated amount of time to save the CBC money in return for concessions at the negotiating table. Some suggested that we'd been locked out to make up in wages what the CBC had lost during the NHL lockout the previous year. I was told with great confidence that the lockout would be over by the first of October, just in time for the CBC to prepare for the NHL broadcasts (whoever told me that wasn't far off; the lockout was over by October 4). Such rumors were to be expected on a picket line and were best taken with a large grain of salt.

Several years later, in his book *Tower of Babble*, former Executive Vice-President Richard Stursberg laid out his thinking. He believed that technological changes made the lockout necessary. The CBC needed to move online; multi-tasking would be critical. But the labour dispute had to be timed just right. The unions could not be allowed to strike as the new TV season debuted. That's when Stursberg would be presenting his new programming strategy. Nor could the strike be allowed to mess up the upcoming hockey season, with the NHL itself just emerging from a lockout. That's why SET locked us out in August—so that they could control the timing themselves.

Of course, people like me were not privy to Stursberg's thinking. We were basically just pawns. I shared my opinions about it all in my CBC Workerbee blog, but it was mostly nonsense. That's okay—I wasn't really trying to convince anyone. I was just venting. And it felt good. I was part of a healthy blogosphere, a vibrant online community of locked-out workers.

A manager I knew stopped to say hi, one of the frontline operations managers who would spend the lockout holding the CBC together. A gust of wind whipped my placard up, striking her in the face before I could catch it.

"Sorry!" I said, aghast, afraid she might think I'd done that deliberately.

She thought no such thing. We chatted, me pressing her for information, mostly. I wanted to know who was doing what inside. I especially wanted to know who was working Radio Master Control. She demurred.

"Oh, come on!" I persisted. "What's the big deal?"

"I can't tell you. I've already gotten into trouble once." She skittered away, and I felt bad for harassing her.

I continued to circle the Toronto Broadcast Centre, observing my Canadian Media Guild friends on the line with grim satisfaction. How I'd longed for them to get a taste of what CEP members had had to go through (twice). For years I'd harboured a fantasy of the Guild enduring a job action in the dead of winter while my union stayed warm inside. I dreamed of approaching Guild members and putting my arm around them and saying, as sincerely as I could muster, "How's it goin'? Have you heard anything?" as several had done with us so often in previous job actions. Well now here they were finally getting a taste of it all. Except that I was stuck outside with them, yet again.

At least it wasn't the dead of winter.

The following day I visited TD bank. They agreed to defer my mortgage. Between my picket pay and Lynda's salary we would be okay for a while. Having been through this all before I was pretty relaxed about it.

At home my family couldn't pry me off the computer.

"I've just got too much I want to write," I blogged.

I blogged late into the night, relating stories picked up on the line. Like the one about the manager and his friend. After his shift, the manager emerged from the Broadcast Centre, spotted his friend on the picket line, and began to walk with him. Naturally, he didn't carry a picket sign. Doing laps around the Broadcast Centre, they lost track of time. The next day the manager's boss gave him heck for picketing. But he hadn't been picketing. He'd just been hanging out with his buddy. Albeit on a picket line.

There are plenty of opportunities for people to get in trouble on picket lines.

A memo surfaced. It became known as the "don't feed the animals" memo:

"...there should be no other managers or other non-CMG staff visiting the line, nor should there be any attempts to "improve the mood" on the line, by providing food or drink, for example. It's very important, if there is a lock-out, that we bring a quick resolution to the work stoppage. A quick resolution will be helped by picketers focusing on the reality of their situation. Making things more comfortable for the picketers does not support this goal."

This did not go over well on the line but turned out to have been written before the lockout. Once the labour dispute actually began, management reconsidered its position:

...we need to keep in mind that these are our colleagues and friends, and they will be our colleagues and friends when things return to normal and we're all back to work...We should interact with them as we would any colleague or friend with whom we are having a disagreement—with respect and openness. Don't hesitate to communicate as normally as possible with picketers on the line but with the following advice:

- Do not get drawn into anything which might be perceived as negotiating directly with employees

- Do not display any animosity and do not react to animosity

- Show empathy for their personal situations

- And communicate our resolve to do what we think is right for the organization


On Friday, September 2, I picked up ten hours on the line. Halfway through, one of the picket marshalls introduced himself to me as Dave. Picket Marshall Dave asked me if I would mind being a picket captain. I accepted. The job kept me rooted to one spot. I passed the time hobnobbing with two burly security guards that the CBC had hired to keep peace on the line. I never learned their real names: I'll call them Biff and Dirk. Biff and Dirk were only too happy to reveal their martial arts experience and share war stories in which spine injuries and dislocated jaws figured prominently, injuries not restricted to the security guards. They were from the same company that had openly attempted to intimidate CEP members during the previous strike at the CBC.

"You seem much more approachable this time," I told them.

"It was the nature of the company to be more intimidating in the past," Biff told me. "We're kinder, gentler thugs now."

They told me that they were only security guards temporarily, on their way to becoming firemen and police officers. They expressed respect for our picket line's restraint and good sense.

"What would happen if we got it into our heads to storm the entrance or perform a sit-in?" I asked. "There's only three or four of you."

"We can sense when something like that's brewing," Biff said. "We'd bring in about fifty more guys in heavy protective gear and gear up. We wouldn't be afraid to knock some heads."

Biff described himself as a "nice guy" but clearly relished the notion of physical violence. "It's the adrenaline rush," he confessed.

When I first started blogging the lockout in mid-August, there had been about twelve bloggers. By September 7, there were over fifty. Not all were active. Many posted once a week, if at all.

Everybody had a different approach. Some goofy, hostile, serious, others ambivalent, over-the-top, or poetic. I tried to be funny and informative but sometimes came off rather earnest. On Thursday, September 8, I posted about my father. He had been a teacher on Prince Edward Island and had belonged to a union most of his working life. As a kid, I had asked him, "Could you guys ever go on strike?"

"No," he told me. "With us it could only ever go to binding arbitration. In a civilized country, in a civilized age, you should go about your business in a civilized fashion."

One quarter century before my employer locked me out, my father's union and the government of Prince Edward Island (Canada's smallest province) had employed binding arbitration to resolve their dispute. Why in all the time since hadn't such civilized notions spread to the rest of the country?

I broached the subject on the line. I was reminded that CBC and the Guild had had fifteen months during which to come up with an agreement, and they had not been able to. There was no reason to believe that binding arbitration would work.

But I still believed that it could.

On Saturday, September 10, I picketed sixteen hours, starting at 5:30am. It was dark when I started and dark when I finished. Early on I chatted with news announcer Bob McGregor.

"I was the last man out when the lockout was declared," he told me. "A manager wanted me to read only one minute of the news at midnight, but I insisted on reading the entire newscast before allowing myself to be escorted out. It was the professional thing to do."

Bob let me take his picture for my blog. Sadly, he passed away a few short years after the lockout. CBC.ca used that photo on a story about him.

September wound down. The nights started to get chilly. I heard talk of setting up oil barrels. I was adamantly opposed. I figured I was already slowly dying from having breathed the creosote-soaked wood we'd burned the last two times out. And those oil barrels stank, they really did. If we started using them we'd be forced to throw out all our clothes afterward. Why not deal with the cold simply by dressing warmly?

I needn't have worried. On Monday, October 3, news rolled in that management and the Guild had come to an agreement. The lockout was over.

Tuesday on the line the feeling was that the union had won. Word was our communication strategies and morale had been the envy of the labour world. This hadn't been the result of any great strategy on our part. It was just (I thought) the inevitable result of throwing fifty-five hundred of the most creative people in the country out on the street. The Guild had successfully fostered a festive atmosphere on the picket line, boosting morale exponentially. Who doesn't like hanging out with friends on sunny days while enjoying concerts in the park? I believed that we'd just experienced something unique, and that I might actually miss the lockout when it was over.

And I did.

# XXXIX

## The Adventures of Apocalypse Al

Back inside we picked up where we'd left off.

J. Michael Straczynski's *The Adventures of Apocalypse Al* had been one of the few projects from The Great Radio Drama Submission Call that had not been cancelled. Greg Sinclair directed it. Greg DeClute was the recording engineer. I was assigned to do sound effects.

*The Adventures of Apocalypse Al* is the story of a tough female private eye out to save the world. Not quite our world. A world of imps, zombies, techno-wizards, trolls, an undead ex-boyfriend, and more in that vein. It consisted of twenty approximately five-minute long episodes. Cynthia Dale (*Street Legal*) played the female private eye, the eponymous Apocalypse Al. Other memorable actors included Colm Feore (*The Umbrella Academy; Bon Cop Bad Cop*) and Chuck Shamata (*The Day After Tomorrow; Cinderella Man*). Chuck was so good that Straczynski wrote him additional dialogue on the spot. I convinced Sinclair to cast Matt Watts in a cameo as a ticket taker in an amusement park. Matt's sardonic delivery was pitch perfect.

Early on in the project I admitted to Straczynski that I was a fan of his work. That I loved *Babylon 5*, had read his column in *Writer's Digest* for years, and was familiar with his work in comics. Straczynski seemed to enjoy talking about his career. He wouldn't answer all my questions, though. For instance, between the first and second season of *Babylon 5* the lead actor, Michael O'Hare (playing Commander Jeffrey Sinclair) was replaced by **Bruce Boxleitner** (playing Captain John Sheridan). Exactly why O'Hare dropped out of the show was a mystery. Straczynski had written about the transition in online forums but had stopped short of explaining it.

Referring to this, I said, "You weren't very forthcoming about the transition from Sinclair to Sheridan, why that happened."

"No, I wasn't," he said.

"So, I won't ask you about it, then."

"No, you won't," he said.

After O'Hare's death of a heart attack in 2012, Straczynski revealed that O'Hare had left the series due to severe mental illness. To protect O'Hare's career, he'd promised O'Hare he'd keep it a secret until his death. And he did.

What Straczynski seemed to enjoy most was cracking wise. Just about everything out of his mouth was a joke. It was important to him to be the funniest man in the room. He almost always was.

There was a crazy amount of sound effects on *Apocalpyse Al*. Only one did I have any trouble with: the sound of Al's car. It was supposed to be a muscle car. Probably I should have done what I'd done with *Cherry Docs*: I should have taken a tape recorder out on the street to record somebody's sports car. But it wasn't like we were making a feature film. I didn't have an unlimited budget and tons of time. I was forced to rely on the radio drama department's fairly extensive (though not quite extensive enough) sound effects library.

Mixing the show in Studio 212, we reached the first scene featuring Al's car. Greg DeClute hit play on Pro Tools. We all heard the sound of Al's car revving up through the control room's enormous SOTA speakers.

Straczynski said, "What's that?"

"That's Al's car," I said.

"Al's driving a lawnmower?" This was vintage Straczynski.

I didn't like the sound I'd chosen either, but it was the best I'd been able to find. Clearly, I needed to do better.

"Lose it," Straczynski said.

I deleted the unsatisfactory sound effect.

Straczynski suggested that we move on.

I was surprised. I needed to find another sound effect to replace the one I'd deleted. Officially, we only had that day to mix the episode we were working on. We couldn't move on until I'd addressed the problem.

Pointing at the Pro Tools mix window, which now featured a gaping hole where the sound of the car had been, I said, "What about this hole?"

"I'm looking at it," Straczynski said, looking straight at me.

After a few seconds of uncomfortable silence, we moved on. I would have to wait to fix the car sound effect.

The mix took much longer than an ordinary radio play. Mainly this was because it was a high production piece with plenty of sound effects and lots of sonic treatments. But it was also because we often took a lot of time to discuss each scene. We debated placement of sound effects. We debated whether to include footsteps. We debated which scenes should include music. The music was excellent. Although composed largely (if not entirely) on synths, it was lush and full and complemented the material wonderfully, successfully evoking *Apocalypse Al*'s fantastical, private eye universe. Straczynski didn't believe in placing music underneath scenes that were supposed to be funny. He felt that it got in the way of the humour. We left a lot of music cues out.

The mixes took so long that we ran out of our officially allotted time. I was just supposed to be the sound effects guy on this one, but because Greg DeClute wasn't available the department asked me to come in on the weekend to finish the mix. Greg Sinclair wasn't available either, so it wound up being just me and Straczynski.

We spent a lot of time talking. And when I say talking, I mean Straczynski telling me stories. It didn't help us finish the mix, but I wasn't complaining. He was as engaging as ever. He told me (for instance) about a film script he was working on, about a woman reuniting with her son who had been missing, only to discover that the boy wasn't actually her son at all. This was a pet project of Straczynski's. He'd spent many years researching it. I didn't think much of it at the time, but a couple of years later Clint Eastwood directed a movie starring Angelina Jolie about exactly that. Sure enough, Straczynski had written the script for the movie that became *Changeling*.

On Sunday, our last day working together, Straczynski said, "Listen. I know I crack a lot of jokes. I want to apologize if at any point I crossed the line or was offensive."

There had just been the one crack about the car sound effect which I'd opted not to take personally. I had enjoyed Straczynski's company. "I started this process a fan, and I'm finishing it as a fan," I told him. We shook hands, parted ways, and lived happily ever after.

Not exactly. We still hadn't finished the damn mix. By this time both Gregs were off on other projects, so I spent the next couple of weeks mixing *The Adventures of Apocalypse Al* all by my lonesome in SFX 3. Occasionally Sinclair popped in, listened to my work, and suggested tweaks.

When it was finally done, I thought, well, that's great. Maybe now we can finally live happily ever after. *The Adventures of Apocalypse Al* was just about the most populist piece of entertainment we'd ever produced. I figured it would go a long way toward attracting a younger demographic. *The Hitchhiker's Guide* crowd. To help promote it, I posted about it on my blog. Jesse Willis, who ran a site called SFFAudio.com, promoted it. Another site, Babylonpodcast.com, picked up on it. Straczynski himself talked it up, telling one blog (Dave Does the Blog) about it, who reported, "The CBC will be broadcasting a 12-episode (sic) radio series by Joe [Straczynski, not me] called *The Adventures of Apocalypse Al*, a noir sf comedy along the lines of *Men in Black* or *Hitchhikers Guide*. Joe notes that it will eventually migrate to US radio and CD."

Imagine my astonishment when, after all our hard work and what must have been a considerable investment of money (at least in radio drama terms), the Powers That Be decided not to broadcast the show at all. Not even a single episode.

Why?

I don't know. I wasn't a part of that decision-making process, and every single person that was is now long gone from CBC Radio.

Blogger Jesse Willis started an online campaign that he called **Free the Adventures of Apocalypse Al**. It didn't work. *The Adventures of Apocalypse Al* was shelved, and never aired. Years later the legal department came around asking me about the project. It seemed Straczynski wanted the rights to the show and was willing to pay. I don't know how much money changed hands. I made copies of the production from the existing masters. I assume they were passed on to Straczynski, but I don't know for sure, as we haven't stayed in touch.

On March 14, 2014, Jesse Willis reported the following on his SFFAudio site:

> Nearly 10 years ago I began reporting that J. Michael Straczynski had been asked to write a radio play for CBC Radio One. Later, we learned that Cynthia Dale had been cast in the title role. And still later that the show was in production. And it was indeed recorded. But it never aired. Over the years the campaign to get it aired plodded along—but without any success. Then a couple of years ago word of a comics version came about. [On June 10, 2014, Straczynski and Image Comics released a comic book version of *The Adventures of Apocalypse Al* with artists Sid Kotian and Bill Farmer.] Now, after the comics version is actually out (the first issue was dated February 2014) I am stunned to report that there is indeed now a new audio drama available. I should point out that this is an entirely NEW recording (not the one Canadian taxpayers paid for but never heard) and we don't know yet if the remaining 3/4 of the story will be produced for audio.

The new audio version of *The Adventures of Apocalypse Al* was produced by Patricia Tallman. Tallman had been one of the actors on *Babylon 5*. The cast of this new version included Patricia Tallman herself as Allison Carter, Robin Atkin Downes, Fred Tatasciore, and Stephanie Walters. Robin Atkin Downes was also the sound effects editor/designer.

I've never heard this version, and probably never will, though I am curious whether Robert Atkin Downes managed to find a decent muscle car sound effect.

# XL
## Live Effects for a Dead Dog

I have nothing against sound effects per se.

I love sound design, for instance—taking sound effects from different sources and electronically creating worlds out of them that you could fully believe in. But as I've mentioned before I never really enjoyed performing sound effects live with actors. It just wasn't my specialty. We had a couple of guys—Anton Szabo and Matt Willcott—who did specialize in it. They were good at it. Then Matt retired and the rest of us had to divvy up the job. Myself, I preferred recording, or producing, or jabbing forks into my eyes. Anything other than performing sound effects live with actors.

When I was assigned to do sound effects for the *Dead Dog Café* I was dismayed, but concealed my feelings from *Dead Dog* producer Kathleen Flaherty. I didn't want to let her down.

Making matters worse, I had been shipped a Compaq Armada laptop from Edmonton especially for the *Dead Dog Café* recording sessions that wasn't making me happy. It had audio software on it called Dalet. At the time I didn't much care for Dalet because after working in the radio drama department for a while I had become a snob. I considered Dalet's editing capabilities inferior to programs like Sonic Solutions and Pro Tools. But really this was ill-informed. Dalet's strength was its ability to network. Toronto boasted a network of over four hundred Dalet computers and twenty-some servers upon which we relied for most of our radio production, live and otherwise. The system was stable and worked well most of the time. And I would come to change my mind about Dalet's editing capabilities after receiving instruction from trainer Brian Dawes, who taught me that Dalet was actually quite powerful once you knew what you were doing.

I was forced to use the laptop because it had been preloaded with many of the music and sound effects cues that I would be required to play back during the taping sessions, and I didn't have time to come up with an alternative. On the plus side, someone had taken the time to make my life easier by prepping the laptop for me—probably radio technician Eric Wagers, from Edmonton, who had originally performed sound effects for the *Dead Dog Café*.

I went into the taping session with a sense of dread, afraid that I wasn't prepared, that everything would go wrong. We were taping on a Sunday morning. Greg DeClute helped me bring in props on the GO Train. He brought his son's hockey sticks and I brought some umbrellas belonging to my daughters. In the studio, I wheeled out the *Dead Dog Café* door—the one with the bell attached to it, held together with duct tape and wire—along with several other props. The cast arrived. Gracie (Edna Rain), Jasper Friendly Bear (Floyd Favel), and Tom King (playing a version of himself), along with someone new to the show, a young woman named Portia Jumping Bull (played by Tara Beagan).

I had prepared my sound effects weeks earlier by reading the scripts and getting a sense of the sounds required. I deleted all the dialogue, leaving myself a list of sound cues. Any cues that were kind of vague, I referred back to the script to determine the context. Most cues were obvious. Like, say, "plunger." How many different kinds of plungers are there?

Shortly before our recording session I reviewed my list. Seeing a plunger on the list I thought, well, we don't have any of those kicking around the studio. I'd better bring one in from home. I found one, disinfected it, stuck it in my bag, and carried it all the way in on the train along with the umbrellas and Greg's hockey sticks. I placed it close by so that when the script called for it, I'd be able to grab it easily.

We started recording a scene. The actors read their lines. We got to the sound cue that said, "SFX: Plunger!" I grabbed the plunger and begin vigorously plunging the floor, making "thwocking" sounds that I considered really quite outstanding.

Producer Kathleen Flaherty immediately called a halt to the proceedings. "Cut! Joe, what on earth are you doing?"

"Making plunging sounds. Is it working?"

It was not.

Turned out the cue was actually calling for a plunger to test Tom King's blood sugar level. It was a medical device. Which was obvious when I took a closer look at the script.

Fortunately, the *Dead Dog Café* was a comedy show, and everyone working on it had a good sense of humour. We had a laugh about it and moved on. And I learned to read my scripts more carefully.

We had a guest on the show that day—Margaret Atwood. As I've written earlier, I'd once spent four days at Atwood's house recording her interviewing Victor-Lévy Beaulieu (and vice versa). She didn't appear to remember me. There was no reason she would have—it wasn't like we'd stayed in touch, exchanging Christmas cards. But she was friendly and enthusiastic.

I never did warm up to performing sound effects with the cast. And not just because I'd made a silly mistake with a plunger. Whenever I was assigned to perform sound effects live with actors I almost always felt apart from them. Ill-at-ease. Often, the actors all knew one another. At the very least they could relate to one another. I was a part of the cast in that I had to perform with them, but I was not one of them. I was just this guy off to one side smashing plates and tinkling teacups.

Still, it was a privilege to be there. Tom King told us stories in between takes. He talked about his recent weight loss. Upon learning that he had diabetes, he'd dramatically adjusted his diet. For instance, he took great care not to eat bananas that were overly ripe. Of special interest to me, he talked about the craft of writing.

"I like to ask my students to write passages with no adjectives," he told me.

I tried to do it in this chapter and thought I had succeeded until my editor informed me that, "this chapter has adjectives of quality ("different," "great,"), and of quantity ("most," "twenty-some"), subjective complements that are adjectives ("was vague," "was powerful" etc.), and some plain, old adjectives like "good," "recent," and "special.")

To which I would add "difficult."

(As in, "Tom's challenge was more difficult than I expected.")

# XLI
## *Funny Boy*

*Funny Boy* is the coming-of-age story of a young man attempting to come to terms with his sexual identity and his family and community in the years leading up to the Sinhalese-Tamil riots. CBC Radio broadcast the radio play version of *Funny Boy* live the afternoon of Sunday, November 26, 2006, the first time we'd done such a thing in quite a while. It was directed by Canadian film director Deepa Mehta. Mehta's involvement and the fact that the broadcast pre-empted normal programming (including the news, which was considered quite a coup for the radio drama department) meant that *Funny Boy* was a bit of a Big Deal for us.

I was the broadcast recording engineer on the show, in charge of the overall sound. This was a challenge because we broadcast *Funny Boy* live-to-air at the same time as it was performed in front of a live audience of about 100 people, after having already performed it three nights prior.

Deepa Mehta's involvement got us ink in the papers. As a film director, she brought a unique sensibility to the project. She had a keen interest in the theatrical aspect of the production, with a strong emphasis on visuals—not exactly a priority for radio. My own overarching concern was that everything sound as good as possible for the broadcast. This initially resulted in a clash between the two of us. When we first set up, I placed microphones in the actors' faces, where I expected to get the best pickup. I hadn't given any thought whatsoever to how things would look for the theatrical audience. As far as I was concerned, they were there to watch a radio show, and that's what radio shows looked like.

During the first two rehearsals I had my hands full just trying to make things sound right. Fortunately, I had Greg DeClute along. It was Greg's job to mix the live music. His presence reduced my stress level considerably. But both of us struggled to make the production sound good in the smallest theatrical space in Soulpepper's new digs. Because there wasn't a whole lot of room, the musicians were forced to play directly next to the actors, resulting in a lot of bleed-through. We wound up carting two large sound baffles to the site from the Toronto Broadcast Centre to get some separation. Also, the actors sounded quite "boomy" in that environment. It was crucial to get them as close on mic as possible. Then I had to get them to stop "popping" all their "p's." (This happens when air, expelled from mouths while speaking plosives, strikes microphone capsules. It creates a horrible sound that you don't want to hear on air.) Pop filters sorted that out easily enough. But then I had to figure out how to get the actors to stop hitting their microphones and pop filters with their hands during their more exuberant scenes, not to mention how to reduce (ideally eliminate) the sound of them handling their scripts.

The actors were professional, though. By Saturday night we had all of these problems sorted out. We also managed to strike a balance between the requirements of radio and performance of the play live in front of a theatrical audience. It took some experimentation, but I found mic placements that did not obscure actors' faces and still sounded good. Deepa had the stage looking attractive with carpets and vanities, a simple but effective lighting scheme, and the actors all dressed in elaborate costumes. In the end I believe we all got what we needed.

Elizabeth Bowie, our Associate Producer, kept the production running smoothly. Among other responsibilities, she called the show for me on broadcast day, making sure that my hands were on the right faders at the right time. Sound effects guru Anton Szabo performed his sound effects wizardry flawlessly, and Mike, the technician at the venue (whose last name I'm afraid I never caught), capably handled the PA in the house.

On November 24, the week before the broadcast, the *Toronto Star* ran an article about it. This was great promotion for the CBC and the radio drama department in particular. Typically, no mention was made of the technical crew doing the work, other than to say that we'd managed to source authentic sounds of Sri Lankan birds.

Which is something, I guess.

# XLII
## *Canadia*

During the making of *Steve the Second*, Matt Watts conceived of another science fiction comedy project. *Canadia: 2056* tells the story of an American midshipman embedded on the only Canadian starship supporting an American fleet on their way to fight an intergalactic war. Tom Anniko directed a pilot starring Pat Kelly.

The pilot received a lukewarm reception from the Powers That Be, who requested another version, this time with Matt Watts in the lead. I was excited about Matt in the role because he had brought such a great presence to the *Steve* series. Otherwise the cast was pretty much identical.

Tom Anniko wasn't available to direct the second pilot, so I got my second chance to direct a radio play (my first having been *Birth* with Michael Lennick). I decided I wanted to try something I'd never tried before as either a director or a recording engineer. I decided I wanted to attempt the granddaddy of all travelling shots. I'd recorded modest travelling shots in the past, such as the one Greg Sinclair and Saul Rubinek had designed for *Barney's Version*. I'd also recorded travelling shots on location in Montreal with a boom microphone for producers Bill Lane and Tom Lopez on their murder mystery series *Recipe for Murder*. But I didn't feel like I'd ever really hit one out of the park.

As we were planning the second pilot for *Canadia: 2056*, I suggested to Matt that he write a *West Wing/Hill Street Blues* style travelling shot off the top of the episode. He did, crafting a scene where our hero Max Anderson is escorted by Commander Favreau (played by Stephanie Broschart) from one end of the ship Canadia to the other. To do so, Favreau leads Anderson through a series of radically different acoustic environments. It was a great opportunity to take our listeners on an acoustic tour of the starship Canadia.

Unfortunately, Matt and I never got a chance to discuss exactly how to block the scene before we recorded it. I had originally thought that I might grab a boom and a Tascam and follow the actors around the studio floor, but when the time came, I opted instead to record the actors in place with the rest of the cast swirling around them.

Racing against the clock in post-production, I lost my nerve and simplified the scene to a static (audio) shot of Anderson and Favreau talking (and supposedly walking) against a simple ambient background track. It didn't work at all. When Matt heard the rough mix, he was horrified.

"Still needs a bit of tweaking," I admitted.

I resolved to try to fix it later.

Mixing the show late one night in SFX 3, I realized that I didn't have all the sound effects I needed for one scene. I dispatched Matt to fetch some sound effects on CD for me. Fetching the CDs meant that Matt had to pass through five different environments to the room where we kept the sound effects CDs. Each of those environments (which included a large hallway, a studio, a small central equipment room, a smaller hallway, and an office) featured radically different acoustic ambiances. On the way, it occurred to Matt that the travelling shot could be made to work by breaking it up into five distinct ambient sound sets.

Matt and I set off on a trek across the Toronto Broadcast Centre armed with an AKG stereo microphone and our Edirol digital recorder. We passed through as many radically different acoustic environments as possible and I recorded it all, about fifteen minutes worth. Afterward, I loaded the material into my Pro Tools mixing session and cut it down to a minute and a half, the length of the travelling shot. We placed doors at strategic points during the scene and built wildly different sound effects beds for each section, including a set of stairs, an engine room, an interior construction site, and so on.

I electronically "treated" the actors' voices (and accompanying sound effects) depending on where they were supposed to be. For instance, I used a Pro Tools plugin called TrueVerb to make the actors sound realistically like they were in a stairwell. Although as I've mentioned before I'm leery of using footsteps in radio plays for fear of it becoming all about the footsteps, I added a "soupçon" of footsteps here and there to help sell the movement.

We think it worked.

I was quite pleased with the entire episode, actually. And I was not the only one. On the strength of the second pilot, management ordered ten episodes of *Canadia: 2056*. I was enormously excited about the prospect of producing and recording the series. It was, to me, the culmination of all my ambitions. My whole career had been leading to this moment.

But it wasn't to be.

# XLIII
## The Story of *Q*

This is the story of *Q*.

Weekday afternoons on CBC Radio One typically had a listenership of about two hundred and twenty thousand people. It had been this way for years. It didn't matter what you programmed in that time slot—you could play 1 kilohertz tone and the listenership would stay at two hundred and twenty thousand people, it seemed—but CBC Radio needed more listeners than that, so the programmers placed a show called *Freestyle* in that time slot and to everyone's astonishment the listenership promptly dropped even further, to one hundred and eighty thousand people.

Something needed to be done. Something was. A big study, which they called the Arts and Culture study. Based on this research the programmers decided that they needed to replace *Freestyle* with an Arts and Culture show. It would be a national show. A flagship show. They would pour tons of resources into it. It was a Big Deal. There was only one problem. They wanted me to work on it. And I didn't want to have anything to do with it. I had no idea that it was supposed to be the Next Big Thing.

The Director of Arts and Entertainment, Kim Orchard, called me into her office early one Friday afternoon in January 2007 and asked me if I would like to become the tech for this new arts show. She said I could have some time to think it over. I returned to my workstation and thought it over. I didn't have to think long.

I had zero interest in taking on the job. I was happy making radio plays. Matt Watts and I were about to produce ten episodes of *Canadia: 2056*. It was a dream come true for me, the pinnacle of everything I'd been working toward. In my mind, this new arts show would be little different than the old arts show, *The Arts Tonight*. *The*

*Arts Tonight* had been a fine show—I had worked on it many times back in the late eighties with its first host (and one of my favourite on air personalities) Shelagh Rogers—but becoming the tech of a show like that would essentially be dialing my career back about ten years.

Those of us in the trenches knew that this show was coming down the pike. No one I knew wanted to work on it. We all thought it would be a disaster. We had heard that Jian Ghomeshi was going to host it. He had been the host of *50 Tracks*, which had been a big success, he'd fronted the band Moxy Fruvous, he'd hosted a television show, and he'd done a stint on *Sounds Like Canada*. He had a reputation for being difficult to work with. And I thought, I don't need that crap.

I returned to Kim Orchard's office almost right away.

"I'm not really interested in working on the show," I told her. "I wonder if we can work something out."

"No," she said. "I'm not interested in working out any deals. You know it's up to me to decide where you work."

"I know."

"In fact," she said, "If I want to, I can make you go and record news."

"Yes, I'm aware of that," I said, feeling increasingly uncomfortable.

"I could simply reassign you to the show," she said. "Except that now I don't know if I want to."

I chuckled nervously.

"I want a highly motivated team," she told me. "I don't want a malcontent on the show."

"Have you known me to be a malcontent?" I asked.

"I have known you to be nothing but a malcontent," she said. "Always complaining about your lot in life, you and the whole department, you all have this sense of entitlement, and frankly I don't even think any of you work very hard."

"Is there something wrong with trying to improve your lot in life?" I asked.

"You do it through hard work and shining through."

"How do you feel about my work since you've been in the department?"

"I'm not familiar with it. There are four of you. I have no idea who does what."

"Okay, where does that leave us?"

"You go away, you think about it, and if you can come back to me on Monday and tell me with great enthusiasm that you want to be a part of this show then maybe, MAYBE I'll let you be a part of it."

I left Orchard's office feeling insulted. I decided I had no interest in working for her in any capacity anymore. I immediately went to a different department, CBC Sirius Radio, and asked the boss there, Mark O'Neill, if he'd take me on. Mark had heard my radio play *Captain's Away!* and was familiar with my work. He said yes. So as far as I was concerned when I left work that Friday afternoon I wasn't working for Arts & Entertainment anymore. I was working for CBC Sirius Radio.

I met with Orchard again on the Monday.

"I hear you've arranged a transfer to CBC Sirius Radio," she said. "Congratulations."

"Thank you," I said.

"I hope you enjoy your thirty thousand dollar a year pay cut."

That prospect hadn't occurred to me.

"Right," I said. "So when do you want me to start on the new arts show?"

And that was the end of that.

Looking back at this incident after several years in management myself, I realize that Orchard had every right to reassign me to a different show. Every right. She just went about it the wrong way. I told James Roy (who had returned to his core function of Executive Producer of Radio Drama) about the whole affair. He remarked that he could have gotten me to work on the show happily. I'm not sure that I would have been happy about it, but I'm pretty sure that he could have gotten me to work on the show with a lot less drama. By listening to me and addressing my concerns to the extent that he was able. In other words, by treating me with respect.

The upshot is that when I started my work on the radio show that would become *Q* I was quite upset. I loved the medium of radio drama. At the time it was all I wanted to do. Orchard took me out of something I loved and made me a part of something I wanted no part of. I wasn't the only one. Of the staff selected for the new arts and culture show, one promptly quit, one transferred to Winnipeg, and at least two didn't want to be there. Furthermore, they could not find an executive producer who wanted anything to do with the show. Kim Orchard had been right: strictly speaking, in this context, I actually was a malcontent.

But I was also a professional.

I knew that I had to ditch the way I was feeling. I knew that the bitterness I was harbouring—and it was genuine bitterness— wouldn't disappear overnight.

I was sitting in a swing space working on preparations for the new show when I received an email from Tom Anniko. He was pleased to announce the appointment of Greg DeClute as the producer/ recording engineer of a ten-part science fiction/comedy radio series— *Canadia: 2056*, the series that I had helped Matt Watts create and that I had been looking forward to producing. I swore aloud. The only other person in the room, Jesse Wente, looked up. I explained the situation to Jesse. But there was nothing to be done about it.

A few days later Greg and I travelled home together on the GO Train. "Matt and I were talking," he said. "We'd like you to story edit *Canadia*."

I was still seething about the whole affair. "Not interested," I told him.

About a week after that, Greg said, "Matt and I still think—"

"No," I interrupted him.

A few days later Greg caught up to me in the hall. "I know you don't want to hear this. But Matt and I really think you're the guy to story edit the show."

By then I had finally calmed down sufficiently to recognize the generosity of the offer. "Is Tom okay with it?"

"He is."

I took a deep breath. I had wanted to be the producer/recording engineer, not the story editor. "All right. I apprcciate you guys asking. Count me in."

The going rate for freelancers at that time was $500 per episode. The department paid me $150 per episode. They hadn't wanted to pay me at all, but Greg and Matt went to bat for me. Still, as both Greg and Matt (and probably Tom) no doubt knew, in the end I probably would have done it for free.

I did my best not to let on to my new colleagues how I was feeling about working on the new Arts and Culture show. I knew better than to come to work sullen. It's easy to have a good attitude when things are going your way; the trick is to have a good attitude when things are not going your way. I did my best, and gradually the bitterness subsided.

Eventually they found an Executive Producer willing to take a chance on the new show. Lo and behold, it was Mark O'Neill, who had been willing to hire me to work on CBC Radio Sirius. (James Roy would eventually take on Mark's role as Program Manager with Sirius.) Having Mark aboard was a good sign. Ultimately, we wound up with nine people in total to make this new national Arts and Culture show. One recording engineer, one executive producer, one host, three producers, and three associate producers. They threw us all into a room named Skybox Three in the Rogers Centre's Renaissance Hotel. (The Rogers Centre, called SkyDome at the time, is an all-purpose stadium located just behind the CN Tower in downtown Toronto.) "Make us a radio show," they told us.

The sessions were expertly facilitated by veteran radio producer Chris Straw. We talked. We talked for days. All we knew was that it had to be an arts and culture radio show and that it would be personality driven. But we didn't know what any of that meant. Low culture? High culture? Both? What is low culture and high culture? What about sports? Is sports considered culture or recreation? Interviews were a given, but how long should they be? Are interviews on the phone okay or should they all be high-quality lines? Would we be the arts show of record? What does that even mean? Do we break stories? Do we talk about Paris Hilton? If so, how much? What about Margaret Atwood? How do we open the show? How do we close the show? What do we even call the damn thing?

To help us figure things out we took a bunch of courses. We all had plenty of experience making radio but you never stop learning. We took courses on critical thinking. Things like: do we trust this source? Is this story really news? We took a course on ethics. Such as: when are we in conflict of interest? And we took courses on interviewing.

Gradually, I came to realize that I was actually part of something special. And that Kim Orchard had really paid me quite a compliment by placing me on such a show. Though it would take me years to admit it, she had done me a favour.

In time we got the show figured out. High culture AND low culture. High impact guests when possible. Interviews about eight minutes long—longer when warranted. Live music every Friday, maybe more. No Paris Hilton. Lots of energy. Plenty of short, flexible elements so we could mix things up on the fly. We had it all figured out. Everything except for a name.

We'd been racking our brains for weeks trying to come up with a name. It was really important to us that we choose the name, not management. It seemed like the front-runner for management was the name "Radar," and "Radar" just didn't work for us. We needed something better. The problem was the show was so broad that we couldn't come up with a name that encompassed everything the show was about. And then one day, out of the blue, someone had it:

"Awesometown."

Yeah, that lasted about five minutes.

We did a pilot with the name "Radar." The pilot was quite a wild ride.

We produced it live-to-tape with a small audience present. Musician Tomi Swick performed live with a friend. We had a guest in New York and another on the phone and yet another live in studio. All of which wouldn't have been so bad if we'd had the studio booked to do some setup, but the studio we used was booked right up until we were to start recording the pilot. Worse, Tomi Swick and his pal were late to the studio (not their fault, I was told), the upshot being that I had zero time to test anything. Which is not good when you're going live and dealing with the idiosyncrasies of an unfamiliar studio.

We got into the pilot okay but the first guest following Tomi Swick was on the phone and I discovered at the last minute that the studio phones didn't work. My first thought was that I had overpatched the phone inputs with Tomi's mic or guitar, but that wasn't it, so we put off the phoner until later in the show and reworked the show on the fly. I had way too much script in front of me—one of many details I'd have to sort out before we took the show live for real—and I kept having to move the script to get at the console. Before long I was completely lost and had to rely on Mark O'Neill (who was studio directing) for where we were and what was coming up next.

Finally I figured out that someone had turned the phones in the studio off—there was an obscure piece of gear allowing you to do that near the floor on one of the racks—so I turned them back on and we were able to get the phoner happening. Had I been able to get in the control room before the show to test things I would have figured that out, but during the chaos of the show it took a bit longer.

Still, despite how rock-and-roll it felt in the control room, the pilot wound up sounding okay on tape. We knew that we would get better organized in time, and I'd eventually learn all the ins and outs of Studio 203.

And one day the show would have a proper name.

But what?

It was pretty clear that if we didn't come up with a name soon that one would be foisted upon us by management and it would probably be the dreaded "Radar." So we hunkered down and for the umpteenth time wrote our top choices on the whiteboard.

We stared at all the names for a while, discussing various possibilities, but we still couldn't agree on any of them. One of the names on the board was "The Cue," suggested by Producer Matt Tunnacliffe. Somebody else suggested "Studio Q." It might have been Matt as well. We all sort of liked both, but they weren't quite right somehow. After staring at the board intently for a bit longer, it occurred to me that the letter "Q" all by itself was kind of intriguing.

"What about just the letter 'Q'?" I suggested. "All by itself?"

I figured that the notion would, as usual, quickly be dismissed and we would continue to disagree and the show would wind up being called either "The Ticket" or "Radar," the two current front-runners.

Much to my surprise the suggestion was not dismissed out of hand. Instead, everybody quickly warmed to the idea. Why? Well, as mentioned earlier, a part of the problem was that we couldn't figure out a name that encompassed both arts and culture, let alone both low and high arts and culture. We needed an inclusive name that could come to mean those things, something enigmatic. Also, "Q" could stand for many things: Question, inQuisitive, Query. Thought of as cue, it's a theatrical term, such as an actor's cue, or cue to cue. Standing in a "queue" to see a play, movie or concert. In radio it can mean "cue up." It lends itself to a certain playfulness: "And now for the Q-news." "Time now for our daily Q-tip," and so on. A nice, stylized "Q" looks great on a coffee mug or T-shirt. What really clinched the name was when Jian realized that he could easily make rhyming couplets out of it. "The sky is blue; you're listening to $Q$."

To this day, it means a lot to me that I came up with $Q$ (albeit based on Matt's suggestions). The circumstances under which I joined the show were not ideal. Being responsible for the name gave me big time buy-in on a show that I initially wanted no part of. And however you look at it, getting to choose the name of a new, prominent national radio show was undeniably cool.

We had the name all sorted out, but a week before the show's debut we still didn't really know whether it was going to work. I remember tense meetings with the team and Jian. Jian felt that there was too much interference from management. He didn't feel like he was able to make the show he wanted to make. There were different sensibilities at work. Jian and the Executive Producer weren't quite clicking. And we hadn't even begun talking about certain issues.

As the engineer, I was responsible for the sound of the show.

From the beginning I had been advocating for a theme package. I wanted to hire a composer and a band and get them to write all the music for the show. In the drama department we hired composers all the time so it was a no brainer for me, but for some reason the team balked at the idea.

For the pilots we'd been using an edit of "Spanish Bombs" by the Clash for the opening theme. It wasn't bad. It was basically a loop of the first four bars of the song. But it didn't have the panache we were looking for. I felt it would have been much classier to use music written especially for the show. At the last minute, Mark O'Neill agreed with me and hired Luc Doucet to write a theme. Now, the show debuted on a Monday, and Luc Doucet's band recorded the theme on the Friday. They recorded it. They didn't mix it. And they didn't record it to the proper specifications. We needed an intro, beds, backtime music.

On Sunday—the day before we debuted—I received a CD with all the raw tracks, unmixed. I was working on something else that day, teaching University of Toronto students the art of making radio plays, and I didn't even start mixing the theme until seven o'clock that night. By ten o'clock my ears were gone. A bad case of threshold shift. I could barely tell what I was listening to. I was completely fried and nobody else was around and I couldn't for the life of me tell if my mix was working or not. To make matters worse, I'd mixed what I thought was the lead guitar track foreground, but when I referred to the track sheet I saw that it wasn't supposed to be the lead, another guitar track was supposed to be the lead. I'd been thinking that the lead guitar wasn't going to work anyway because Jian wouldn't be able to talk over it, so I remixed it down, converted the mix to MP3 and sent it to Jian and Mark, and went home, exhausted.

The next morning, Monday April 15, the day the show premiered, the first thing Mark said to me was, "We got some remixing to do." It was two hours before show time. I'd been half expecting that, but my heart sank because I didn't know how much remixing he wanted to do, and it was 9:30am and we were debuting in two and a half hours. Plus Loreena McKennitt was on the show performing live, and I had to finish setting up for her. You could say I felt a tad stressed.

This is where some stellar leadership came into play. I really didn't think we'd get the theme done in time. I told Mark that we should go with the "Spanish Bombs" theme. But Mark, with nerves of steel, said, "No, no, we'll pull this off."

And somehow, we did. Fortunately, the remix was just a matter of swapping the guitar leads, which took all of ten minutes. Unfortunately, we then had to recut the theme, looping the middle section without the guitar lead to give Jian a place to talk without the guitar competing with his voice. There was a bit of back and forth between me, Mark and Jian before we established the correct length of the various components of the theme, and some hasty editing, but miraculously we finished just in time for me to go set up for Loreena's live music hit.

One hour after we finished mixing _Q_'s brand-new theme we used it for that day's show. Three weeks later I tweaked it slightly. And the show continued to use that version of the theme for several years afterward.

That first day the show debuted on the dot at 12:06 pm (we broadcast live to Sirius Radio, then the show was repeated to the Maritimes at 1:06, then Ontario at 2:06 and so on throughout the rest of the country). Loreena McKennitt was lovely to work with and she sounded terrific—even a meatball recording engineer like me couldn't make someone of her calibre sound bad.

Shortly into the show we found out that a promo we had recorded before the show was messed up. It was supposed to be played back out of Master Control to certain parts of the country within the hour, so we had no choice but to deal with it. At 12:30pm the show paused for one and a half minutes for a regional news update. During that time we were off the air. We decided to squeeze fixing the promo into that one and a half minute, if you can imagine. We finished fixing the promo with ten seconds to spare before going back on the air (I do not recommend trying that at home, kids).

We had a special recording from Margaret Atwood that we

wanted to play during the show. It was Margaret telling Jian "not to mess up... the arts are important!" Unfortunately, the recording was done in stereo and we were using a mono computer program (Dalet) to play back our audio material. Playing back a stereo file required exiting Dalet and loading a stereo version of the program.

"Do we need to play any mono files after the Atwood clip?" I asked Matt Tunnacliffe, now our regular studio director.

"No," he told me.

When the time came, I exited the mono Dalet program, loaded the stereo program, and played the Atwood clip. It was about thirty seconds long. During the Atwood clip we learned that through some quirk of fate it would be necessary to play a mono file after all directly after the stereo file. So, when the Atwood clip finished, I immediately got out of the stereo program and began loading the mono program. Jian started reading the intro to the mono clip. The mono program loaded at the exact same time as he finished, giving me precisely one second to load the mono clip and fire it. Insanity! But it all sounded good on air (I think).

You'd think that would have been enough stress for the day.

You'd be wrong.

There was a newscast at one o'clock during which we enjoyed a brief break. According to our information on this first day, the newscast was supposed to be six minutes long. There was a countdown clock in the studio that told us when we were supposed to be back on air. It gave us a twenty-second countdown. At 1:04:40 we were enjoying this brief respite, sitting back enjoying our cigars, anticipating another whole minute and twenty seconds before going live again, when suddenly Mark O'Neill cried out. He was staring at the countdown clock in horror. Looking up, I saw that the clock was counting down one minute early.

Was the clock wrong? Were we going to be live at 1:05? We hastily decided to trust the clock and start the show. I called Radio Master Control at the same time to ask them if the clock was right. I needed an answer before 1:06, because if the clock was wrong, we would have to restart the show at 1:06. Master told us that as far as they knew the clock was right. We carried on with the show. Afterward we learned that we had been given the wrong information, and that the start time for part three of the show had indeed been 1:05.

The remainder of the show went like a charm. Afterward I told everyone present that I needed a stiff drink of scotch. No one got me one, damn them. I was fairly shell shocked. But the show had ROCKED! Or so they told us.

And I seriously considered installing a wet bar in the studio.

# XLIV
## Recording Artists

At first, I had wanted nothing to do with the show that became *Q*. Only after much time passed did I realize that it had actually been a boon. Rather than dialing my career back ten years as I had feared, *Q* came to represent a kind of pinnacle of that career. I helped create a brand-new show for CBC Radio, and not just any show, but a flagship show. I *named* the damned thing. I enjoyed meeting all the fascinating guests. I liked the excitement, the fast pace, and challenges of live radio. But the part I came to like the most was the music.

In my time with *Q* we featured on average three bands a week. Initially I found this intimidating. I had recorded musicians here and there over the years but never to this extent. As so often was the case in my career with CBC Radio, it was sink or swim. Fortunately, I had help. My colleagues continued to be generous with their assistance. This time it was music recording engineer Rob Selmanovic who helped me the most. Rob taught me how to organize my music pickups. He provided many tips on mics, vocal treatments, outboard gear and so on. Like other key figures throughout my career such as John Johnston, John McCarthy and Greg DeClute, Rob was unstintingly generous with his knowledge.

Because of the limitations of the studio, which in those days was small and consisted of an analog Studer 963 console with only a few mic inputs and limited outboard gear, we tried to keep the music sessions modest. We discouraged bands from bringing in full drum kits. Sometimes only a couple of members of the band showed up, such as Jim Cuddy and Greg Keelor of Blue Rodeo or Josh Finlayson and Andy Maize of The

Skydiggers. Still, bands often brought every member of the band and plenty of instruments, and I had no choice but to roll with the punches.

Fortunately, it didn't take much to make these musicians sound good. Often I just needed to hang functioning microphones in front of them. They did the rest. One of my first sessions featured jazz singer (and arranger, producer and actor) Emilie-Claire Barlow. She sang "O Pato (The Duck)" accompanied solely by electric guitar. I couldn't believe how good the pickup sounded, which had nothing to do with my ability as a recording engineer; it was all Emilie-Claire Barlow's considerable gifts as a recording artist.

Sometimes we pre-recorded artists before the show and played back the recorded version during the show. Other times we featured the artists live on the show. Every Friday we included a live musical act. In my time with *Q* we featured Fine Frenzy, Jully Black, Oubijou, Luc Doucet, Stars, Brett Dennan, Suzanne Vega, KT Tunstall, Jenn Grant, Kevin Drew, Patrick Watson, Bedouin Soundclash, Ron Sexsmith, James Hunter, Basia Bulat, Regina Spektor, and many others. Most pickups were fairly straightforward. Some were rather more memorable. Ryan Adams once showed up with three bandmates well into the live show, forcing us to perform a sound check during a brief newscast, after which Ryan and his buddies proceeded to knock it out of the park.

Other times these sessions were memorable for different reasons. Such as the day I recorded the band Travis.

The band and their entourage showed up just before two pm. I was eating my lunch in the studio after having finished the live broadcast for the day. The plan was to record an interview and one song live-to-tape to be broadcast the following day.

A whole bunch of people came into the studio; I had no idea who was in the band and who wasn't. I knew little about the band except that there's nobody actually in the band named Travis (apparently the name is taken from Harry Dean Stanton's character in the film *Paris, Texas*). I shook a few hands, then allowed them to settle into the booth while I gobbled down the rest of my microwave dinner. Then I went in to help the musicians set up.

The band's management had requested a couple of vocal micro-phones and two direct boxes to plug an acoustic guitar and a bass guitar into. (Direct boxes allow you to plug an instrument directly into a console so you don't have to mic it). I had those all set up and ready to go. Although the entire band had showed up, only two of them were actually going to sing and play, lead singer Fran Healey and bass guitar player Dougie Payne.

"Could you mic my acoustic guitar instead of using a direct box?" Fran asked me.

"Sure," I said. "Actually, I prefer using a mic. I only used the direct box because that's what your technical specifications asked for."

"Somebody change the tech specs!" he called out.

"I'll put an SM57 on it," I suggested.

He said, "How 'bout that AKG 414 you've got hanging over the piano?"

"Sure," I said, and set it up.

In the control room I waited for Fran to finish tuning, then attempted to set levels as they rehearsed a song. Too many people were yapping in the control room. I couldn't hear a damned thing. I told them all politely but firmly to pipe down. Fran was com-plaining about something. I turned all the mics off so I could go into the booth and speak to them privately.

"I couldn't hear anything, I had to tell everyone out there to shut the hell up," I told them.

They laughed and said, good on ya.

Fran told me he wanted a bit of reverb on himself and a lot on Dougie. Dougie was supposed to sound kind of ghostly. No problem, I told them, but I was thinking: damn it, all I have is a Yamaha REV 5, a reverb unit that dates back to the eighties. I can't stand the sound of the thing and have been complaining about it since day one. It would have to do.

There was something wrong with the sound of Fran's guitar. It was distorting. I checked all my levels and the trim and couldn't see the problem. I'd never had a guitar distort that I could recall. I decided to swap out the 414 microphone on the theory that maybe it was overloading. This happens sometimes on condenser microphones if they're getting too much acoustic information; they just can't handle it. It's called capsule distortion. At least that's what I call it. But for a guitar to cause capsule distortion is kind of nutty; it usually happens when vocalists (or actors) are really belting it out.

I would usually mic guitars for the show with an SM57 and I'd had good luck with them. We had Brad Deneen on a few days earlier and somebody had written in to compliment me on the sound of his guitar, so I thought I would try it now. But when I went into the booth to swap out the microphones, somebody followed me in. This fellow spotted a Neumann U-87 and suggested that I use it instead. Fran introduced him as "our producer."

Now, the fact that he was a producer didn't impress me much. Most producers I knew, while being perfectly acceptable human beings, didn't know much technically. In fact, they often had half-baked technical notions. I told this fellow that I didn't want to try the U-87 (even though it's an awesome microphone) because, like the AKG 414, it was a condenser microphone.

"What's wrong with that?" he asked.

"We might be getting capsule distortion," I told him, confident that he wouldn't know what I was talking about.

"On a guitar?" he said.

This had two immediate consequences. First, I realized that this guy might actually know what he was talking about. Second, I instantly felt like an idiot, because the truth is it was highly unlikely that we were getting capsule distortion from a guitar.

"Okay, I'll try it," I told him.

He said, "I don't mean to get in the way."

I said, "Not a problem, tell me anything you want. I don't mind, really." I still had no idea who he was.

"There you go, butting in, making everyone tense," Fran said to the newcomer.

"No really, I don't mind. It's not a problem," I said.

Which was the truth. I didn't get my back up at all when people piped in. It made them feel a part of the process and I could potentially learn something. I didn't have much ego invested in engineering. When it came to recording music, I was just a meatball engineer. I told the guy as much and invited him to stand behind the console to help me with the mix.

We tried the song again with the U-87. Fran's guitar was still distorted, damn it. There were other issues as well. My helpful new friend had me tweak all the levels, and he thought Fran's lead vocal was peeking out of the mix too much. He wanted more compression on it. This was a problem. I didn't have separate compression on the various vocals. I am aware that ideally you have access to separate compression on everything but I didn't have that many compressors. It was a radio studio, not a recording studio, and because we usually had to do things fast I tried to keep it simple.

There wasn't much I could do about Fran's lead vocal except try to keep the guitar and bass up. Except the guitar was still distorted. I was starting to feel under the gun. We needed to start the interview. My new friend suggested there was a problem with the strip on the console. I agreed and plugged the guitar into a different strip. It corrected the distortion, but I still wasn't happy with the sound of the U-87 on the guitar. We were running late, so I had to let it go.

I was starting to regret allowing this fellow to help. Although I am no crackerjack music engineer, when I did a mix on the fly I pretty much had to trust my instincts. He was taking the mix in a different direction than I would have and it wasn't sitting properly. I had no doubt that if he was sitting at the board, he could have made it work. But he wasn't sitting at the board, I was. I had been forced to forgo what I would have done and second-guess myself. Second-guessing rarely makes anything better. Plus I was embarrassed about the distorted guitar and the lack of compression, and (as Fran had predicted earlier) I was starting to feel a tad tense.

In this fellow's defense, he had apologized for interfering and I had invited him repeatedly to help. And in his mind I was probably butchering the recording.

We decided that the sound we had would have to do. The plan was for Fran and Dougie to play the song at the end of the interview.

Halfway through the interview, Jian asked Fran and Dougie why their superstar producer was tagging along. Only then did I realize that this producer fellow helping me might be someone special in the world of rock music.

They played the song and I wasn't really happy with the sound. It wasn't awful but it wasn't great. I was too embarrassed to even look at the producer. He made a couple of suggestions about levels and I tried to follow them.

"I'm sorry it probably wasn't as good as you would have liked," I told him.

He clapped me on the shoulder and shook my hand, and I thought, well at least he's a decent guy.

Fran and Dougie were decent, too. They thanked me sincerely and shook my hand on the way out. I listened to the mix afterward with another engineer and we decided that it wasn't quite as bad as I'd feared. My $Q$ mates seemed to think it was okay.

Shortly afterward I was standing overlooking the CBC atrium when a friend looked out and said, "Geez, is that Nigel Godrich over there?"

I told him I'd just worked with him and asked him just who the heck this Nigel Godrich fellow was, anyway. Turns out Nigel Godrich is a producer and recording engineer well known for his work with Radiohead. He's also worked with Paul McCartney, Beck, R.E.M, Roger Waters, and U2.

All of which I was awfully glad I hadn't known until then.

# XLV
## Moving On

Six months into my gig on *Q*, John McCarthy came calling. John had been pivotal to my career once before by inviting me to join the radio drama department. He'd also become a good friend and mentor. By this time, John was running Radio Operations in Toronto. He was what we called the Plant Manager. I told people that meant that he was in charge of the rhododendron in the corner. Nobody ever laughed. Probably I should have picked a funnier kind of plant.

Anyway, one day he came looking for me. "I'm posting a job," he said. "I'd like you to apply."

"What job?"

"Supervisor, Audio Systems."

I was skeptical. Audio Systems was the radio maintenance department. "I'm not a maintenance technologist. I don't know anything about maintenance."

"You've spent your entire career operating audio equipment," John told me. "You're the client. The maintenance guys wouldn't be able to blow smoke up your ass. You may not know how to fix it, but you know what needs to be fixed."

I thought back through my career. The Audio Systems maintenance team had always done an excellent job of maintaining our studios and equipment, making it possible for people like me to do my job. Guys such as Paul Cutler and Chad Mounteny kept Radio Master Control humming twenty-four hours a day seven days a week. Others such as Don Paterson, Frank Finistauri and Kyle Kutasewich heroically maintained our high-end studios 211, 212 and Glenn Gould Studio; the consoles in those studios (Neve Capricorn, Euphonix System 5, Neve VR) could be notoriously temperamental. Nobody could beat Loan Huynh, Ori Joseph and Kalle Naelapea when it came to maintaining our many and varied radio studios used for packaging and live broadcasts. And John Baldwin, Deraj Ramnares, Ralph Frampton and Ivan Jovanovic kept the aging Dalet desktop radio system running smoothly.

I recalled all the problems I'd had with equipment over the years. The maintenance team had never been the issue; it had been the equipment itself. Blown power supplies, old consoles, dirty patch bays. The 963 Studer console in *Q*'s studio, Studio 203, had certainly been a challenge. I remembered the frustration of not being able to help a musician struggling with his headphone feed because the auxiliary output hadn't worked properly. Consoles like that were end-of-life. It was a challenge even getting parts for them. Maybe as a supervisor I could give the Audio Systems team the support they needed, and help to get that equipment fixed, or better yet, replaced.

Had I still been making radio plays I never would have considered moving to management. I wanted to be a recording engineer/ producer, not a manager. But those ambitions had been well and truly thwarted. I had nothing to lose. And I was curious. Could I even survive in management?

And yet...

"You should be asking Greg, not me." I told John.

I had always assumed Greg DeClute to be John's protégé.

John shrugged. "He's not interested."

I checked in with Greg. "It's not the right time," he informed me. "They can get rid of a manager in a heartbeat. Right now, I'm protected by the union. I'll think about management later, when I'm a little closer to retirement."

I appreciated his concerns, but I didn't feel the same way. I felt I'd be safe reporting directly to John. I would have stormed the beaches of Normandy with that guy. I applied for the job. There were three other candidates. Despite John having tapped me on the shoulder for the job there was no guarantee I'd get it.

The day of the interview I put on my best suit. (I only had two; the other one dated back to high school.) Although half decent—it was an Armani—it barely fit. (I was a little thicker than when I'd purchased it a decade earlier.) It was also out of style. But in the wardrobe of a radio technician that consisted almost entirely of jeans and T-shirts, it was the best I could do. It must not have been too bad. Shortly before the interview one of the schedulers looked me up and down. "You clean up nicely," she said.

That helped.

Jian spotted me. "Death in the family?"

"Something like that." I didn't want him to know about the interview.

John McCarthy and Zachary Kourous represented Radio Operations during the interview. Catherine Gregory stood in for Radio News, one of Audio System's clients. I don't remember a single question or answer. I do remember being completely comfortable in the presence of these three. Of course, John was a bona fide mentor, and I knew Catherine as a warm, friendly person with an unassailable reputation. Zach and I were also well-acquainted, having attended a year of CBC French courses together. We'd become friends in our choppy French. It was actually weird speaking English with him now.

Long story short, I got the job.

To my astonishment, Kim Orchard held a going away party for me. There was cake and punch. She even made a little speech, telling those present that "Joe is leaving a big pair of shoes to fill." I considered that very gracious of her. (My replacement, Alain Derbez, proved more than capable of filling my allegedly big shoes.)

It would be another month before I'd start my new job. I spent that month on *Q* in a terrific mood. We did a couple of remotes for the show in Moosejaw and Regina. The Moosejaw edition of *Q* went well, though both Jian and I made mistakes. We had created a makeshift studio in a café. I was playing back some IDs and themes from a laptop. I didn't have a mouse because someone had swiped mine for another computer. Getting ready to play an ID, I placed the cursor over the start button. The ID started to play of its own accord, interrupting Jian.

"Ah, don't I have more time?" he said to me, the nation, and the live audience, forcing me to stop playing the ID in progress. It was embarrassing, but that's live radio for you.

And Jian accidentally called Moosejaw "Toronto," which the live audience thought was hilarious, but Jian went with it, making it a running joke throughout the show. My mistake had been clumsy, ugly. Jian's had been hysterical. Still, afterward, everyone commended me on a job well done.[3]

On Monday we broadcast out of a proper studio in Regina. I visited the station Sunday afternoon to check it out and was dismayed to discover that the console was a Studer On Air 2000, an early digital console that I'd never used before. I spent the afternoon figuring it out. The following day the show went fine.

Back home in Toronto—on Tuesday, October 23, 2007—I engineered my last edition of $Q$, and the last live radio show I would ever tech. I managed to hit all the right buttons. The next day Alain Derbez took over. I knew that $Q$ would be in good hands with him, and he wound up doing the show far longer than I ever did.

On Wednesday it felt strange watching Alain engineer the show. I kept wanting to leap in and push the buttons myself. Our musical guest was Murray McLauchlan. When one of our associate producers introduced Murray to Alain instead of me, I felt a pang. But it was only right. Alain was doing the show now, not me. I would just have to get used to it. I hadn't wanted anything to do with this show, and now here I was missing it. $Q$ hadn't been what I'd thought it would be. It had been far more challenging and rewarding than I'd expected.

Just over a week later—eight months into my gig on $Q$ and almost twenty years into my career at the CBC—I was no longer to do anything technical.

It was time to move on.

---

3 On October 26, 2014, several years after I left Q, the CBC fired the show's host, Jian Ghomeshi. "Information came to our attention recently that in CBC's judgment precludes us from continuing our relationship with Jian," a CBC spokesman said at the time. Subsequent events are a matter of public record.

# XLVI
## Cue Backtime

Backtimes are instrumental pieces of music used to end radio shows, or parts of radio shows. They're often jazz, but they can be anything, so long as they're instrumental. That way the host can talk over the music without struggling to be heard over the sound of someone singing. We figure out how long the music is (say, three minutes) and then start the piece three minutes and one second before the end of the show, so that when the music finishes—a nice, hard out signifying the end—there's a second of silence before whatever comes next, be it a promo, or a net cue, or the news, or what have you.

If you listen carefully you can hear the backtime music I've selected playing underneath this bit. Some Pat Metheny, maybe, to take us out.

Endings can be challenging, especially in live radio. When your show is over, it's over. You can keep on talking but nobody outside the studio will hear you. The computer has switched away. Maybe you had more to say, maybe you weren't done talking. You were in the middle of a sentence and you didn't notice the second hand had reached the top of the clock. Or you had somebody on the phone and you couldn't get them to stop talking in time.

More than one host has been cut off by the computer.

Once, a radio host of a call-in show posed a lengthy question to a guest on the phone. He went on and on.

"Can you repeat the question?" the guest asked.

"No, I can't, actually," the host laughed. "Because we're all out of time."

Endings can be challenging. I could go on but I don't want to get cut off. Soon, Radio Master Control will switch to another source.

What comes next? A network ID, maybe Lorna Jackson—"You're listening to CBC Radio One"—or perhaps an hourly newscast with Ken Haslam, followed by a brief weather report and then *Quirks & Quarks* with Jay Ingram. In radio, something always follows. For me, what came next was a whole other career with the CBC, this time as a manager.

But that's a whole other book.

Music up and out...

# Glossary

For those unfamiliar with various broadcasting terms, here are a few select definitions:

**acoustic chamber**: A small enclosed recording space with sliding glass doors located in Studio 212 (the drama studio) in the Toronto Broadcast Centre. It was used to replicate specific acoustic environments such as the interior of cars. No longer in existence.

**analog audio**: The word analog itself (sometimes spelled analogue) means something comparable (analogous) to something else. In the case of sound, analog means recordings in a format (such as tape or vinyl) capable of reproducing continuous, uninterrupted vibrations comparable to the original sound waves.

**audio console**: An electronic console used to combine audio from separate sources (such as microphones and musical instruments) and send that audio elsewhere, such as for broadcast or to a public address system or to record it. Sometimes called a "Board" or a "Mixing Desk."

**Audio Systems**: What the CBC radio maintenance team used to be called.

**backtime**: An instrumental piece of music used to end a radio show or part of a radio show over which the announcer speaks.

**baffles**: An object or device used to reduce sound. We used large sound baffles on wheels in Studio 212 to create smaller acoustic environments simulating living rooms, offices etc. on the large studio floor.

**board**: See audio console.

**bounce**: Create a two-track (stereo) version of a sound file from multiple tracks.

**Canadian Broadcasting Corporation (CBC)**: Canada's public broadcaster, a federal Crown Corporation funded by (but operating at arm's length from) the Canadian government. "CBC" refers to the English language service; Radio-Canada refers to the French language service. CBC/Radio Canada also broadcasts in multiple aboriginal languages.

**Canadian Radio Broadcasting Commission (CRBC)**: Canada's first public broadcaster. It came before the CBC (Canadian Broadcasting Corporation).

**capsule distortion**: When a microphone overloads creating an unpleasant sound because it is receiving too much acoustic information (i.e., everything is too loud for the microphone).

**carbon granule microphone**: The first type of microphone. Essentially granules of carbon in an enclosure, one side of which is a thin metal or plastic diaphragm that compress the carbon granules when struck by sound waves. Capable of producing high level audio signals with very little power. Used in early AM radio and early telephones, and still used today in certain applications.

**cart**: An industry standard endless-loop tape cartridge developed in 1952 under the brand name Fidelipac. From the fifties until the late nineties, radio stations used them to play every kind of audio material from music to stings to station IDs to sound effects.

**compression**: A low concentration of air particles moving through space.

**compressor**: A type of audio gear or software used to reduce dynamic range, which is the difference between low and high levels in a piece of audio.

**condenser microphone**: A type of microphone that requires power (called "phantom power") to function. Generally higher quality than dynamic microphones and used to record more delicate sounds.

**confidence clock**: A clock in a studio connected to Radio Master Control with a countdown timer and a light (typically red) to let you know when you're going to be on and off air.

**console**: See Board.

**continuity**: When audio can pass successfully from one location to another, such as from a studio to Radio Master Control.

**cue speaker**: A small speaker on an audio console for auditioning audio before using that audio for a broadcast or recording. Also called pre-fade listen, or PFL.

**Dalet**: A networked desktop audio editing system used by CBC Radio from 1996 until it was replaced by DaletPlus twenty years later.

**DaletPlus**: The networked desktop audio editing system that replaced Dalet, essentially a more sophisticated version of Dalet.

**daytimer**: AM radio stations that are only permitted to broadcast during daytime hours because of the potential for their signals to interfere with other radio stations at night, when solar radiation is reduced, and medium wave radio signals can propagate much farther.

**Digital Audio Tape (DAT or R-DAT)**: A signal recording and playback medium that was developed by Sony in the mid-eighties. It appears similar to a compact audio cassette and uses 4 mm magnetic tape enclosed in a protective shell, but it is half the size at 73 mm × 54 mm × 10.5 mm.

**D-Cart**: Also called Digital Cartridge Editing System. A digital audio editing platform developed by the Australian Broadcasting Corporation in the early nineties that CBC installed in 1993 and used until replacing it with Dalet in 1996.

**dead air**: Unintentionally broadcasting silence.

**Dead Room**: An acoustic environment in Studio 212 with no hard surfaces for actors' voices to reflect off, simulating an outdoor environment.

**delay system**: A system to record everything CBC Radio broadcasts to Atlantic Canada that plays that content back an hour later for the Eastern Time Zone, and so on to time zones further west until the content has been played back for the entire country. In this way every Canadian can hear their favourite show at exactly the same time, subjectively at least.

**destructive interference**: When longitudinal sound waves are 180 degrees out of phase and cancel one another out, resulting in no sound.

**Dialogue Edit**: A small CBC Radio studio used primarily for editing dialogue tracks for radio plays.

**digital audio**: A means of reproducing sound waves by accurately measuring and recording sufficient sonic information over a specific period of time to record the information as a sequence of numerical samples.

**direct box**: Instruments such as guitars can be connected directly to audio consoles via these small electronic devices, eliminating the need to mic the instruments.

**discrepancy**: A deviation from the broadcast schedule as it was supposed to air. For example, when an announcer doesn't show up for their show in time, resulting in dead air. Sometimes called "Fault."

**distortion**: When the original shape of a sound wave is altered, often by increasing the gain. This can sound good with musical instruments, but it usually sounds bad with voices.

**double-ender**: When an interviewer back in the studio talks to a guest on the phone while an audio technician records the guest out in the field. Afterward, back in the studio, a tech eliminates the poor phone-quality recording of the guest, replacing that recording with the high-fidelity recording done in the field.

**dubbing**: Making a copy of a piece of audio.

**dynamic microphone**: Dynamic microphones operate by suspending a coil of wire connected to a diaphragm inside a magnetic field. When sound vibrates the diaphragm, the coil vibrates and produces an electrical signal.

**dynamic range**: The difference between low and high levels in a piece of audio.

**equalization**: Increasing or decreasing the volume of different frequencies of a selection of audio.

**Euphonix System 5**: A high-end digital audio mixing console. The Euphonix System 5-B replaced the Neve Capricorn in Studio 212 in the summer of 2003. We liked it so much that in December of that year we put one in our Music Mobile recording truck.

**fader**: A device used to increase or decrease the volume of audio. Physical faders typically slide along a track in a console. Virtual faders in digital consoles appear on screen.

**fault**: See Discrepancy.

**feed**: Audio content distributed across Canada, and sometimes to and from other countries, to be used on various CBC Radio shows.

**feedback (acoustic)**: An unpleasant screeching noise usually considered undesirable (except in certain kinds of music) created when a microphone picks up an audio signal and broadcasts it via a speaker back into that same microphone at sufficient gain and at just the right frequency to ensure a feedback loop. Also known as the Larsen effect after the Danish scientist Søren Absalon Larsen, who first discovered the principles of audio feedback.

**foley**: Creating sound effects for radio plays, television and film. Named after sound effects artist Jack Foley, who originated the technique for film.

**gain**: How loud the audio (input) is before it's processed.

**hourlies**: CBC Radio newscasts broadcast at the top of very hour, four and a half minutes long, and read by a single news announcer.

**ISDN (Integrated Services Digital Network)**: At CBC Radio we used ISDN units to broadcast remotes. They were basically high falutin' phone lines. We'd plug the output of our remote console into an ISDN unit, which would in turn be connected to a phone line to transmit the audio back to the Toronto Broadcast Centre, from where it would be broadcast. The official definition is "a set of communication standards for simultaneous digital transmission of voice, video, data, and other network services over the digitalised circuits of the public switched telephone network."

**lavalier mic**: A small microphone intended to be unobtrusive, usually with a clip allowing it to be attached to clothing.

**lining up**: Making sure the audio from a studio can reach Radio Master Control before a broadcast. Involves a time check as well to confirm the studio clock is showing the correct time and ensure the broadcast starts on time.

**mix**: Adjusting multiple sound elements into a pleasing whole via an audio console by a sound engineer, such as for a piece of music or a radio play, either live or for a recording.

**mixing desk**: See audio console.

**MS Stereo**: Stands for Mid/Side microphone recording. A way to record in stereo that allows recording engineers to control the width of the stereo spread and that can be adjusted after the recording. Patented by EMI engineer Alan Blumlein in 1933.

**Nagra**: The world's first portable tape recorder, invented by Polish inventor Stefan Kudelski, and introduced in 1951. Heavily used in the film industry from the sixties to the nineties. "Nagra" is Polish for "will record."

**Neutral Room**: A room in Studio 212 that could be used to replicate multiple neutral interior acoustic environments.

**Neve Capricorn**: A high-end digital audio mixing console. Used in Studio 212 until it was replaced by the Euphonix System 5-B console in the summer of 2003.

**NGCN (Next Generation Converged Network):** Developed by Rogers Cable Communications and Evertz Microsystems for the CBC to replace existing landlines, and launched in 2011, the NGCN network carries audio, video, and data content between CBC locations.

**packaging**: Putting a radio show together for broadcast later.

**phantom power**: Provides power via microphone cables to condenser microphones and active direct boxes.

**pickup**: Recording material either in a conventional studio or in a remote setting. It also means an actor or announcer redoing a line either because they've made a mistake or want an alternative take.

**polarity**: Two possible choices that are mutually exclusive. In sound, polarity is a question of direction of flow of electrical current.

**pot:** Short for potentiometer, and another word for fader.

**potentiometer:** A position sensor used to measure displacement in any direction. Potentiometers that slide up and down (faders) measure linear displacement and potentiometers that turn (rotary pots) measure rotational displacement.

**presentational radio:** Presenting content to listeners in a straightforward, unambiguous manner, such as on a newscast or interview show.

**pre-tape**: Taping material for broadcast before the actual show.

**Pro Tools**: Professional digital audio editing software sold by Avid Technology.

**public address system (PA):** A system of speakers, amplifiers, microphones and other assorted equipment to broadcast audio material such as voice and music in public spaces, either indoors or out.

**quarter-inch tape machine**: Devices to record and playback audio using quarter-inch tape. Sometimes called reel-to-reel machines. The workhorses of CBC Radio, usually four to a studio, during their heyday before the advent of digital desktop radio (D-Cart, Dalet, DaletPlus).

**radio**: See Chapter Three.

**Radio-Canada:** The French language service of the Canadian Broadcasting Corporation.

**Radio Master Control**: The central hub, through which most CBC Radio shows pass before hitting the transmitters and the radios of the nation.

**radio play**: A story told by means of sound often employing multiple actors accompanied by sound effects and music.

**radio technician**: An individual whose job it is to record, manipulate and broadcast sound.

**rarefaction**: A low concentration of air particles moving through space.

**Recording Room**: A room in the basement of the Jarvis Street Radio building where radio technicians received and recorded audio feeds for later broadcast and for archival purposes. The room existed in the Toronto Broadcast Centre as well until the adoption of digital technology when it was replaced by a digital virtual recording room.

**recording engineer**: The individual responsible for the technical portion and overall sound of a recording session. At CBC Radio this includes recording, editing and mixing.

**reference tone**: A continuous tone, usually 1 Kilohertz (1K) used to "line up" audio equipment (adjust playback and record levels). Reference tone is also used to ensure that the audio signal is travelling successfully from one location to another (i.e., one studio to another). This is referred to as "establishing continuity."

**remote**: A broadcast or recording outside of a conventional studio, often for a special event.

**representational radio**: Content representing something other than what it actually is, such as the fiction of a radio play.

**Rev 5**: Yamaha REV 5 Digital Reverberator. A type of outboard audio gear capable of producing multiple types of reverberation. In other words, it can make a person or music sound like it's in different-sized rooms anywhere from a closet or a theatre. Popular in the eighties.

**reverb**: Short for reverberation, reverb is the sound we hear bouncing back from various surfaces in our environment not including the source of the sound.

**rotary pot**: A device used to increase or decrease the volume of audio on a console, like faders only round. "Pot" is short for potentiometer.

**Shure FP42 mixer**: A small portable stereo mixer with four inputs and two outputs, great for remotes.

**sound check**: Testing a sound system before a performance or broadcast to ensure that everything works and sounds good.

**splitting the board**: Using an audio console for more than one purpose at time, such as recording a pickup with the main inputs and outputs while simultaneously dubbing separate content using auxiliary busses.

**sting**: A brief piece of sound or music used to punctuate a radio program and/or separate two different sections of a radio program in a pleasing way.

**streeter**: Short, snappily edited interviews with people out in the real world, "on the street."

**Studer 963**: An analog console, quite common in CBC Radio packaging and live studios from the nineties on until the advent of digital consoles.

**Studer On Air 2000**: A digital audio console.

**swap tone**: Low frequency, barely audible tone added to the end of a recording on quarter-inch tape for automation systems to detect to trigger a "swap" to the next tape containing additional programming.

**Switched 56**: A high-quality telephone line.

**top and tail**: Inserted leader tape before and after audio for broadcast on quarter-inch tape to make it easier for technicians to cue them up.

**travelling shot**: A scene in television, film or radio in which the camera/microphone follows characters on the move without interruption.

**two-way**: A recording involving a host in a studio in one location and a guest (usually in a studio) in another.

**video switcher**: Hardware used to switch between different audio and video sources such as television cameras, used during live or live-to-tape television productions.

**video tape recorder (VTR):** Hardware used to record and play back video and audio from magnetic tape.

**voice track**: A track in editing software containing voices, either actors, guests, or otherwise.

**voice tracking**: Recording the voices of actors, performers, announcers and guests.

**VU Meter**: Stands for "volume unit" meter. Displays a representation of the level of audio in audio equipment.

**volume**: How loud audio is after it's been processed (i.e., put through a piece of gear such as an amp or speaker).

**wallbox**: Usually located near the floor in studio performance spaces, wallboxes provide a means of plugging microphones and other audio gear to the console in the control room.

# Acknowledgements

A lot of people have helped me throughout my career. Here are a few that I feel merit special mention. Ralph Carruthers at Three Oaks Studio Radio—Ralph really created something special there. Lowell Huestis, Paul H. Schurman and Paul M. Schurman of CJRW 1240 Radio in Summerside for putting me on the air. John McCarthy and Greg DeClute at the CBC deserve special mention for all they've taught me about radio over the years, and also for their help on this book. Thanks to Avery Olive for designing this book. And special thanks to Arleane Ralph, whose eagle eye and penetrating insights never fail to impress me, along with her generosity. Finally, thanks and much love to my wife Lynda and my beautiful daughters Erin and Keira.

# About the Author

Joe Mahoney has worked full-time for the *Canadian Broadcasting Corporation* for over three decades in many roles including recording engineer, producer, and several operational management roles.

# Recommended Reading

I found the following books helpful while writing this memoir:

*A Promised Land* by Barack Obama

*Adventures in the Screen Trade* by William Goldman

*An Astronaut's Guide to Life on Earth* by Chris Hadfield

*an outlaw and a lady* by Jessi Colter

*Bambi VS Godzilla* by David Mamet

*Born Standing Up* by Steve Martin

*Endurance* by Scott Kelly

*H is for Hawk* by Helen Macdonald

*Kitchen Confidential* by Anthony Bourdain

*Off the Record* by Peter Mansbridge

*On Writing: A Memoir of the Craft* by Stephen King

*Secret Life: The Jian Ghomeshi Investigation* by Kevin Donovan

*Talking to Canadians* by Rick Mercer

*The Tower of Babble* by Richard Stursberg

*Two Towns in Provence* by M. F. K. Fisher

*Understanding Audio* by Daniel M. Thompson

# Index

www.ingramcontent.com/pod-product-compliance
Lightning Source LLC
Chambersburg PA
CBHW020150090426
42734CB00008B/763

* 9 7 8 1 0 6 9 0 9 6 5 9 3 *